Get the eBook FREE!

(PDF, ePub, Kindle, and liveBook all included)

We believe that once you buy a book from us, you should be able to read it in any format we have available. To get electronic versions of this book at no additional cost to you, purchase and then register this book at the Manning website.

Go to https://www.manning.com/freebook and follow the instructions to complete your pBook registration.

That's it!
Thanks from Manning!

Kubernetes Secrets Management

Kubernetes Secrets Management

ALEX SOTO BUENO
ANDREW BLOCK

MANNING
SHELTER ISLAND

Manning Publications Co.
20 Baldwin Road
PO Box 761
Shelter Island, NY 11964

Development editor:	Patrick Barb
Technical development editors:	Conor Redmond
Review editor:	Aleksandar Dragosavljević
Production editor:	Andy Marinkovich
Copy editor:	Christian Berk
Proofreader:	Jason Everett
Technical proofreader:	Mike Haller
Typesetter and cover designer:	Marija Tudor

ISBN 9781617298912
Printed and bound by CPI Group (UK) Ltd, Croydon, CR0 4YY

brief contents

contents

preface

As technologists, we are naturally drawn to seeking out innovative ways of solving problems—whether that be through the use of new or existing approaches, frameworks, or technologies. One such technology both authors have been enthralled with over the last few years is Kubernetes. While Docker brought containers to the masses, it was Kubernetes that provided an extensible platform for running containers at scale.

We approached Kubernetes from different ends of the spectrum: one from an infrastructure mindset, understanding what it takes to build a Kubernetes cluster, and the other focusing on applications, looking to take advantage of the capabilities provided by the underlying infrastructure. There are several interwoven themes that apply to both infrastructure and application-focused individuals; one such area that remains a constant, whether using Kubernetes or not, is security.

Security is one of those topics that, while essential, often gets deprioritized or overlooked compared to other areas of interest. What we have found while working with organizations and developers is that they may not understand what types of resources require protections or how they can go about securing them. Those who have started working with Kubernetes are also surprised to learn that Kubernetes itself had very little in terms of security when it was first released. The protection mechanism that became known as Secrets was developed as a solution to provide some form of protection for sensitive assets prior to the initial 1.0. As a result, Secrets provide a minimal level of security, which may come as a surprise, given the name of the resource.

The combination of being potentially unfamiliar with the types of assets that should be secured and how to secure them, the false sense of security offered by the native Kubernetes features, and a myriad of solutions becoming available in this space spells a potential recipe for disaster. Our goal with this book is emphasizing the shift left mentality, in which security becomes a key concern when working with Kubernetes and addresses the capabilities and pitfalls of the included tooling, alternate solutions, and ways these can be incorporated within different parts of the delivery process. We don't intend—and wouldn't be able—to address all possible security options, but the concepts and implementations discussed in *Kubernetes Secrets Management* should enable you to be more successful and secure when working with Kubernetes.

acknowledgments

During these challenging times, I'd like to acknowledge Santa (fly, fly), Uri (thanks for all the conversations), Guiri (Vive Le Tour), Gavina, Gabi (thanks for the beers), and Edgar and Ester (yes, it's Friday); my working teammates Edson, Sebi, Natale, Ana-Maria, Elder, and, of course, Burr and Kamesh (you will be on our team wherever you are)—we are the best team in the world! Also, thanks to Jonathan Vila, Abel Salgado, and Jordi Sola for the fantastic conversations about Java and Kubernetes.

Special thanks to all the reviewers who read our manuscript and provided such valuable feedback: Alain Lompo, Atila Kaya, Chris Devine, Clifford Thurber, Deepak Sharma, Giuseppe Catalano, John Guthrie, Jon Moore, Michael Bright, Mihaela Barbu, Milorad Imbra, Peter Reisinger, Robin Coe, Sameer Wadhwa, Satadru Roy, Sushant Bhadkamar, Tobias Ammann, and Werner Dijkerman; your contributions helped improve this book.

Last but certainly not least, I'd like to acknowledge Anna for being here; my parents, Mili and Ramon, who bought me my first computer; and my daughters Alexandra and Ada, "sou les ninetes dels meus ulls."

—ALEX SOTO BUENO

Writing a book can be a challenging ordeal while also juggling other responsibilities amid a global pandemic. I would like to acknowledge those that helped reinforce various security concepts, including Raffaele Spazzoli, Bob Callaway, and Luke Hinds. In addition, all those in in the Open Source community who helped build knowledge and stayed connected during these challenging times.

But, most importantly, I would like to acknowledge my parents, AnneMarie and A.J., for their pillar of support that keeps me grounded and focused no matter the adversity.

—ANDREW BLOCK

about this book

Kubernetes Secrets Management was written to help you understand how to manage secrets during development, and release an application to the Kubernetes cluster. We begin with an introduction to Kubernetes and setting up the environment in which to run the examples presented in the book. After the introduction, we discuss managing secrets during development time and storing them correctly, either in the code repository or inside the Kubernetes cluster. Finally, we show a cloud Kubernetes-native way of implementing continuous integration and delivery as well as managing secrets in the pipeline.

Who should read this book?

Kubernetes Secrets Management is for senior developers with minimal experience in Kubernetes who want to expand their knowledge about Kubernetes and secret management. This book is also for operators who want to learn how to manage secrets, including how to configure, deploy, and store these secrets appropriately. While plenty of docs and blog posts to this effect exist online, *Kubernetes Secrets Management* brings together all that information to one clear, easy-to-follow text, so readers can understand security threats step-by-step, and how to address them.

How this book is organized: A roadmap

This book has three parts that cover eight chapters:

Part 1 explains the fundamentals of security and secrets and the basic Kubernetes concepts essential for understanding the rest of the book.

- Chapter 1 introduces what is and is not a secret, why it is important to keep secrets secret, as well as an overview of Kubernetes.

- Chapter 2 further introduces Kubernetes, its architecture, and the basic concepts for deploying an application with secret data. It also discusses why standard Kubernetes Secrets do not provide sufficient security.

Part 2 covers several security issues you might encounter during the development and deployment of an application to Kubernetes and how to fix them. Moreover, part 2 covers using secret storage to manage application secrets outside of the Kubernetes infrastructure.

- Chapter 3 introduces tools and approaches that can store Kubernetes Secrets securely at rest and illustrates the benefits of declaratively defining Kubernetes resources.
- Chapter 4 covers the encryption of secrets at rest inside the Kubernetes cluster as well as their integration with a key management service.
- Chapter 5 focuses on the importance of using a secrets management tool, such as HashiCorp Vault, to securely store and manage sensitive assets for applications deployed to Kubernetes. It also demonstrates how both applications and Vault can be configured to provide seamless integration with one another.
- Chapter 6 expands on the idea, introduced in chapter 5, of using an external secrets management tool—this time focusing on cloud secrets stores, including Google Secret Manager, Azure Key Vault, and AWS Secrets Manager.

Part 3 introduces a way of implementing Kubernetes-native continuous integration and delivery with Tekton and Argo CD and managing secrets correctly.

- Chapter 7 covers delivering quality applications rapidly to hit the market sooner and, better yet, managing the secrets correctly throughout the pipeline, so no secrets leak in this phase of development.
- Chapter 8 covers using continuous deployment and GitOps methodology to deploy and release services to a Kubernetes cluster by using Argo CD to deliver quality applications rapidly, while correctly managing the secrets throughout the pipeline, and ensuring no secrets leak in this phase of the development.

The reader may skip the second chapter if they have a good knowledge of Kubernetes (e.g., Deployments, Services, volumes, and ConfigMaps) and minikube.

About the code

This book contains many examples of source code both in numbered listings and in line with normal text. In both cases, source code is formatted in a `fixed-width font like this` to separate it from ordinary text. Sometimes code is also **in bold** to highlight code that has changed from previous steps in the chapter, such as when a new feature adds to an existing line of code.

In many cases, the original source code has been reformatted; we've added line breaks and reworked indentation to accommodate the available page space in the book. In rare cases, even this was not enough, and listings include line-continuation markers (➥). Additionally, comments in the source code have often been removed from the listings when the code is described in the text. Code annotations accompany many of the listings, highlighting important concepts.

You can get executable snippets of code from the liveBook (online) version of this book at https://livebook.manning.com/book/kubernetes-secrets-management. The complete code for the examples in the book is available for download from the Manning website at www.manning.com, and from GitHub at https://github.com/lordof thejars/kubernetes-secrets-source.

liveBook discussion forum

Purchase of *Kubernetes Secrets Management* includes free access to liveBook, Manning's online reading platform. Using liveBook's exclusive discussion features, you can attach comments to the book globally or to specific sections or paragraphs. It's a snap to make notes for yourself, ask and answer technical questions, and receive help from the author and other users. To access the forum, go to https://livebook.manning .com/book/kubernetes-secrets-management/discussion. You can also learn more about Manning's forums and the rules of conduct at https://livebook.manning.com/ discussion.

Manning's commitment to our readers is to provide a venue where a meaningful dialogue between individual readers and between readers and the authors can take place. It is not a commitment to any specific amount of participation on the part of the authors, whose contribution to the forum remains voluntary (and unpaid). We suggest you try asking the authors some challenging questions lest their interest stray! The forum and the archives of previous discussions will be accessible from the publisher's website for as long as the book is in print.

about the authors

ALEX SOTO BUENO is a Director of Developer Experience at Red Hat. He is passionate about the Java world, and software automation, and believes in the open-source software model. Alex is the co-author of *Testing Java Microservices, Quarkus Cookbook, Securing Kubernetes Secrets,* and contributor to several open-source projects. A Java Champion since 2017, Alex is also an international speaker, radio collaborator at Onda Cero, and teacher at Salle URL University. You can follow Alex on Twitter (@alexsotob) to stay tuned to what's going on in Kubernetes and the Java world.

ANDREW BLOCK is a Distinguished Architect at Red Hat who works with organizations to design and implement solutions leveraging cloud native technologies. He specializes in continuous integration and continuous delivery methodologies to reduce delivery time and automate how environments are built and maintained. He is also the co-author of *Learn Helm,* which introduces how to package applications for deployment in a Kubernetes environment. Andrew is also a contributor to several open-source projects and emphasizes the benefits of working together to build and maintain Communities of Practice. Andrew can be found on Twitter at @sabre1041 where he frequently shares the latest and greatest headlines and tips in the field of emerging tech.

Part 1

Secrets and Kubernetes

Whether working through an infrastructure or application lens, the operation of these assets is driven via the use of configuration properties; some of which may contain sensitive values. In the first part of this book, we will introduce the fundamentals of managing of secrets within Kubernetes.

Chapter 1 provides guidance for identifying the traits commonly found in secrets and their role within Kubernetes. Chapter 2 focuses on the primitives of Kubernetes, its architecture, and the basic concepts for deploying an application with sensitive data. After reading part 1, you will have the skills to identify configurations containing sensitive content along with the knowledge of the primary limitations of the Kubernetes Secret resource.

Kubernetes Secrets

1

This chapter covers

- Focusing on security
- Taking full advantage of the Kubernetes ecosystem
- Differentiating between what is and is not considered a Secret
- Bringing it all together
- Getting started with the tools you will need for success

Enterprise software systems rely on accurate configuration data to support their normal operation. Configurations take many forms and can be set up in a variety of ways, depending on the use case and context. These configurable properties could include details to support the application framework or the normal operation of the program.

While many of these properties are intended to be viewed by any party, there are certain attributes, such as passwords, that should only be seen or accessed by certain individuals or components. These sensitive forms of data are called *Secrets*, and protecting these Secrets is a top priority for Kubernetes administrators and developers. As one might expect with any complex system, Kubernetes configurations employ a myriad of properties to support normal operation, some which may contain sensitive information that, if exposed, would risk the integrity of the entire platform.

Over time, an increasing number of options have become available for managing configurations in Kubernetes, but most trace their history to the two primary methods for storing configurations within the platform: ConfigMaps and Secrets. While each resource provides a way for storing configuration material through the use of key–value pairs, the primary difference between the two is that Secrets are designed to hold confidential data along with supporting more complex data types, such as binary assets instead of plain text values. It's important to note that some of these data types may contain sensitive properties.

However, the included Kubernetes Secrets resource is just the tip of the iceberg as it relates to secrets management within Kubernetes. Additional tools and approaches have evolved to supplement the native capabilities of Kubernetes Secrets. One of the driving forces behind the evolution of these tools is the fact that the native Kubernetes Secrets resource does not provide the level of security one might need or expect from a secrets management system.

Instead of making use of a proper encryption algorithm, values stored within Kubernetes Secrets are merely Base64 encoded, meaning their values can be easily decoded by a malicious attacker; this encoding scheme was employed for the purpose of storing binary data rather than providing any form of security. But, what makes these alternate tools superior to the native Kubernetes Secrets resource? Is it because they provide a more robust encryption mechanism, are more intuitive to use, or integrate well into the target system or end application? Maybe. These are all factors that need to be considered when choosing from your available options.

In many cases, there is no *correct* answer. Everyone, whether an individual developer or a multinational organization, assesses security in a different way. What may be fine for one may not be fine for the other, especially when there are security regulations that must be followed. Understanding not only the importance but also the various methods that can be used to protect sensitive assets within Kubernetes are the goals of this book. Upon completion you will have a better understanding of the role Secrets play in a Kubernetes environment within applications as well as with the technologies and approaches that can be used to properly manage sensitive resources and support the underlying infrastructure.

1.1 *A focus on security*

Security is a continuously evolving topic. Every week, news of a new vulnerability is reported with an intrusion no doubt to follow. One of the reasons for adopting a container-native strategy is that many benefits come with cloud-native application development and operation. However, security, in many cases, is still seen as an afterthought and is lower in priority than some of the other aspects of cloud-native development. The fundamental shift to how systems are built and deployed gives organizations an opportunity to reflect on how they prioritize work and some of the factors that should go into how infrastructure and applications are designed. Organizations are beginning to take note of the importance of security and *shifting left* to include it earlier in the development process. It also gives them the opportunity to reflect on their current security practices and contemplate how they want to design and deliver their strategies and policies moving forward.

Adopting concepts like the principle of least privilege, which limits the amount of access granted to resources to only the minimum necessary privileges to accomplish a task, embraces the importance of managing access to sensitive resources. Applying role-based access control (RBAC) to restrict access to authorized users is one of the most common approaches for applying this principle. But keeping an eye on security should not be viewed as a *one and done* task that only occurs at the planning and initial implementation phase. It is important for these policies to be reviewed on an ongoing basis to confirm whether any actor still needs access to a desired resource. This continual assessment is not only a good practice, but it also increases overall security.

1.2   Taking full advantage of the Kubernetes ecosystem

As one can probably imagine, proper secret management in a Kubernetes environment goes far beyond the simple deployment of Pods and Services. More advanced topics, such as *sidecars*—which are separate containers sitting alongside the primary container to provide supplementary capabilities along with admission webhooks that can react to various changes within the platform—push Kubernetes to the limit to achieve secure solutions. The true extensibility of the platform is demonstrated through Custom Resource Definitions (CRD), which extend the base set of Application Programming Interface (API) resources and can be used for managing secure assets among other ways of supporting how secrets can be managed and accessed.

But it is not always the technology itself that moves projects forward and opens up opportunities. Tireless efforts from members from the open source community in collaboration with various organizations have dedicated their time and resources to provide solutions in this space, allowing additional options and approaches to become available for providing the most secure operating environment possible.

1.3   Not everything is a Secret

While it is important to have a security-first mindset, one must be considerate of the effort it takes to properly perform secrets management. For example, if you developed an application that sends alerts based on the current temperature once a configurable threshold was reached, such as if the temperature of a refrigerator reached 5 degrees Celsius, would this threshold of 5 degrees Celsius truly be considered a sensitive resource? Probably not. The time, resources, and effort to fully secure and manage assets must be taken into account, as the administrative overhead and ongoing lifecycle may outweigh the benefits.

The mindset that every configurable value should be treated the same is a common fallacy hindering many teams. Determining which values can remain in plain text and which others require protection is an exercise that should be performed by all teams. Defining a standardized method for identifying sensitive resources will help align not only how application teams approach secrets management, but it will also promote making more informed decisions and reducing wasted time.

1.4 *Bringing secrets management and Kubernetes together*

Secrets management has been a challenge long before the days of Kubernetes. The process can be laborious and will most likely involve careful planning and consideration. So what steps should you take? Let's break down each section from the bird's-eye perspective depicted in figure 1.1, which will aid in understanding the steps you will need to examine.

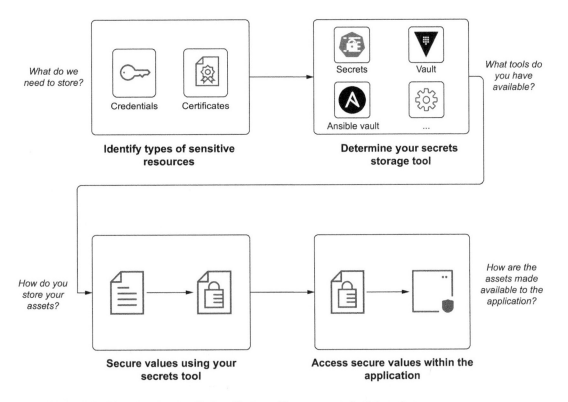

Figure 1.1   The steps involved in handling sensitive resources in Kubernetes

First, prior to any sort of implementation or execution, there should be an agreement on what types of configurable material is present as well as those that are to be deemed sensitive (figure 1.2).

In some cases, the answer is fairly straightforward, such as a password to a database. For others, it may not be so easy. Take an example of a web application that makes a connection to the same backend database. Would the database hostname be considered sensitive material? To some, it may be, as there could be a desire to obfuscate the location in order to reduce the potential attack vector. However, if the location referred to a common shared database used by members of a team in a development environment, it may not. Many battles have been fought, won, and lost throughout this process, and the answer does, in fact, vary.

Once there has been an agreement on the types of properties deemed sensitive,

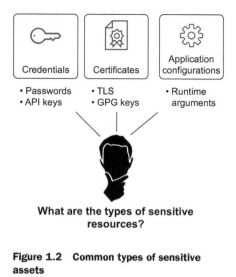

What are the types of sensitive resources?

Figure 1.2   Common types of sensitive assets

the next step is determining how they should be stored. There are several factors that should be taken into account:

1   What are the available secrets management solutions?
2   How is the sensitive asset intended to be used?
3   What application framework is being used, and what are the options for injecting external configurations?

In a Kubernetes environment, the Secret resource is a natural default, as it provides some form of protection and is included in every distribution of Kubernetes. But, what else is available? Figure 1.3 depicts the two primary approaches.

Kubernetes Secrets

1. Kubernetes Secrets are the de facto method for storing sensitive material in Kubernetes.

Third-party tools

2. Alternate methods can be used to both store and secure sensitive material for use in Kubernetes.

Figure 1.3   Typical utilities for storing sensitive Kubernetes assets

If the framework for your application or component offers a secrets management system, it may be a viable option to leverage this native feature. Many cloud providers also offer their own key management system (KMS) as well as a managed service option. This is highly appetizing when operating in cloud environments. Other solutions, such as HashiCorp Vault, provide a key management system that can be deployed anywhere, whether in the public cloud or elsewhere.

After determining the secrets management solution you will move forward within the particular implementation, the next step is to store assets within the tool. While the process of storing resources can vary depending on the tool, most expose an API-based interface that can be used to integrate at a variety of levels. The API becomes the focal point for interacting with the secrets management solution, and for convenience, a Command Line Interface (CLI) option or a user interface exposed through a web browser abstracts the underlying interaction with the API. These options all aid in the storage of secrets and can be achieved in a manual fashion or integrated into a continuous integration or continuous delivery (CI/CD) process to achieve repeatability and consistency (figure 1.4).

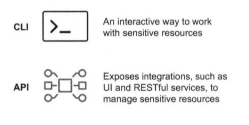

CLI   An interactive way to work with sensitive resources

API   Exposes integrations, such as UI and RESTful services, to manage sensitive resources

Figure 1.4   Common methods for interacting with secrets management tools

The final, and arguably most important, step is retrieving the stored resource out of the secrets management tool for use by the application. Thanks to the power of Kubernetes, there are a variety of options and approaches that can be used for this. Ultimately, it boils down to two distinct steps:

1 Translating the value from its protected form to plain text
2 Exposing the value, so it can be consumed by the application

The process in which stored values are converted back to their plain text representation is dependent on the secrets management tool in use. In many cases, the same approach used to store the values can be used, just in reverse. Things can get interesting, depending on how you make these values available to applications. Most simply, as with standard Kubernetes Secrets, a reference is made to the stored Secret in the Kubernetes manifest being created, where the asset is then exposed to applications as either an environment variable or contained within a file on the file system of the application. However, if more advanced secrets management tools are used, or there is a desire for more dynamic capabilities to further restrict how values are exposed to applications, additional options may be available.

Certain tools can be co-located alongside running applications within the aforementioned sidecar containers to interact with the secrets management store and inject sensitive values into applications for consumption. Alternatively, at deployment time, the Kubernetes manifest of the application can be modified by the platform to decouple how values are injected in a dynamic fashion. Furthermore, approaches in which the sensitive value is never exposed in plain text and is accessed directly by the application in memory are also available. From start to end, regardless of the approach, you need to carefully plan and think through assessing the necessary tools, requirements from the application, and the overall time and effort it will take to implement the solution.

1.5 *Tools to get started*

To guide you along your journey throughout this book, you will make use of several tools that not only interact with a Kubernetes cluster but any of the secrets management solutions being discussed. It is important to have an environment that allows for the installation and configuration of software. At a minimum, to interact with a Kubernetes cluster and manage the Kubernetes Secret resource, the Kubernetes command-line tool (*kubectl*) will be needed. As you work through some of the alternate solutions in the secrets management space, additional tools will be introduced. So without further delay, let's get started!

Summary

- Configurations take many forms—some of which may be sensitive in nature—to support both application and infrastructure contexts.
- Values stored in Kubernetes Secrets are not encrypted but, instead, Base64 encoded and easily decoded.
- The principle of least privilege embraces only enabling the minimum level of access necessary.
- The Kubernetes container orchestration platform contains primitives to enable approaches for managing secrets.
- Concepts and approaches will be introduced in subsequent chapters to enable readers to properly manage secrets in Kubernetes.

An introduction to
Kubernetes and Secrets

2

This chapter covers

- Understanding the basic architecture of a Kubernetes cluster
- Deploying an application to Kubernetes
- Managing application configuration externally
- Using Kubernetes Secrets to store sensitive information

Because secrets management begins with the initial configuration and the security needs of the application, it's important to fully understand the initial setup process. In this chapter, you will learn more about how to manage configurations, both insecure and secure, by deploying a simple RESTful Web Service that returns a greeting message.

> **NOTE** You'll need a Kubernetes cluster to run the implementations in this book. You can use any Kubernetes distribution provided by a public cloud or made to run it locally.

The examples in this book are tested using a minikube cluster. Minikube allows you to run Kubernetes locally in a *single-node* Kubernetes cluster inside a virtual machine (VM) on a laptop. Follow the instructions in appendix A to install your Kubernetes cluster, and then return to this chapter to get started.

We'll start by reviewing some basics about Kubernetes architecture and configuration. If you are already well versed in Kubernetes, the next few pages, in which we'll establish the initial configuration for your web service, should be very familiar. We'll dive into Kubernetes Secrets after we complete the default setup.

2.1 Kubernetes architecture

The first thing to understand about Kubernetes architecture is there are two kinds of Nodes—master and worker Nodes—and in typical production deployments you might have several Nodes of each kind.

> **IMPORTANT** The Kubernetes community has started changing the names of the Nodes, using more inclusive language (e.g., control plane and secondary Node); we truly support this change, but the version of minikube used in this book, has not yet implemented this change. To be aligned with minikube output, master and worker Nodes are used in this chapter.

Figure 2.1 shows an overview of a Kubernetes cluster and the relationship between master Nodes and worker Nodes. The worker Node(s) is responsible for running your workloads, such as developed services or databases, and the master Node(s) manages the worker Nodes and decides where workloads are deployed.

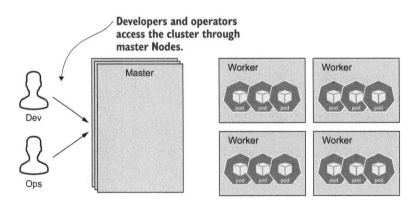

Figure 2.1   Overview of Kubernetes architecture with master and worker Nodes

The minimum number of Nodes required to conform to a Kubernetes is just one master Node acting as the master and worker Node. Although this might not be the typical use case in production, it is typical when developing in the local machine. Usually, in production, you will have between three and five master Nodes and several worker Nodes, the number of which may depend on the number of workloads to deploy and the degree of redundancy you expect in your application. Let's explore what is inside master and worker Nodes.

2.1.1   *What is a master Node?*

A *master Node* is responsible for executing several tasks in a Kubernetes cluster; for example, it decides where the application is deployed, detects and responds to abnormalities, stores the application configuration parameters, and, by default, is the place secrets (or sensitive information) of the application are stored.

A Kubernetes cluster must have at least one master Node, but typically in production environments you may have more than one for redundancy. You will find the next four elements inside each master Node:

- kube-apiserver—This is the frontend for Kubernetes and exposes the Kubernetes API to the Kubernetes users. When an operator runs a command against the Kubernetes cluster, it does so through the api-server.
- etcd—This is a key–value database used to store all cluster data. Every time you get information about the cluster, that data is retrieved from etcd.
- *scheduler*—This is the process responsible for selecting a Node for running workloads on. Factors taken into consideration when selecting the Node on which to deploy your workload might depend on its requirements, such as hardware, policy constraints, affinity and anti-affinity rules, data locality, and so on.
- *controllers*—The main task of controllers is monitoring specific Kubernetes resources.

There are four major controllers:

1 *Node controller*—This controller is responsible for monitoring and acting when any Node goes down.
2 *Replication controller*—This controller is responsible for ensuring your workloads are up and running all the time.
3 *Endpoint controller*—This controller makes it possible to access the workloads with a static IP and DNS name.
4 *Service account and token controllers*—This creates default accounts and tokens for new namespaces.

Figure 2.2 shows all the elements that comprise a master Node.

Now that you know the parts of a master Node, let's see the parts of a worker Node.

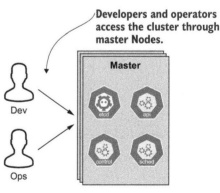

Figure 2.2   Elements of a master Node (kube-apiserver, etcd, scheduler, and controller)

2.1.2   What is a worker Node?

A *worker Node* is the instance where your workloads are deployed and run. Since workloads in Kubernetes are software containers, the container runtime is hosted inside each worker Node.

Each worker Node is composed of the following three elements:

- *kubelet*—This is an agent that ensures containers are running in a Pod.
- *proxy*—This is a network proxy that implements part of the Kubernetes `Service` concept.
- *container runtime*—This is responsible for running containers.

At the time of writing this book, the following runtimes are supported: `Docker`, `containerd`, `crio-o`, and any implementation of the Kubernetes Container Runtime Interface (CRI). Figure 2.3 shows all the elements that compose a worker Node. Now that you have a good understanding of the Kubernetes architecture, let's start using Kubernetes from a developer or operator's point of view.

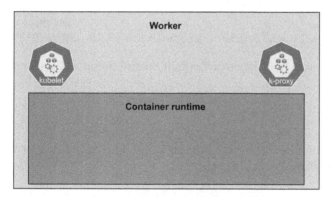

Figure 2.3   Elements of a worker Node

2.2   Deploying workloads in Kubernetes

So far you've seen the architecture of a Kubernetes cluster, but as developers, you will want to deploy a web service, a database, a message broker, or any other element required by your application into Kubernetes. You will explore how a developer can interact with Kubernetes by deploying a simple application that returns a welcome message. Also, you want to be able to configure them externally from the platform or be able to access them using a network protocol.

2.2.1   Deploying a workload

One of the most important Kubernetes resources to deploy a workload to the cluster is a *Pod.* Pods are the smallest deployable unit in Kubernetes, composed of a group of one or more containers. Each container in a Pod shares IP, storage, resources, and lifecycle.

Pods are the units where business workloads are running (e.g., a service API, a database, and a mailing server). An analogy helpful for understanding what a Pod is, is thinking it's a sort of VM (of course it isn't) that runs processes, where each process shares the resources, network, and lifecycle of the VM. In a Pod, it's the same concept, but instead of running processes, it runs containers.

There are many ways to deploy a Pod in a Kubernetes cluster, but one of the most common is describing the deployment in a YAML file and applying it using the kubectl CLI tool. To create a YAML file containing the Pod definition, open a new terminal window, and in a new directory create a file called greeting-pod.yaml, defining the container image that belongs to the Pod, as shown in the following listing.

> **Listing 2.1 Creating a Pod**

```
apiVersion: v1          Sets the file
kind: Pod           ◁── as type Pod
metadata:
  name: greeting-demo     ◁──   Gives a name
spec:                           to the Pod
  containers:
  - name: greeting-demo                          Sets the container
    image: quay.io/lordofthejars/greetings-jvm:1.0.0   ◁──  image to run
```

Once you have created the file, you can apply it to the cluster using the kubectl apply subcommand:

```
kubectl apply -f greeting-pod.yaml
```

> **IMPORTANT** Minikube doesn't require you to authenticate to access the cluster. But depending on the Kubernetes implementation, you may need to authenticate before running this command.

You need to wait until the Pod is allocated into a Node and it is ready to be accessed. To do that, use the kubectl wait subcommand in the terminal:

```
kubectl wait --for=condition=Ready pod/greeting-demo
```

Now validate that the Pod is allocated correctly by getting the Pod's status:

```
kubectl get pods
```

A Pod is allocated into a Node and starts correctly, as the final status is Running.

```
                                        Possible statuses are Pending,
                                        Running, Succeeded, Failed,
NAME            READY   STATUS    RESTARTS   AGE   Unknown, Terminating,
greeting-demo   1/1     Running   0          18s  ◁── ContainerCreating, and Error.
```

Let's do an experiment and delete the Pod you created to see what's happening with its lifecycle:

```
kubectl delete pod greeting-demo
```

Wait a few seconds until the Pod is terminated, and then get the Pod status:

```
kubectl get pods
```

The output (if you've waited enough time) will show you the `greeting-demo` Pod is no longer available:

```
No resources found in default namespace.
```

You can run the `kubectl get pods` as many times as you want, but the Pod will always disappear forever. So a Pod itself might not be useful in most of the cases because if the service dies for any reason, it will become unavailable until you redeploy it again manually.

The process executed when a service dies (or stops) in an unexpected way (e.g., if the Node where it is running is down, the network is down, or an application has a fatal error) is restarting the service to minimize the downtime of the application. Before Kubernetes, the process of restarting the service was done (semi)manually, but with Kubernetes a service running in a Pod is restarted automatically if it is created with a Deployment or ReplicaSet.

2.2.2 *Deployment objects*

Up until now when a Pod has died, it has not restarted automatically; this is the nature of a Pod. If you want to add some resiliency to the Pod lifecycle, so it restarts automatically when there is an error, then you need to create a `ReplicaSet`.

Usually, a ReplicaSet is not created manually but through a `Deployment` resource. A `Deployment` always has a ReplicaSet associated with it, so when a service is deployed using a `Deployment` resource, it explicitly has a ReplicaSet that monitors and restarts a Pod in case of an error, as shown in Figure 2.4.

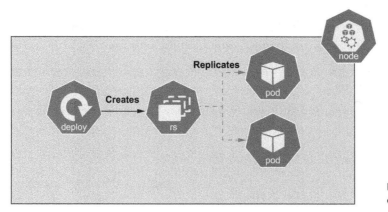

Figure 2.4   Nature of a Deployment

To create a Deployment, create a new file called `greeting-deployment.yaml` in the terminal window opened before. A Deployment file contains more elements than a Pod file. You will need to set the number of Pod replicas required at the time you start. A typical value is `1`, but it could be any other number.

A deployment must also define the container image that belongs to the Pod and the listening port of the container. The Deployment file is shown in the following listing.

Listing 2.2   Creating a deployment

```
apiVersion: apps/v1
kind: Deployment
metadata:
  name: greeting-demo-deployment        ◁──┐ Deployment
spec:                                         name
  replicas: 1
  selector:
    matchLabels:
      app: greeting-demo
  template:
    metadata:
      labels:                          ┌─ Labels set
        app: greeting-demo      ◁──────┘  in the Pod
    spec:                                      ┌─ Containers section, as seen
      containers:      ◁─────────────────────┘  in the Pod definition
      - name: greeting-demo
        image: quay.io/lordofthejars/greetings-jvm:1.0.0
        imagePullPolicy: Always
        ports:
        - containerPort: 8080
```

Once you have created the file, you can apply it to the cluster using the `kubectl apply` subcommand:

```
kubectl apply -f greeting-deployment.yaml
```

You need to wait until the Pod is allocated into a Node and is ready to be accessed. To do that, use the `kubectl wait` subcommand in the terminal:

```
kubectl wait --for=condition=available deployment/greeting-demo-deployment
    --timeout=90s
```

Confirm the Pod is started and allocated correctly by getting the Pod status:

```
kubectl get pods
```

You should get something like the following output:

```
NAME                                            READY   STATUS    RESTARTS   AGE
greeting-demo-deployment-854c4f4f69-xh5v6       1/1     Running   0          18s
```

Run the following command to get the Deployment status:

```
kubectl get deployment
```

The output of a Deployment is slightly different than that of a Pod. In this case, the `available` field is the most important one, as it shows you the number of replicas that are up and running. Since you set replicas to 1 in the example, only one Pod is available through this Deployment:

```
NAME                       READY   UP-TO-DATE   AVAILABLE   AGE
greeting-demo-deployment   1/1     1            1           5m50s
```

Now repeat the previous experiment, and delete the Pod to see what's happening with its lifecycle now. First of all, you need to find the Pod name created in the previous deployment file by running the `kubectl get pods` command:

```
NAME                                        READY   STATUS    RESTARTS   AGE
greeting-demo-deployment-7884dd68c8-4nf6q   1/1     Running   0          14h
```

Get the Pod name, in your case `greeting-demo-deployment-7884dd68c8-4nf6q`, and delete it:

```
kubectl delete pod greeting-demo-deployment-7884dd68c8-4nf6q
```

Wait a few seconds until the Pod is terminated, and get the Pod status:

```
kubectl get pods
```

Now the output is different from the previous section when you only created one Pod. Notice that now there is a new Pod running. You can see that the Pod is new by checking two fields: the name of the Pod, which is different than in the previous case, and the age, which is nearest your time:

```
NAME                                        READY   STATUS    RESTARTS   AGE
greeting-demo-deployment-7884dd68c8-qct8p   1/1     Running   0          13s
```

The Pod has `Deployment` with a `ReplicaSet` associated; therefore, it has been restarted automatically. Now that you know how to deploy your workloads correctly, it is time to see how you can access them.

SERVICES

So far, you've deployed an application to the Kubernetes cluster; however, each Pod that belongs to a Deployment gets its own IP address. Since Pods are, by definition, ephemeral, they are created and destroyed dynamically, and new IP addresses are assigned dynamically as well. Reaching these pods via IP addresses might not be the best choice, as they might be invalid in the future.

A Kubernetes service is the way to expose a set of Pods with a stable DNS name and IP address, which will load balance across them. With the `greeting-demo` Deployment from the previous example done, it is time to create a service, so we can access it.

But before that, we'll introduce the concept of labels in Kubernetes. A *label* is a key–value pair associated with Kubernetes resources with the main purpose of identifying those objects from the user's point of view. For example, you could set a Deployment with a custom label to identify it as a Deployment that belongs to the production environment.

If you look carefully at the previous Deployment, you'll see there is a label defined with the key app and value greeting-demo applied to all Pods created:

```
template:
  metadata:
    labels:
      app: greeting-demo
```

The set of Pods targeted by a Service is usually determined by the labels registered in the Pods. Now you'll expose the Pods created in the previous Deployment using a service that selects the Pods with the app: greeting-demo label.

Create a new file called greeting-service.yaml in the working directory. The service definition should configure the port mapping between containerPort defined in the Deployment (8080) and the exposed port you choose to be exposed by the service. Moreover, you need to define the selector value setting the labels of greeting-demo Pods. The service file should look like the one shown in the following listing.

Listing 2.3   Creating a service

```
apiVersion: v1
kind: Service
metadata:
  name: the-service
spec:
  selector:
    app: greeting-demo
  ports:
    - protocol: TCP
      port: 80
      targetPort: 8080
  type: LoadBalancer
```

Once you have created the file, you can apply it to the cluster using kubectl apply subcommand:

```
kubectl apply -f greeting-service.yaml
```

Since you are using minikube, there will be no external IP to access the service, and the minikube address must be used. You can validate there is no external IP associated with the created service by running the following command in the terminal window:

```
kubectl get services
```

You should see that the external IP of the the-service service remains in Pending status.

```
NAME            TYPE          CLUSTER-IP    EXTERNAL-IP   PORT(S)        AGE
kubernetes      ClusterIP     10.96.0.1     <none>        443/TCP        35d
the-service     LoadBalancer  10.102.78.44  <pending>     80:30951/TCP   4s
```

In the terminal window, run the following command to set the connection values as environment variables to access the service:

```
IP=$(minikube ip)
PORT=$(kubectl get service/the-service -o jsonpath=
⇒"{.spec.ports[*].nodePort}")
```
← **The access port is randomly assigned, not using the exposed port set in your service definition.**

Next you can query the service by using `curl` tool:

```
curl $IP:$PORT/hello
```

The greeting application returns a `Hello World` message as response to the request.

> **IMPORTANT**   In the case of running Kubernetes in a public cloud, an external IP will become a real IP in a few seconds. You can get the external IP value by getting the service configuration:

```
kubectl get services

NAME     TYPE           CLUSTER-IP      EXTERNAL-IP     PORT(S)          AGE
myapp    LoadBalancer   172.30.103.41   34.71.122.153   8080:31974/TCP   44s
```

CLEAN-UP

Before you can jump to the following concept, it is time to delete the application you've deployed in this section. To do that, you can use `kubectl delete` command:

```
kubectl delete -f greeting-deployment.yaml
```

The service deliberately isn't deleted, as you will have a use for it later on.

2.2.3   Volume

A Kubernetes *volume* is a directory containing some data that is accessible to the containers running inside Pods. The physical storage of the volume is determined by the volume type used. For example, the `hostPath` type uses the worker Node file system to store the data, or `nfs` uses the *NFS* (Network File System) to store the data.

Kubernetes volumes is a vast topic, as it is related to persistence storage, and it is outside the scope of this book. You will use volumes in this book but only as a way of mounting ConfigMaps and Secrets. If you are not familiar with these, don't fear; we'll cover them in the following sections.

2.3   Managing application configuration

In the previous sections, you've seen how to deploy an application to a Kubernetes cluster with a welcome message *hardcoded* into the application. In this section, you will set the welcome message of the application externally from a configuration parameter.

2.3.1   ConfigMaps

A *ConfigMap* is a Kubernetes object used to store nonconfidential data in map form. One of the advantages of a ConfigMap is that it lets you externalize environment configuration data from the application code, setting specfic values depending on the cluster, as seen in figure 2.5.

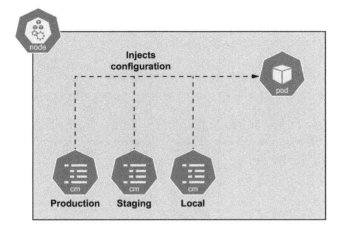

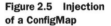

Figure 2.5   Injection of a ConfigMap

The configuration map can be injected into a Pod to be consumed as an environment variable or a volume. The application that has been deployed in the previous sections of this chapter returns a default welcome message (Hello World), but this welcome message is decoupled from the code, so you can set it externally. Listing 2.4 shows the logic in the service that loads the welcome message to get back to the caller.

First of all, the code checks if there is a GREETING_MESSAGE environment variable set. If there isn't one set, then it tries to load a properties file located at /etc/config/conf.properties with the greeting.message key defined inside the file. Otherwise, the default message is returned to the caller.

Listing 2.4   Greeting service

```
final String envGreeting = System.getenv("GREETING_MESSAGE");

if (envGreeting != null) {
  return envGreeting;
}

java.nio.file.Path confFile = Paths.get("/etc/config/conf.properties");
if (Files.exists(confFile)) {

  final Properties confProperties = new Properties();
  confProperties.load(Files.newInputStream(confFile));

  if (confProperties.containsKey("greeting.message")) {
    return confProperties.getProperty("greeting.message");
  }

}

return "Hello World";
```

Let's start configuring the application externally, using a ConfigMap.

ENVIRONMENT VARIABLES

One of the ways to get a value from a ConfigMap is injecting it as an environment variable into the Pod. Then you can get the environment variables in your applications using whatever methods the programming language provides you.

The most important part of a ConfigMap resource is the `data` section. This is the field where you will define the configuration items in the form of key–values. Create a ConfigMap resource named `greeting-config.yaml` with `greeting.message` as the configuration key and `Hello Ada` as configuration value, as shown in the following listing.

Listing 2.5   Creating a ConfigMap

```
apiVersion: v1
kind: ConfigMap
metadata:
  name: greeting-config
data:
  greeting.message: "Hello Ada"
```
**Configuration values set
as key–value properties**

This ConfigMap creates a configuration item with a new welcome message. Apply it like any other Kubernetes resource to the cluster using `kubectl apply`:

```
kubectl apply -f greeting-config.yaml
```

The ConfigMap is created, but it is just a configuration element. You now need to change the previous deployment file, so it gets the configuration from the Config-Map, and inject it inside the container as an environment variable.

Create a new file called `greeting-deployment-configuration.yaml` in the working directory. This Deployment file will look similar to the one you created previously, except it will contain an `env` section, which sets the environment variable (`GREETING_MESSAGE`) to be created inside the Pod. The value of the environment variable is taken from the `greeting-config` configuration map created previously. The file should look like the one shown in the following listing.

Listing 2.6   Creating a deployment with ConfigMaps

```
apiVersion: apps/v1
kind: Deployment
metadata:
  name: greeting-demo-deployment
spec:
  replicas: 1
  selector:
    matchLabels:
      app: greeting-demo
  template:
```

```
metadata:
  labels:
    app: greeting-demo
spec:
  containers:
  - name: greeting-demo
    image: quay.io/lordofthejars/greetings-jvm:1.0.0
    imagePullPolicy: Always
    ports:
    - containerPort: 8080
    env:
    - name: GREETING_MESSAGE        ◁──┐ Defines the name of the
      valueFrom:                        environment variable to use
        configMapKeyRef:                           Sets the name of the
          name: greeting-config   ◁──┘             ConfigMap to use       Sets the key that
          key: greeting.message           ◁──────────────────             will get the value
```

Apply it to the cluster by running the `kubectl apply` command:

```
kubectl apply -f greeting-deployment-configuration.yaml
```

The `GREETING_MESSAGE` environment variable is created inside the `greeting-demo` container, with `Hello Ada` as value. Since your application is aware of this variable, the message sent back is the one configured in the ConfigMap under the `greeting .message` key. Now check it: with `IP` and `PORT` environment variables already set, as explained in section 2.2.2 you can query the service and see the message has been updated to the configured one:

```
curl $IP:$PORT/hello
```

`Hello Ada` is returned as a response, as it is the message configured in the ConfigMap. Now that you've seen how to configure your application using a ConfigMap and injecting the values as environment variables, let's move on to injecting this configuration value as a file.

VOLUME

So far, you've seen that a ConfigMap can be injected as an environment variable, which is a perfect choice when you are moving legacy workloads to Kubernetes, but you can also mount a ConfigMap as a file using volumes. Since the application can be configured using a properties file, you'll write a new properties file inside the container using a ConfigMap and volumes.

Create a ConfigMap resource named greeting-config-properties.yaml in the working directory. To define the properties file, in the `data` section, set the filename required by your application (`conf.properties`) as a key and the content of the properties file embedded as a value. The new Deployment file is shown in the following listing.

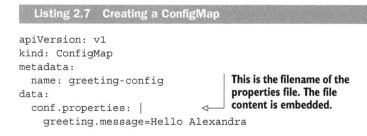

Listing 2.7   Creating a ConfigMap

```
apiVersion: v1
kind: ConfigMap
metadata:
  name: greeting-config
data:
  conf.properties: |
    greeting.message=Hello Alexandra
```

This is the filename of the properties file. The file content is embedded.

Apply it to the cluster by running `kubectl apply` command:

```
kubectl apply -f greeting-config-properties.yaml
```

Now you need to materialize the config.properties file from the ConfigMap to the container. For such a task, you need to define a Kubernetes volume in the container definition and store the content placed in the ConfigMap inside it.

Create a new file named `greeting-deployment-properties.yaml` in the working directory. In the Deployment file, you need to define two big things: the volume configuration and the ConfigMap where content is retrieved.

In the `volumeMounts` section, set the name of the volume (`application-config`) and the directory where the volume is mounted. Your application will read the configuration properties file from /etc/config. The second thing you need to do is link the ConfigMap to the volume, so the configuration file will be created inside the defined volume with a specific name (`conf.properties`) and the content that was defined in the ConfigMap. Figure 2.6 shows the relationship between both elements.

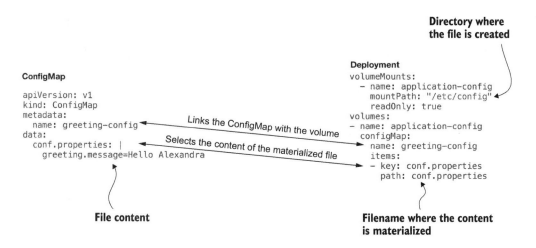

Figure 2.6   Injecting ConfigMaps

The Deployment file injecting configuration in a volume is shown in the following listing.

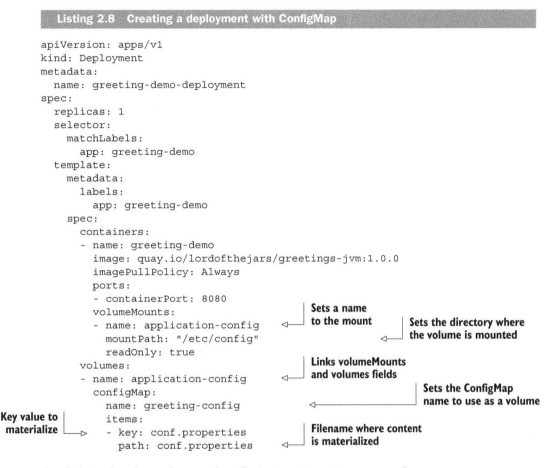

Listing 2.8   Creating a deployment with ConfigMap

```
apiVersion: apps/v1
kind: Deployment
metadata:
  name: greeting-demo-deployment
spec:
  replicas: 1
  selector:
    matchLabels:
      app: greeting-demo
  template:
    metadata:
      labels:
        app: greeting-demo
    spec:
      containers:
      - name: greeting-demo
        image: quay.io/lordofthejars/greetings-jvm:1.0.0
        imagePullPolicy: Always
        ports:
        - containerPort: 8080
        volumeMounts:
        - name: application-config          ⟵  Sets a name to the mount
          mountPath: "/etc/config"          ⟵  Sets the directory where the volume is mounted
          readOnly: true
      volumes:
      - name: application-config            ⟵  Links volumeMounts and volumes fields
        configMap:
          name: greeting-config             ⟵  Sets the ConfigMap name to use as a volume
          items:
          - key: conf.properties            ⟵  Key value to materialize
            path: conf.properties           ⟵  Filename where content is materialized
```

Apply it to the cluster by running the `kubectl apply` command:

```
kubectl apply -f greeting-deployment-properties.yaml
```

The container that is started contains a new file at the /etc/config/conf.properties directory, and the file content is the one embedded in the ConfigMap. Now check that the configured value in the properties file is used by the service. With IP and PORT environment variables already set as explained in section 2.2.2 you can query the service and see that the message has been updated to the configured one:

```
curl $IP:$PORT/hello
```

A `Hello Alexandra` message is returned, as it is the value configured in the Config-Map. You can use both approaches to inject all configuration values from a Config-Map into a container, but what is the best approach? Let's explore some use cases to determine how best to proceed.

THE DIFFERENCES BETWEEN ENVIRONMENT VARIABLES AND VOLUMES

In this section you will explore when to use environment variables and when to use volumes. The *environment variables* approach is usually used when working with a legacy application that can be configured using environment variables and you can't or don't wish to update the source code. The *volumes* approach can be used when working with greenfield applications or applications configured using a file. The configuration process is easier with the volumes approach if the application requires to set multiple configuration properties, as you configure all of them at once in the file. Moreover, the content of a volume is refreshed by Kubernetes if the ConfigMap gets updated. Of course, your application needs to handle this use case and provide a reload configuration capability too. Keep in mind that this sync process does not happen immediately; there is a delay between the change, and the kubelet syncs the change as well as the time to live (TTL) of the ConfigMap cache.

> **TIP** If refreshing the configuration values is a key feature of your application, there is a more deterministic approach you may take: using the Reloader project. `Reloader` is a Kubernetes controller that watches changes in Config-Maps and Secrets and performs rolling upgrades on Pods with their associated `Deployment`, `StatefulSet`, `DaemonSet` and `DeploymentConfig`. It has the advantage that it works in both the environment variables and volumes approaches, and you do not need to update the service source code to handle this use case, as the application is restarted during the rolling update. However, there is the drawback of having to install the `Reloader` controller inside the cluster.

So far, you've seen the first of the two Kubernetes approaches for injecting configuration data into a container. But ConfigMaps content is not secret nor encrypted, as it is in plain text. This means the data has no confidentiality. If you are trying to configure a database URL, port, or database configuration like timeouts, retries, or packet size, you can use ConfigMaps without much concern regarding the security issues. But what about with parameters such as database username, database password, and API key, for which confidentiality is very important? For these parameters, you will need to use the second type of Kubernetes object that can inject configuration data into a container.

2.4   *Using Kubernetes Secrets to store sensitive information*

Let's move the example forward: suppose that after some testing, you decide that the greeting message is sensitive information, and as such you need to store it as a Kubernetes Secret. A *Secret* is a Kubernetes object used to store sensitive or confidential data, like passwords, API keys, SSH keys, and so on. Secrets are similar to ConfigMaps in that both approaches are used to inject configuration properties inside a container; however, the former approach is secure, while the latter is not. They are created in similar manners (with the difference being the `kind` field, which specifies the type of object), and they are similarly exposed inside a container (as environment variables or mounting as a volume). But obviously, there are some differences, which we will explore in the following sections.

2.4.1 Secrets are encoded in Base64

As discussed in chapter 1, one of the big differences between Secrets and ConfigMaps is how data is stored inside `etcd`. Secrets store data in Base64 format; ConfigMaps store data in plain text.

Let's dig deeper into Base64 format. *Base64* is an encoding schema that represents binary and text data in an ASCII string format, converting it into a radix-64 representation. For example, in Base64 format, `Alex` text data is converted to `QWxleA==`. It is very important to keep in mind that Base64 is *not* an encryption method, so any text encoded in Base64 is a masked plain-text.

Now create a Secret containing a greetings message you'd like to keep confidential. The Secret object is similar to the ConfigMap object but contains two possible ways of setting data: `data` and `stringData`. `data` is used when you want to encode configuration values to Base64 manually, while `stringData` lets you set configuration values as unencoded strings that are automatically encoded. Let's create a Secret named `greeting-secret-config.yaml` in the working directory, as shown in the following listing, containing the secret message in the `stringData` field.

Listing 2.9   Creating a Secret

```
apiVersion: v1
kind: Secret
metadata:
  name: greeting-secret
type: Opaque
stringData:
  greeting.message: Hello Anna
```
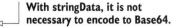
With stringData, it is not necessary to encode to Base64.

Apply it to the cluster by running `kubectl apply` command:

```
kubectl apply -f greeting-secret-config.yaml
```

Now that the Secret has been created, you need to change the deployment file, so it gets the message value from the Secret created in the previous step, and inject it inside the container. In the same way, you can inject configuration properties from ConfigMaps as environment variables or as volumes.

You'll write a deployment file that injects the secret as an environment variable in a similar manner to how you did in the ConfigMap section, but in this case, instead of using the `configMapKeyRef` key, you will use `secretKeyRef`. Create a new file called `greeting-deployment-secret-env.yaml` in the working directory, as shown in the following listing.

Listing 2.10   Creating a deployment with a Secret

```
apiVersion: apps/v1
kind: Deployment
metadata:
  name: greeting-demo-deployment
spec:
  replicas: 1
  selector:
    matchLabels:
      app: greeting-demo
  template:
    metadata:
      labels:
        app: greeting-demo
    spec:
      containers:
      - name: greeting-demo
        image: quay.io/lordofthejars/greetings-jvm:1.0.0
        imagePullPolicy: Always
        ports:
        - containerPort: 8080
        env:
        - name: GREETING_MESSAGE
          valueFrom:
            secretKeyRef:
              name: greeting-secret
              key: greeting.message
```

Defines the name of the environment variable to use

Uses secretKeyRef instead of configMapKeyRef, as it happens with ConfigMaps

Sets the name of the Secret to be used

Sets the key that will get the value

Apply it to the cluster by running the `kubectl apply` command:

```
kubectl apply -f greeting-deployment-secret-env.yaml
```

Now check that the secret value is used by the service when a request is sent. With `IP` and `PORT` environment variables already set in the terminal, as explained in section 2.2.2, you can query the service and see that the message has been updated to the configured one:

```
curl $IP:$PORT/hello
```

`Hello Anna` is returned, since it is the value of the secret you configured for this application. Of course, don't do this in production; a secret is something you should never expose in the public API, but for this exercise, we thought it was a good way to show how secrets work. You can also inject a secret as a volume, in a similar way as you did with ConfigMaps.

In this case, the `items` field is not specified; hence all the keys defined in the Secret object are mounted automatically. Since the key of the mounted directory is `greeting.message`, a file named `greeting.message` is created at the configured volume with `Hello Anna` as the data content.

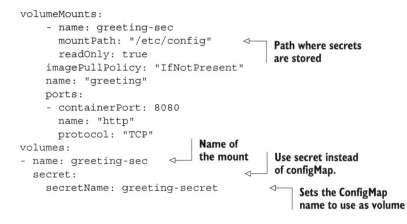

```
volumeMounts:
  - name: greeting-sec
    mountPath: "/etc/config"        ◁──┐ Path where secrets
    readOnly: true                      │ are stored
  imagePullPolicy: "IfNotPresent"
  name: "greeting"
  ports:
  - containerPort: 8080
    name: "http"
    protocol: "TCP"
volumes:                       ┌── Name of
- name: greeting-sec   ◁───┘   the mount    ┌── Use secret instead
  secret:                          ◁─────┘ of configMap.
    secretName: greeting-secret        ◁──┐ Sets the ConfigMap
                                           │ name to use as volume
```

Now you know the basics of secrets, the difference between ConfigMaps and Secrets, and how to inject them into a container. But this is the basic stuff; there are still many things you need to do before you can say your application is managing the secrets correctly.

As a reader you might be wondering, "Why is a Secret named *Secret* if it is not really secret at all? It is not encrypted; it's just encoded in Base64." That is a fair question, but keep reading to the end of this chapter to fully understand the reasoning behind it.

2.4.2   *Secrets are mounted in a temporary file system*

A Secret is only sent to a Node if there is a Pod that requires it. But what's important is that a Secret, even though it is mounted as a volume, is never written to disk but in-memory using the `tmpfs` file system. `tmpfs` stands for *temporal filesystem*, and as its name suggests, it is a file system, where data is stored in volatile memory instead of persistent storage. When the Pod containing the Secret is deleted, the kubelet is responsible for deleting it from memory as well.

2.4.3   *Secrets can be encrypted at rest*

Data at rest is the term for data persisted that is infrequently accessed. The configuration properties fall in this category (Secrets are configuration properties too), as they are usually stored in files and accessed once at boot-up time to be loaded into the application. *Encryption* is the process of converting plain text data into ciphertext. After the text is ciphered, only authorized parties can decipher the data back to plain text. *Encryption data at rest* then is the process of encrypting sensitive data at rest.

Among other things, all data from ConfigMaps and Secrets is stored inside `etcd` and is unencrypted by default. Notice that all these elements are data at rest, and some should be protected. Kubernetes supports encryption at rest by ciphering secret objects in `etcd`, adding a new level of protection against attackers. We know this has been a really quick introduction to this topic, but we will explore it in greater depth in chapter 4, as this is an important concept for secrets and Kubernetes.

2.4.4   *Risks*

You may think that by using Kubernetes Secrets, you are managing your secrets correctly, but you are not. Let's enumerate all the possible security breaches a hypothetical attacker could exploit to steal your secrets.

IS IT MORE SECURE TO INJECT SECRETS AS ENVIRONMENT VARIABLES OR AS VOLUMES?

Maybe you're wondering whether it's best to inject a Secret as an environment variable or as a volume. Intuitively, you might think injecting as a volume is safer than as an environment variable because if an attacker were to gain access to the Pod, listing an environment variable would be easier than searching through the whole file system to try to find the secret files. And that's a fair point, but the following example will show how, in terms of security, when there is unwanted access to the Pod, both environment variables and volumes offer a similar level of security.

Let's suppose an attacker gains access to a running Pod, and the Secrets are injected as environment variables. The attacker could list all environment variables by running the `export` command in a shell:

```
export

declare -x GREETING_MESSAGE="Hello Anna"        ⟵┐ The Secret
declare -x HOME="/"                                is compromised.
declare -x HOSTNAME="greeting-demo-deployment-5664ffb8c6-2pstn"
...
```

The attacker would easily be able to figure out the values of your secrets.

The other option is using volumes. Since any arbitrary directory can be mounted, you may think you are safe because an attacker should need to know where the volume is mounted. Well yes, that's true, but sadly there is a way to find that easily.

If the attacker gains access to a running Pod with Secrets mounted as a volume, they could list all the mounted file systems by running the `mount` command in a shell:

```
mount | grep tmpfs

tmpfs on /dev type tmpfs (rw,nosuid,size=65536k,mode=755)
tmpfs on /sys/fs/cgroup type tmpfs (ro,nosuid,nodev,noexec,relatime,mode=755)
tmpfs on /etc/sec type tmpfs (ro,relatime) /      ⟵┐ Volume mount
...                                                  with Secrets

ls /etc/sec        ⟵┐ Lists the
                      Secret's keys
greeting.message

cat /etc/sec/greeting.message       ⟵┐ Prints the
                                       Secret's value
Hello Anna
```

There is no perfect solution. One of the advantages of using volumes instead of environment variables is that some applications might log the current environment variables at boot-up time, which, at the same time, can be sent to a central logging system, meaning any security breach in the logging system will expose the secret value.

Is securing Kubernetes Secrets a hopeless task? Of course not. First you need to calibrate the chances of an attacker getting access to your Pods, Nodes, and infrastructure. Second there are some actions that you can apply to limit access to a Pod—for example, removing rights for executing kubectl exec or kubectl attach.

SECRETS ARE STORED IN ETCD

As you read in section 2.1.1, etcd is a key–value database where all Kubernetes objects are stored, and of course, ConfigMaps and Secrets are no exceptions. The process when a Secret is created is as follows:

1 A developer or operator creates a new Secret resource and communicates with Kubernetes API service to apply it (kubectl apply -f …).
2 The Kubernetes API service processes the resource and inserts the Secret inside etcd, under the /registry/secrets/<namespace>/<secret-name> key.

This process is shown in figure 2.7.

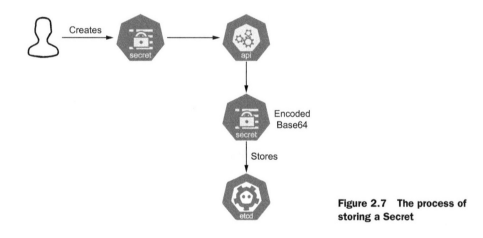

Figure 2.7   **The process of storing a Secret**

etcd is, after all, a database. Therefore you need to take some aspects into consideration:

- Access to etcd must be restricted to admin users. If it isn't, etcd could be queried by anyone to get the Secrets.
- The contents of the etcd database are persisted to disk. Since Secrets are not encrypted by default, anyone with access to the disk can read the etcd content.
- Performing disk backups is a normal operation, but be aware of what's happening with backups, as they contain sensitive information that is not encrypted by default.

- etcd is an external service that is accessed by the Kubernetes API server using the network. Make sure to use SSL/TLS for peer-to-peer communication with etcd (*data in transit*).

BASE64 IS NOT ENCRYPTION

To reiterate once again, as it can be a cause of misinterpretation, Base64 is not an encryption method but an encoding method. It is important to remember that Secrets are not encrypted by default, and you need to enable the Encryption Data at Rest feature to store your Secrets encrypted into etcd. This will be covered in greater detail in chapter 4.

ACCESSING PODS

As you've seen before, if an attacker gets access to the Pod, it is relatively easy to steal Secrets, even if you are using environment variables or volumes. There is another type of attack, related to this one, you should prepare for: an attacker who can create a Pod can injecting and reading Secrets. In chapter 5, we'll discuss preventing this kind of attack.

SECRETS AT SOURCE CODE REPOSITORIES

A Secret can be created using the kubectl CLI tool.

```
kubectl create secret generic greeting-secret \
              --from-literal=greeting.message=Hello
```

Most of the time, you configure the Secret via a file (either a JSON or YAML), which might have the secret data encoded in Base64 and not ciphered. There are some risks associated with this approach, as Secrets can be compromised in the following situations:

- Sharing the file in an insecure way (e.g., email)
- Committing the file into the source repository
- Losing the file
- Backing up the file without any security

ROOT PERMISSIONS

Anyone with root permission on any Node can read any secret from the API server by impersonating the kubelet. You also need to take care of the infrastructure (worker nodes) to avoid a direct attack from the operating system.

You've finished implementing a basic strategy for dealing with secrets and Kubernetes, but your work with secrets isn't complete, as you've yet to tackle most of the risks you've identified in this section. Let's start from the ground up; chapter 3 discusses managing secrets from the beginning, which is how to create and manage the Kubernetes resource file following the best security principles. Stick around because things are about to get interesting.

Summary

- A Kubernetes cluster is composed of master and, optionally, worker Nodes.
- Any Kubernetes resource and current status of the cluster is stored at the `etcd` instance.
- We discussed deploying an application to Kubernetes.
- We covered configuring an application externally with ConfigMaps, either as an environment variable or as a file.
- Secrets are not so different from ConfigMaps in terms of construction and usage.

Part 2

Managing Secrets

Now that you have a basic understanding of Secrets and Kubernetes, part 2 focuses on the ways these assets can be managed and how they can be applied in the context of a Kubernetes cluster.

Chapter 3 provides an overview of different approaches to storing Kubernetes Secrets securely at rest, including supporting tooling to assist in the process. Chapter 4 focuses on storing secrets securely inside a Kubernetes cluster, including the capabilities at an infrastructure level to support encryption. Chapter 5 introduces a secrets management tool for storing and managing sensitive assets. Finally, in chapter 6, the concepts from the prior chapter are expanded to integrate cloud secrets stores.

Securely storing Secrets

3

This chapter covers

- Capturing Kubernetes manifests to store in version control systems
- Enabling secure secret storage at rest
- Using Kubernetes Operators to manage Kubernetes resources, including Secrets
- Incorporating security considerations into Kubernetes package managers
- Implementing key rotation to improve your security posture

Chapter 2 provided an overview of the key architectural components of a Kubernetes environment as well as the way workloads are deployed and methods for injecting configurations via ConfigMaps and Secrets. But once resources have been added to a Kubernetes cluster, how are they managed? What happens if they were inadvertently removed? It becomes increasingly important for them to be captured and stored for potential later use. However, when working with resources that may contain sensitive information, careful thought and considerations must be taken into account. This chapter introduces tools and approaches that can be used to store Kubernetes Secrets securely at rest and illustrates the benefits of declaratively defining Kubernetes resources.

3.1   *Storing Kubernetes manifests at rest*

One of the benefits of cloud-native technologies is that resources can be built, deployed, and configured on demand. With only a few clicks of a mouse or keystrokes, entire architectures can be constructed with minimal effort. If you are just getting started with Kubernetes, excitement blossoms as you realize just how easy it is to build complex applications. You may even feel driven to show a parent, friend, or co-worker. But as you demonstrate your work, you may be asked how it can be replicated. It is at that point that it becomes crucial for each Kubernetes resource, including those that contain sensitive values, to be properly managed and stored for later use.

In chapter 2, we covered the two primary methods for creating resources in a Kubernetes environment:

1. Using the Kubernetes CLI (kubectl), translating inputs provided via command line arguments.
2. Explicitly stating the configuration of resources using a YAML or JSON formatted file.

The former, in which the Kubernetes CLI provides the translation for you, is known as the *imperative method*. For example, when you used the `kubectl create secret` subcommand to create the secret for your deployment in the last chapter, the Kubernetes CLI determined how to interpret the input you provided and send a request to the Kubernetes API to create the secret. While this approach simplifies the initial setup and configuration of resources, it also poses challenges into their long-term supportability. The `kubectl create secret` command is not idempotent, and rerunning it a second time will result in an error. This can be seen by executing the following, which will attempt to create a secret called `greeting-secret` and will result in an error, as a secret with the same name in the `default` namespace you created in chapter 2 already exists:

```
kubectl create secret generic greeting-secret -n default \
  --from-literal=greeting.message=Hello

Error from server (AlreadyExists): secrets "greeting-secret" already exists
```

> **NOTE** If no secret was already present in the `default` namespace, running this command a second time will result in a similar error.

Now instead of using the imperative approach, resources can be represented explicitly in either YAML or JSON format and applied to the cluster using the `kubectl` tool. This approach is known as *declarative configuration* and has benefits to support the long-term lifecycle of resources within a Kubernetes environment.

Declarative configuration is a key trait of a concept that has gained popularity over the last few years: infrastructure as code (IaC). Instead of manually configuring resources or using random scripts, the configurations applied to infrastructure or applications are explicitly defined, which results in the following benefits:

- Reduction of errors
- Repeatability
- Auditing and tracking

The ability to audit and track these configurations is made possible especially when storing manifests in a version control system (VCS), such as Git. Once resources have been captured, their life span, including what and who changed them, can be appropriately tracked. So if a disaster occurred, instead of having to determine what the state of the Kubernetes cluster was at that point, the manifests that have been previously captured and stored can be reapplied, resulting in minimal downtime and effort.

3.1.1 Capturing resources for declarative configuration

When adopting a declarative-based configuration or transitioning from a primarily imperative based approach, there are multiple strategies for capturing the manifests (figure 3.1). Recall that the end result will be a series of YAML or JSON files. While both file types can be applied to a Kubernetes cluster using the kubectl command line tool, YAML-based files are preferred due to their readability.

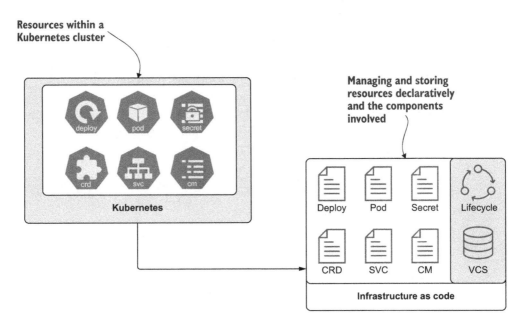

Figure 3.1 Capturing Kubernetes resources as infrastructure as code (IaC)

Two common scenarios can be used to capture manifests for storage in a declarative fashion:

1. Capturing the output from an invocation of `kubectl` imperative commands.
2. Capturing the output of resources already present within a Kubernetes environment.

CAPTURING KUBECTL IMPERATIVE COMMANDS

To aid in the storage of manifests in a declarative fashion, the Kubernetes CLI provides two helpful flags that can be added when invoking imperative commands, such as `kubectl create secret`.

- `--dry-run`—Simulating how resources would be applied to the Kubernetes environment. Kubernetes versions older than 1.18 did not require the use of a parameter, such as `client`, as APIServer dry-run was refactored in newer versions.
- `-o`—Outputting the result of the command in a number of formats, including YAML.

Adding these flags to the imperative secret creation command will output the representation of what would be sent to the Kubernetes cluster without any changes being made to the actual state of the cluster.

```
kubectl create secret generic greeting-secret -n default \
  --from-literal=greeting.message=Hello --dry-run=client -o yaml
```

CAPTURING DEPLOYED RESOURCES

There is still tremendous value to the imperative capabilities of the Kubernetes CLI. It is common to combine imperative invocations and manual configurations in the development process while the details of each resource are tested and validated. Once the configuration is in place, it is recommended to capture these assets, so they can be stored in a version control system to align with IaC principles.

The current state of resources can be queried using the `kubectl get` subcommand. In a similar fashion shown in listing 3.1, the command can be output in a variety of formats. Execute the following command to display the contents of the `greeting-secret` created in chapter 2.

Listing 3.1 `greeting-secret` **secret**

```
kubectl get secrets greeting-secret -o yaml

apiVersion: v1
data:
  greeting.message: SGVsbG8=        ⟵  Base64 encoded value of the
kind: Secret                             literal that was instantiated
metadata:                                when the secret was created
  creationTimestamp: "2020-12-25T00:22:44Z"
  managedFields:
  - apiVersion: v1
    fieldsType: FieldsV1
```

```
    fieldsV1:
      f:data:
        .: {}
        f:greeting.message: {}
      f:type: {}
    manager: kubectl-create
    operation: Update
    time: "2020-12-25T00:22:44Z"
  name: greeting-secret
  namespace: default
  resourceVersion: "27935"
  selfLink: /api/v1/namespaces/k8s-secrets/secrets/greeting-secret
  uid: b6e87686-f4e6-454d-b391-aef37a99076e
type: Opaque
```

As you may notice in the output, there are fields, including `status`, and several fields within `metadata` (`uid`, `resourceVersion`, and `creationTimestamp`, just to name a few) with runtime details from current cluster. These properties are not suitable for storage and should be removed. They can be removed manually or using a tool, such as `yq`—a lightweight YAML processor. An example of removing runtime properties using `yq` is shown in the following listing.

Listing 3.2 Outputting the content of the secret to a file

```
kubectl get secrets greeting-secret -o yaml | \
  yq e 'del(.metadata.namespace)' - | \
  yq e 'del(.metadata.selfLink)' - | \
  yq e 'del(.metadata.uid)' - | \
  yq e 'del(.metadata.resourceVersion)' - | \
  yq e 'del(.metadata.generation)' - | \
  yq e 'del(.metadata.creationTimestamp)' - | \
  yq e 'del(.deletionTimestamp)' - | \
  yq e 'del(.metadata.deletionGracePeriodSeconds)' - | \
  yq e 'del(.metadata.ownerReferences)' - | \
  yq e 'del(.metadata.finalizers)' - | \
  yq e 'del(.metadata.clusterName)' - | \
  yq e 'del(.metadata.managedFields)' - | \
  yq e 'del(.status)' -
```

An overview of how to install the `yq` tool on your machine can be found in appendix B. The output from the prior command can be redirected to a file to enable the storage for versioning within a version control system:

```
kubectl get secrets greeting-secret -o yaml | \
  yq e 'del(.metadata.namespace)' - | \
  yq e 'del(.metadata.selfLink)' - | \
  yq e 'del(.metadata.uid)' - | \
  yq e 'del(.metadata.resourceVersion)' - | \
  yq e 'del(.metadata.generation)' - | \
  yq e 'del(.metadata.creationTimestamp)' - | \
  yq e 'del(.deletionTimestamp)' - | \
  yq e 'del(.metadata.deletionGracePeriodSeconds)' - | \
```

```
yq e 'del(.metadata.ownerReferences)' - | \
yq e 'del(.metadata.finalizers)' - | \
yq e 'del(.metadata.clusterName)' - | \
yq e 'del(.metadata.managedFields)' - | \
yq e 'del(.status)' - \
> greeting-secret.yaml
```

With resources now being described in a declarative manner and eligible to be tracked and visible in version control systems, it becomes even more important for protections to be made to ensure the values cannot be easily determined. Since Secrets are merely Base64 encoded, it is crucial for additional mechanisms to be employed to obstruct the ability to ascertain their values. The remainder of this chapter will introduce and demonstrate tools that can be used to secure Secrets at rest.

3.2 *Tools for securely storing Kubernetes resources*

While the Kubernetes CLI does not offer any additional native capabilities for securing manifests for storage, the popularity of Kubernetes has afforded integration with other cloud-native tools to help solve this challenge. These tools include those that already have the functionality to secure manifests at rest as well as solutions that have been specifically developed for this purpose in a Kubernetes context. As a consumer of Kubernetes, you may be tasked with managing resources that are either focused on the underlying infrastructure or the applications that are deployed within the platform—or maybe both. The tool you will ultimately use depends on your use case. Understanding which tools are available and how they can be used will help you make an informed decision to select the appropriate tool for your specific task.

3.2.1 *Ansible Vault*

A typical deployment of Kubernetes (not including minikube) will need considerations for both infrastructure and application components. These include the physical and virtual resources to support the control plane and worker nodes as well as the configuration of Kubernetes manifests. Configuration management tools are well positioned for this space, as they not only an manage the sometimes complex configurations associated with Kubernetes environments, but they help illustrate and implement IaC concepts.

Ansible is a popular configuration management tool that can be used to manage various aspects of the Kubernetes ecosystem. One of the key benefits of Ansible compared to other comparable tools is that it is well suited for cloud environments, as it is *agentless* (i.e., it does not require a central management server) and communicates via Secure Shell (SSH), a common communication protocol. All you need is the tool on your local machine, and you can get right to work!

INSTALLING ANSIBLE

Ansible is a Python based tool and, as such, is the only prerequisite and can be installed on a variety of operating systems. Given the instructions vary depending on the target operating system, refer to the official documentation (http://mng.bz/2rew) on installing Ansible for your machine.

ANSIBLE 101

Ansible organizes automation directives in a series of YAML files. Directives describing the configurations to be applied to targets are organized into Playbooks, which declare the hosts that configurations should be applied to along with a series of tasks that define the desired state of each target machine. For example, a simple playbook could enforce all Linux machines to have a message of the day (MOTD) presented to all users when they log in. An example Playbook is shown in the following.

Listing 3.3 An example Ansible Playbook

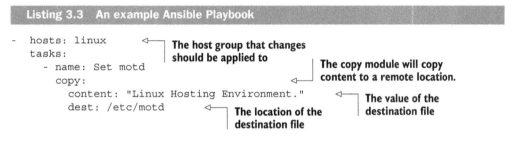

```
-  hosts: linux          The host group that changes
   tasks:                 should be applied to
     - name: Set motd                         The copy module will copy
       copy:                                  content to a remote location.
         content: "Linux Hosting Environment."      The value of the
         dest: /etc/motd        The location of the   destination file
                                destination file
```

Target instances are organized into groups and declared within inventory files; they define how Ansible facilitates the connection, along with any variables that are used during Playbook invocation. Playbooks are then invoked using the `ansible-playbook` command, which will perform the execution of the automation:

```
ansible-playbook <playbook_file>
```

ANSIBLE AND KUBERNETES

Ansible's *bread and butter* is the management and configuration of infrastructure. As the popularity of Kubernetes continues to grow, it is becoming a key component in the infrastructure of many organizations, and as such, integrations between Ansible and Kubernetes are available.

A useful capability of this integration is managing Kubernetes resources, which is achieved using the `k8s` module. Modules are reusable scripts that can be included in Playbooks. In the previous MOTD example, the `copy` module was used to copy content from the local machine to the remote target.

Now you will create an Ansible Playbook to manage the configuration of your Kubernetes cluster by using the `greeting-secret` you already have available on the local machine. Before you begin, prepare your working environment. First, make a copy of the `greeting-secret.yaml` file on your machine and create a new file called `greeting-secret_ansible.yaml`:

```
cp greeting-secret.yaml greeting-secret_ansible.yaml
```

Next create a namespace called `kubernetes-secrets-ansible` to use for this scenario:

```
kubectl create namespace kubernetes-secrets-ansible
```

Next change the namespace preference for your kubectl client to target the newly created namespace:

```
kubectl config set-context --current --namespace=kubernetes-secrets-ansible
```

> **NOTE** When setting the namespace preference, all subsequent commands will query against the targeted namespace.

Now within the same directory that the file `greeting-secret_ansible.yaml` is located, create a new file called `k8s-secret-mgmt.yaml`, with the following content to contain the Playbook.

Listing 3.4 k8s-secret-mgmt.yaml

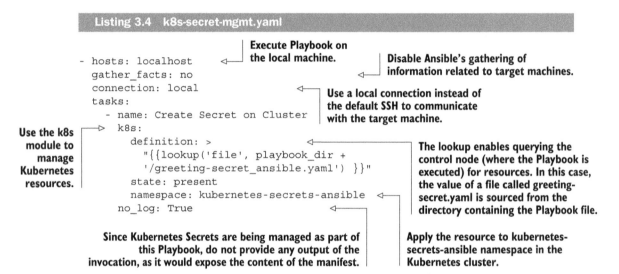

By default, the `k8s` module uses the `kubeconfig` file from the local machine to determine the method of communicating with the Kubernetes cluster. Since you were already authenticated to the minikube instance, this is already taken care of.

Before executing the Playbook, the `openshift` python module must be installed for Ansible to be able to communicate with the Kubernetes cluster. OpenShift is a distribution of Kubernetes, and the `k8s` Ansible module requires the `openshift` module prior to execution. This can be accomplished using pip, which, depending on your operating system, may have been how Ansible itself was installed. If pip is not currently installed, instructions on its installation can be found in appendix C. Add the `openshift` Python module by executing the following command:

```
pip install openshift
```

With the necessary dependencies installed, run the Playbook:

```
ansible-playbook k8s-secret-mgmt.yaml
```

```
[WARNING]: No inventory was parsed, only implicit localhost is available
[WARNING]: provided hosts list is empty, only localhost is available.
➥Note that the implicit localhost does not match 'all'
```

```
PLAY [localhost] ****************************************************************
********************************************************************************
***********************
TASK [Create Secret on Cluster] ************************************************
********************************************************************************
***********************
changed: [localhost]

PLAY RECAP *********************************************************************
********************************************************************************
***********************
localhost                  : ok=1   changed=1   unreachable=0   failed=0
    skipped=0   rescued=0   ignored=0
```

> **NOTE** You can safely ignore the warnings as they do not affect the execution of the Playbook.

As emphasized in the output, the Playbook ran successfully with the secret defined locally, which is now present on the Kubernetes cluster in the `kubernetes-secrets-ansible` namespace. This can be confirmed by running `kubectl get secrets greeting-secret`.

ANSIBLE VAULT

As you might imagine, configuration management tools, such as Ansible, face the same challenges with managing sensitive values. When creating the Ansible Playbook in the prior section, the secret being sourced from the `greeting-secret_ansible.yaml` file contains the Base64 encoded value, and the values are ultimately susceptible to being decoded. Fortunately, Ansible provides the capabilities aid in this situation by enabling the encryption of files that can be decoded at runtime via Ansible Vault.

Ansible Vault allows variables and files to be protected, so they can be safely stored. Unlike Kubernetes Secrets, Ansible Vault uses encryption—not encoding—to avoid being easily reverse engineered (figure 3.2).

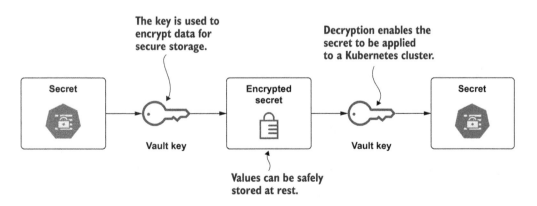

Figure 3.2 The encryption and decryption process using Ansible Vault

As of Ansible 2.10, Ansible Vault only supports `AES256` as the cipher algorithm for encrypting sensitive material. To encrypt the content of the `greeting-secret_ansible.yaml` file containing the secret with sensitive values, use the `ansible-value encrypt` command. You will be prompted to provide a password that can be used to encrypt and decrypt the contents of the encrypted password:

```
ansible-vault encrypt greeting-secret_ansible.yaml

New Vault password:
Confirm New Vault password:
Encryption successful
```

Once the file has been encrypted by Ansible Vault, the resulting file takes the following form.

Listing 3.5   greeting-secret_ansible.yaml

```
$ANSIBLE_VAULT;1.1;AES256
<ENCRYPTED_CONTENT>
```

The result is a UTF-8-encoded file that contains a new line-terminated header followed by the encrypted contents. The header contains up to four elements:

- The format ID (currently only supports `$ANSIBLE_VAULT`)
- The vault format version
- The cypher algorithm
- The vault ID label (not used in this example)

The payload of the file is a concatenation of the ciphertext and a SHA256 digest, as a result of the `hexlify()` method of the Python `binascii` module. The specific details will not be described here, but they are explained thoroughly in the Ansible Vault documentation (http://mng.bz/19rR).

Once a file has been encrypted using Ansible Vault, the `--ask-vault-password` or `--vault-password-file` must be provided when calling the `ansible-playbook` command. To make use of the `--vault-password-file` flag, the password must be provided as the content within the referenced file.

> **TIP** Instead of providing a flag to the `ansible-playbook` command, the location of the Vault password file can be provided by the `ANSIBLE_VAULT_PASSWORD_FILE` environment variable.

Run the Playbook, and add the `--ask-vault-pass` flag, which will prompt for the Vault password to be provided. When prompted, enter the password and press Enter. If the appropriate password was provided, the Playbook will execute successfully.

```
ansible-playbook k8s-secret-mgmt.yaml --ask-vault-pass
Vault password:
[WARNING]: No inventory was parsed, only implicit localhost is available
```

```
[WARNING]: provided hosts list is empty, only localhost is available.
➥Note that the implicit localhost does not match 'all'

PLAY [localhost] **********************************************************
***************************************************************************
***********************
TASK [Create Secret on Cluster] *******************************************
***************************************************************************
***********************
ok: [localhost]

PLAY RECAP ****************************************************************
***************************************************************************
***********************
localhost                  : ok=1    changed=0    unreachable=0    failed=0
    skipped=0    rescued=0    ignored=0
```

If an incorrect value was provided, a message like the following will appear:

```
TASK [Create Secret on Cluster] *******************************************
***************************************************************************
***********************
fatal: [localhost]: FAILED! => {"censored": "the output has been hidden
➥due to the fact that 'no_log: true' was specified for this result"}
```

Since you specified no_log in the task, a more descriptive error will not be provided. To investigate further, you may temporarily comment out no_log to ascertain the ultimate cause of the failure.

By using Ansible Vault to encrypt the contents of the Kubernetes Secret in the greeting-secret_ansible.yaml file, the Playbook and encrypted file can be safely stored in a version control system.

Ansible Vault illustrates how one can manage encrypting and decrypting Kubernetes resources from a client-side perspective. The next section will introduce transitioning the responsibilities to components running within the Kubernetes cluster instead.

3.3 *Kubernetes Operators*

While Ansible Vault satisfies the need to securely store sensitive Kubernetes assets, there are several areas that could be improved upon:

- Those executing the Ansible automation are given the password to decrypt sensitive assets.
- Decryption occurs on the client side. Any sensitive assets are transmitted either in their cleartext value or with a Kubernetes Secret and, thus, are Base64 encoded.

An alternate strategy is leveraging a model where the decryption process occurs completely within the Kubernetes cluster, abstracting the end user or automation process from managing sensitive material as resources are applied. This is the approach implemented by the Sealed Secrets project, where decryption is managed via an operator running within the cluster.

Recall from chapter 2 that a key component of master nodes is that they contain controllers, which are aptly named, as they implement a nonterminating control loop to manage and monitor the desired state of at least one resource within the cluster. When changes to the targeted resource occur, the controller will ensure the state of the cluster matches the desired state.

One of the most common controllers end users are familiar with is a ReplicaSet controller. Deployments are a common method for registering workloads into Kubernetes, and a ReplicaSet is generated automatically whenever a Deployment is created. The ReplicaSet controller will monitor pods associated with the ReplicaSet and ensure the number of active Pods matches the desired state, as defined within the ReplicaSet.

3.3.1   *Custom resource definitions (CRDs)*

Historically, Kubernetes had a fairly small number of resources, such as Pods and Secrets. As the popularity of the platform grew, so did the desire for new resource types, both from core maintainers as well as from users. As any developer can attest to, changes to core APIs are typically a challenging and drawn-out process.

Custom resource definitions (CRDs), a new resource type, were a solution to this issue, as they provided developers the opportunity to register their own APIs and properties associated with these resources, while being able to take advantage of the functionality within the API server without interfering with the core set of APIs. For example, a new resource called `CronTabs` could be defined with the goal of executing tasks at a particular scheduled point in time. An application could be developed to query the API Kubernetes for `CronTabs` resources and execute any of the desired business logic. However, instead of routinely querying the API, what if you could perform many of the same capabilities of the included set of controllers, such as immediately being able to react to state changes, as in the creation or modification of a resource? Fortunately, client libraries and, in particular, client-go for the Go programming language provide these capabilities.

This concept of developing an application to monitor a custom resource and take action against it is known as an *operator*, and this pattern has been widely adopted within the Kubernetes community; it is even implemented by the Sealed Secrets project. The process for developing operators and custom controllers was once a large feat, as developers needed to have intimate knowledge of Kubernetes internals. Fortunately, tools, such as kubebuilder and the Operator Framework have simplified this process (figure 3.3).

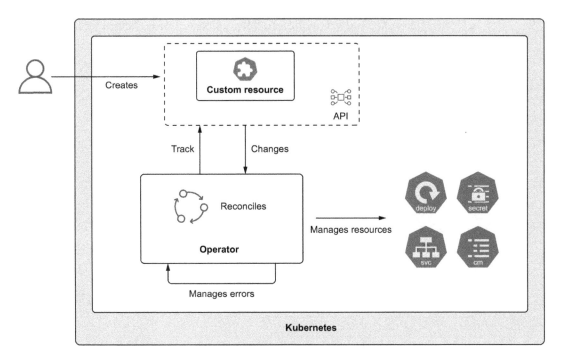

Figure 3.3   An overview of how operators manage resources in Kubernetes

3.3.2   *Sealed Secrets*

Given that the majority of the Sealed Secrets solutions are offloaded to the controller or operator, what actions does it perform? Sealed Secrets contains three distinct components:

- The operator or controller
- A CLI tool called *kubeseal*, which is used by the end user to encrypt Kubernetes Secrets
- A CRD called `SealedSecret`

After the CRD is added to the cluster and the controller is deployed to a namespace, the controller will create a new 4096-bit RSA public–private key pair if one does not exist, which will be saved as a secret within the same namespace the controller is deployed within.

End users use the kubeseal tool to convert a standard Kubernetes Secret into a `SealedSecret` resource. The encryption process takes each value within the Kubernetes Secret and performs the following actions (figure 3.4):

1   The value is symmetrically encrypted with a randomly-generated one-time-use 32-bit session key.

2 The session key is then asymmetrically encrypted with the public key created by the controllers' previously generated public certificate, using Optimal Asymmetric Encryption Padding (RSA-OAEP).

3 The result is stored within the `SealedSecret` resource.

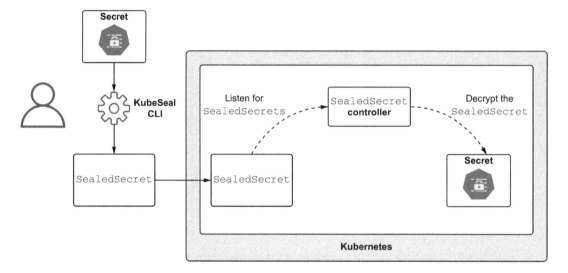

Figure 3.4   The processes and components involved in encrypting and decrypting a secret using the Sealed Secrets project

NOTE   A more detailed overview of the encryption and decryption in use can be found on the Sealed Secret project homepage: https://github.com/bitnami-labs/sealed-secrets.

INSTALLING SEALED SECRETS

The first step of installing Sealed Secrets is deploying the controller to the cluster. While multiple methods are supported, installation via the raw Kubernetes manifests will be used here.

For the purpose of this book, version `v0.13.1` will be used, and steps related to the installation of the controller and associated kubeseal command line tool can be found on the release page within the project repository (http://mng.bz/PoP5).

Similar to the steps you completed in the prior action covering Ansible Vault, create a new namespace called `kubernetes-secrets-sealedsecrets`, and set the namespace preference to target this namespace:

```
kubectl create namespace kubernetes-secrets-sealedsecrets
kubectl config set-context --current \
  --namespace=kubernetes-secrets-sealedsecrets
```

Add the controller to the Kubernetes cluster by executing the following command:

```
kubectl apply -f https://github.com/bitnami-labs/sealed-secrets/releases/
➥download/v0.13.1/controller.yaml
```

By default, the controller is installed into the `kube-system` namespace. Confirm the controller has been deployed successfully by listing the running pods within the `kube-system` namespace:

```
kubectl get pods -n kube-system -l=name=sealed-secrets-controller

NAME                                         READY   STATUS    RESTARTS   AGE
sealed-secrets-controller-5b54cbfb5f-4gz9j   1/1     Running   0          3m43s
```

Next install the kubeseal command line tool. The binary releases along with installation steps can be found on the release page previously referenced in this section. Be sure to follow the steps detailed for your operating system. Once kubeseal has been installed, confirm the CLI has been installed properly and can obtain the public certificate generated by the controller, enabling you to encrypt secrets:

```
kubeseal --fetch-cert
```

◁── **--fetch-cert obtains the current public key certificate.**

```
-----BEGIN CERTIFICATE-----
MIIErjCCApagAwIBAgIRAIOgwJnDRCIcZon5GumMT8UwDQYJKoZIhvcNAQELBQAw
ADAeFw0yMDEyMjgxNjI3MDhaFw0zMDEyMjYxNjI3MDhaMAAwggIiMA0GCSqGSIb3
DQEBAQUAA4ICDwAwggIKAoICAQDosr3qLBJ4YQRiKvQgkQgMN+sCp2mQo8vJbj8z
rOaINXdkD6isHqq80uJ0uJ6ZigFpDmoyOUVlHbkprlngu6d41fBpEW0caREZrcd9
2s8yT2/8yJQ2Q1pZawGl0XjHOFMNEtdk3bvepLWGWcY7QUKJJwHpW5vGVs9xLU34
nnbPK0/dY1O6bnhIfVRgYvomO+IIfSDx3t7OGg/hEm2jp7rkNBIdW0qnH7GwTNVx
6FdD+DGztSgqTMdtt1a7IwRZjfXSf3HAIK0ZY8cq7hsd3+JewSsWwctNCHbeW4Y5
QNjKXcBr9UeReZ6+BOw8p8xSSBYE0DPNLbqccjcjYT/lD/r7Ja2Pb1W4X/tt8Dwc
EccnjGW+3zYdAQulxLN+EZos+hlgFcNAeBHkPwbC9oDAamfsJAihGIWMa/CyBZAm
2eF2aFtU0djDEhrVIuzrw4JKSdatqD0Bu0QOLQl08PM/GnAzDGzZ9jswfdRmjoPS
t20XyRG+9irB4SIv47KjWXulc7h9hYrQWxDlNy/R6TeqirA/hOiBn4ZgaY3xx3+/
tDFJ5YkR+rzEcf+W/5I3SbOzKQ9XvERGVUJUfJbjXoes8JY0qxFZosUyaiwi+xWT
F8R/1k0+OwtH2u1e4pq265I1HBJGQcOpuKpf1U/q1uACncRsi2s+EHA323T7Jkc7
3srk9wIDAQABoyMwITAOBgNVHQ8BAf8EBAMCAAEwDwYDVR0TAQH/BAUwAwEB/zAN
BgkqhkiG9w0BAQsFAAOCAgEAeX4Mf+65e8r2JMTqNKP1XnEYEw/jnq7BpjwxjNxw
AVoF2YdZifi/0U9Xr5SA+uCWYVgRB5wFpZ8trckTaLUiszTeLtlwl1Jouf2VIcbY
N6RF1uHbBEYEyZl7daoF3Sd1stj/oZBPmjEPl2OLus0WpYkGDdy+29fzUz271yA8
P1UE5Uq/7/0P/UIuU9pMQMbciuP0F97ODp/8i2iXyEiXPbe7s+h0GXlsrjyD65Fz
cwc9etAXuHrxcKPyCAtyzW3CmU+WqE6nVCNgwwh4j5r2SEeR3UZVw8Yub45IoZiE
PMcTlfA9e4hw4muKEmygdYCbiFQLsa0G/MtBv+IwpaMPtoY6edjUY+OOpgX7OlI9
ymfnhGLyGqHLbwhZpc3gvJHWCJ9mRkGr66KAHA1+HOlJw/aua0A3Fo2DBP2Ruftu
g3NgE5G6zPnfcalaPjt+Cl7Wu9TfzcIxVtTgM6g+LePgYP3tTRzAMv0DzKHSpBqW
v98pF1cG0vrVk15rLIcAlCMYhP95el4qtfcXwQzKmnQBhW+emaCIudvyFRJdFM2o
f0pSiRYkpLDrqZ2fiqw+eqts80hUDOh9GvJzxtZbOccxTbgaKxX9MtAQllw3vYJx
EHCp06JmUc09GtYCju2gJH29baHWldNDeP/3z9913RmnIWggh4b+G0FmPmB5XOhb
PR4=
-----END CERTIFICATE-----
```

ENCRYPTING SECRETS USING SEALED SECRETS

Now that Sealed Secrets has been successfully installed, encrypt the contents of the `greeting-secret.yaml` created using `kubeseal` in listing 3.2 to create a new file called `greeting-secret_sealedsecrets.yaml` as follows.

Listing 3.6   Encrypting a secret using kubeseal

```
kubeseal --format yaml  <greeting-secret.yaml \
  >greeting-secret_sealedsecrets.yaml -n kubernetes-secrets-sealedsecrets
```

Review the contents of the newly generated `greeting-secret-sealedsecrets.yaml` file in the following listing.

Listing 3.7   greeting-secret-sealedsecrets.yaml

```
apiVersion: bitnami.com/v1alpha1
kind: SealedSecret
metadata:
  creationTimestamp: null
  name: greeting-secret
  namespace: kubernetes-secrets-sealedsecrets
spec:
  encryptedData:
    greeting.message: AgAKGnqEn6MRRsDGoH2lhKTwJ0UVeUaN+Kq0Uyr13ZNnQB/eLFjJ
    ⮑qkzN9+kbnMC9J9ptA2MS2WMIkKnF7cRaX3HloCp/SqgsN3eIhZs6zL4EHcpxUkXTPl
    ⮑83ynwa6oC6z/vAFwwJhKHkQPKJ4yrwOpolbauddL7Oi4fwxqRyK98EHiQ485qv26rK
    ⮑qJgl9q26gsGii0JFyL73OU3/r7nhdzKJ7+eL1EYVqV2Mn95O95ShqVYq970TPpPtLy
    ⮑1MzeA/bT9hhgTmWyBzREZsG+O+knCO3j5NK0QBt7UEEenOlNQBgc5mTFaQ2SBjD9k7
    ⮑MEG979jiPEIOL0LkkLbv2R8cox7HqlEZTOJ0E18ghWwxf3zsxPE2/IJw5WVxcmcAG1
    ⮑O+cy0L+YP36xnaOe15WAtEmWTXk8aVh8SCzaLsYZEoom96Jh8ZGZHMsRuly2gmMUjW
    ⮑4dTGQazeZm+T+q6kJuYxDZ/SDvlui+q9G6IB4joJIRndp16cTxQlqopqhjAO/YZOIc
    ⮑KmAD1YrbXwSNw/Z+X+Y20xZQrp5BMFrvspar+1drNvJ+8/nvhYlo+j3pOMiHI7tyUt
    ⮑5cqxsxhTpZLth5T6/VEt2hBIOQ5AKgJitm6yGnmZKzQwvkHYxGuy15sExI+MJ3LNyO
    ⮑sLTprWzAzSuf/c0KFXM2/fQ+DlysZJsFCDYmiBygcbD65xqLFaQ4oHIcxwhXwmkYnd
    ⮑oA==
  template:          ◄──────────────    The template property adds fields to the
    metadata:                            generated secret. Additional properties, such
      creationTimestamp: null            as labels and annotations, can be included.
      name: greeting-secret
      namespace: kubernetes-secrets-sealedsecrets
```

As an additional security measure, the namespace and name associated with the secret are added as part of the OAEP process, so it is important that the `SealedSecret` resource is generated with this in mind. Finally, verify that the newly created `Sealed-Secret` resource can be added to the Kubernetes cluster. Once added, the Sealed Secrets controller should decrypt the contents and create a new Secret within the same namespace:

```
kubectl apply -f greeting-secret_sealedsecrets.yaml
```

Confirm that a new secret called `greeting-secret` has been created in the `kubernetes-secrets-sealedsecrets` namespace:

```
kubectl get secrets -n default greeting-secret
NAME               TYPE       DATA   AGE
greeting-secret    Opaque     1      20s
```

The Sealed Secrets controller also emits Kubernetes events based on the actions it performs and can be verified by querying for events in the `default` namespace:

```
kubectl get events -n kubernetes-secrets-sealedsecrets

LAST SEEN    TYPE      REASON      OBJECT                       MESSAGE
3m38s        Normal    Unsealed    sealedsecret/greeting-secret SealedSecret
                                                                 unsealed
                                                                 successfully
```

The addition of events provides insight into the lifecycle of resources managed by Sealed Secrets.

Given the tight connection between the `SealedSecret` resource and the associated Secret, if the `SealedSecret` resource is removed, Kubernetes will also remove the referenced Secret. This is due to the fact that the Secret is owned by the `SealedSecret` resource. Kubernetes Garbage Collection will cascade the deletion of resources to any resources that are owned. Additional details related to Kubernetes garbage collection can be found in the Kubernetes documentation (http://mng.bz/JVDQ).

By demonstrating how to make use of Sealed Secrets in our Kubernetes environment, you can feel confident about safely storing the `SealedSecret` resource in your version control system, without having to worry about sensitive assets being easily discovered. In the next section, we will introduce how to manage sensitive assets within Kubernetes package mangers.

3.4 *Managing Secrets within Kubernetes package managers*

As you have seen thus far, Kubernetes provides the primitives for running complex applications: ConfigMaps and Secrets for storing configuration assets, Services for simplifying network access, and Deployments for managing the desired state of container resources. However, one feature Kubernetes does not natively provide is a mechanism for easily managing these resources. This issue becomes increasingly clear as resources begin to accumulate within IaC repositories. Members of the Kubernetes community saw this as a challenge, and there became a desire to better manage the lifecycle of Kubernetes applications in a similar fashion to any other off-cluster application. Traditionally, these are features facilitated by a package manager, such as yum, apt-get, or Homebrew. The result of their efforts led to the creation and eventual popularity of Helm, a package manager for Kubernetes.

Helm simplifies the lives of application developers and consumers of Kubernetes applications by providing the following key features:

- Lifecycle management (e.g., installation, upgrading, and rollback)
- Manifest templating
- Dependency management

Helm uses a packaging format know as *charts*, which contain the Kubernetes manifests that would be associated with an application and deployed as a single unit. Manifests are known as *templates* within Helm and are processed through Helm's templating engine (they are go-template based with additional support from libraries, such as Sprig) at deployment time.

Values are parameters that are injected into the templated resources. The combined set of rendered manifests once deployed to Kubernetes is known as a *release* (figure 3.5).

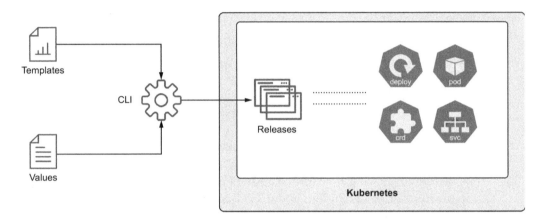

Figure 3.5   A Helm release combines templates and values to create Kubernetes resources

Finally, Helm is managed using a command line client tool that helps facilitate the entire lifecycle of a chart. This will be the primary tool used starting in the next section.

TIP   Additional information related to Helm can be found on the Helm website at https://helm.sh/.

3.4.1   *Deploying the Greeting Demo Helm chart*

The manifests associated with the greeting demo application we referred to in chapter 2 have been packaged into a Helm chart to demonstrate the benefits Helm can provide. In this section you will install the Helm CLI tool, review the Greeting Demo Helm Chart, and deploy it to your Kubernetes cluster.

First download the Helm Command Line tool. Multiple installation options are available, depending on your operating system. The steps and instructions can be found on the Helm project website (https://helm.sh/docs/intro/install/).

Once the Helm CLI has been installed, make sure Git is available on your machine, as it is needed to manage assets in version control within this chapter as well as subsequent chapters. See appendix D for instructions on how Git can be installed and configured.

Now clone the repository containing the Helm chart to your machine:

```
git clone https://github.com/lordofthejars/
➥kubernetes-secrets-source
cd greeting-demo-helm
```

Clone the repository containing the chart.

Change into the chart directory.

Once inside the chart directory, you will notice the following directory structure:

```
── Chart.yaml
├── templates
│   ├── NOTES.txt
│   ├── _helpers.tpl
│   ├── configmap.yaml
│   ├── deployment.yaml
│   ├── ingress.yaml
│   ├── secret.yaml
│   ├── service.yaml
│   └── serviceaccount.yaml
└── values.yaml
```

The Chart.yaml is the manifest for the Helm chart and contains key metadata, including the name of the chart as well as the version. The templates directory contains the Kubernetes resources that will be deployed to the cluster when the chart is installed. The key difference is they are now templated resources instead of the raw manifests you have been working with thus far, as shown in the following listing.

Listing 3.8 secret.yaml

```
{{- if not .Values.configMap.create -}}
apiVersion: v1
kind: Secret
metadata:
  name: {{ include "greeting-demo.fullname" . }}
  labels:
    {{- include "greeting-demo.labels" . | nindent 4 }}
type: Opaque
stringData:
  greeting.message: {{ required "A valid greeting message is required!"
  ➥$.Values.greeting.message | quote }}
{{- end }}
```

Content enclosed within {{ }} is processed via Helm's templating engine.

The include function references named templates present within the _helpers.tpl file. A full overview of templates and the Helm directory structure can be found in the Helm documentation (https://helm.sh/docs/chart_template_guide/named_templates/).

NOTE Additional Kubernetes resources, such as an Ingress and Service Account, are also included in this chart. These are created as part of the typical boilerplate when the helm create command is used. By default, these resources are not deployed during typical usage of this chart but can be if desired by setting the appropriate values.

Parameters associated with the templates are located in the `Values.yaml` file. By browsing through the file, you will notice many key attributes, including the number of replicas as well as the image location and tag. At the bottom of the file, you will notice a property called `greeting.message` with no value specified:

```
greeting:
  message:
```

If you recall the snippet from listing 3.8, this property is injected by referencing the `$.Values.greeting.message` in the `secret.yaml` file in the templates directory. Also of note is the `required` function that enforces a value to be set before this chart can be installed. Values can be specified in a number of ways, including via files or using the command line, and Helm employs precedence to determine which property is ultimately applied. Those defined in the `values.yaml` file have the lowest priority.

Before you install this chart to the Kubernetes cluster, first create a new namespace called `kubernetes-secrets-helm`, and change the current content into the newly created namespace:

```
kubectl create namespace kubernetes-secrets-helm
kubectl config set-context --current --namespace=kubernetes-secrets-helm
```

Next since a value for `greeting.message` must be provided, create a new file called `values-kubernetes-secrets.yaml`, containing the following contents.

> **Listing 3.9   values-kubernetes-secrets.yaml**

```
greeting:
  message: Hello from Helm!
```

Next install the Helm chart by providing a name for the release, the chart location, and a reference to the values file that contains the required property:

```
helm upgrade -i greeting-demo . -f values-kubernetes-secrets.ymal
```

> **NOTE** The `helm upgrade` command was used with the `-i` flag, as it provides an idempotent method for installing Helm charts. If an existing chart is present, it will be upgraded. Otherwise a new installation will occur.

If the installation was successful, an overview of the release is provided along with the rendered contents of the `Notes.txt` file contained from the templates. Curl the IP address and port exposed by the minikube service to confirm the greeting that was set in the Helm value and stored in the `greeting-secret` secret is presented:

```
curl $(minikube ip):$(kubectl get svc --namespace kubernetes-secrets-helm \
  greeting-demo -o jsonpath="{.spec.ports[*].nodePort}")/hello
```

3.4.2 *Using Helm Secrets*

While we were successful in deploying the application as a Helm chart, we are once again faced with the challenge of how to manage sensitive content stored within the values-kubernetes-secrets.yaml file. As you might expect, other members of the Helm and Kubernetes community sought to find a solution to provide security to Helm values, so they can be stored at rest. One of the most popular options available is Helm Secrets, a Helm plugin that provides integration with various secrets management backends. Plugins in Helm are external tools that are not part of the Helm code base but can be accessed from the Helm CLI.

Helm Secrets uses Secrets OPerationS (SOPS), from Mozilla, as its default secrets management driver. SOPS is a tool that encrypts key–value file types, such as YAML, and integrates with cloud (AWS/GCP KMS) and non-cloud secrets management solutions.

For the integration of SOPS as the backend for Helm Secrets, the most straightforward and easiest option to setup for our purposes is leveraging Pretty Good Privacy (PGP). PGP, in a similar fashion to Sealed Secrets, uses asymmetric public/private key encryption to secure the content of files and has been a popular method for transmitting emails securely. At encryption time, a random 256-bit data key is used and passed to PGP to encrypt the data key and then the properties within the file (figure 3.6).

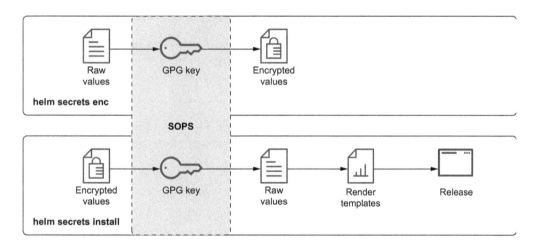

Figure 3.6   Encrypting secrets and using them as part of a Helm release, using Helm Secrets

Now prepare your machine with the software and configurations necessary to protect the sensitive properties of your Helm chart. GNU Privacy Guard (GPG) is an open standards implementation of the proprietary PGP, and the corresponding gpg tool will enable you to manage your keys appropriately. Check appendix E for further instructions on how it can be installed. Once the gpg CLI has been installed, create a new public/private key pair:

```
gpg --generate-key
```

Enter your name and email address. When prompted to enter a passphrase, do not enter any values.

NOTE   While it may seem counterintuitive to leave the GPG passphrase blank, it simplifies the integration with automation tools (some do not support passphrases) as well as reduces the need to manage yet another sensitive asset.

After the public/private key pair is successfully created, you can confirm by listing the keys in the keyring as follows.

Listing 3.10   Listing GPG Keys

```
gpg --list-keys

pub   rsa2048 2020-12-31 [SC] [expires: 2022-12-31]
      53696D1AB6954C043FCBA478A23998F0CBF2A552      <——| GPG Fingerprint
uid           [ultimate] John Doe <jdoe@example.com>
sub   rsa2048 2020-12-31 [E] [expires: 2022-12-31]
```

Make note of the value starting with 5369, as this is the fingerprint for the public key and will be used shortly when configuring SOPS. Next install the Helm Secrets plugin using the Helm CLI:

```
helm plugin install https://github.com/jkroepke/helm-secrets
```

SOPS will also be installed as part of the Helm Secrets installation. Values files managed by the Helm Secrets plugin, by convention, are located in a directory called helm_vars. Create this directory within the greeting-demo chart repository:

```
mkdir helm_vars
```

To complete the integration between Helm Secrets and SOPS, create a new file in the helm_vars directory named .sops.yaml, with the following content:

```
---
creation_rules:
  - pgp: "53696D1AB6954C043FCBA478A23998F0CBF2A552"
---
```

Replace the content next to pgp with the fingerprint for your own public key discovered in listing 3.10.

Next move the values-kubernetes-secrets.yaml file to the helm_vars directory, so it is within the same directory as the .sops.yaml file. This will ensure SOPS decrypts the file appropriately.

```
---
mv values-kubernetes-secrets.yaml helm_vars
---
```

With the integration with SOPS complete and the desired values file in the proper location, use Helm Secrets to encrypt the file as follows.

Listing 3.11   Encrypting using Helm Secrets

```
helm secrets enc helm_vars/values-kubernetes-secrets.yaml

Encrypted values-kubernetes-secrets.yaml
```

Confirm the contents of the `values-kubernetes-secrets.yaml` file are encrypted, as in the following listing.

Listing 3.12   values-kubernetes-secrets.yaml

```
greeting:
    message: ENC[AES256_GCM,data:SYfMBpax8mTOqzPed3ksjA==,iv:OrN/r/WVF+ROR
     ➥BBaiyqyiRyIRS+LPb3gf2q9gU4OVH8=,tag:
     ➥B9NYch4tNruKzBQMKqk00g==,type:str]      ◁── Encrypted value
sops:
    kms: []
    gcp_kms: []
    azure_kv: []
    hc_vault: []
    lastmodified: '2020-12-31T04:21:40Z'
    mac: ENC[AES256_GCM,data:h2fQPc9hzmGMaKIE73aYU2TxbwVYQQLRcYHWh++kAYjK
     ➥zm+o9KibOcsVXz8iRLVbeER62FR4h2AON6ZC8ZxoWW5MxQm
     ➥w729YOQc1nkrgWxsx+ST2ucYmUxn3D4Kqb9X8NSu8P3fPcr
     ➥/Q77fFQ4SK1fLh2Jd92UZt5dJ6hOGJEr0=,iv:cvXEVhZUP
     ➥9uHbYAASbXL8KS3sso34STMZhpG/phzN4U=,tag:PtCoqDf
     ➥Z4C+KN7Qxz55DSw==,type:str]
    pgp:
    -   created_at: '2020-12-31T04:21:39Z'
        enc: |
            -----BEGIN PGP MESSAGE-----

            hQEMA0e7sMUYmEkyAQgAhrnbGtCkbRwEDky1TmWTHXeKhoEx+2bbD8vJ+g9m7hYl
            iDwat80MKu2lGKgnVj2RAMIxwyjaLdoGY+pDXYxUJ5StFojh1bJbkEYKT5KYaGni
            uvkpeYNwLtAZWd6Shjl1vAkVEdMsh3xFtv9ot2uwL/DuxmSvoIR5OxpLwEZSAPgM
            UzsK0SMWQjyIT69oUKlJYd+Nwj0sv1oWJMAkra367EZxKzKKi1eKFZ3QHQ4JVAdp
            +P8ctjQqeWi8bC/wN6PdRGVYfZD8bF3CxgdtYUKHRseNvjX2H6rD60x15FgADx9v
            bGfOu4n5SccgGftgnYI8nXL7vnAntuLREz6XDnLQDNJeAVzDt623nJmlqKGP+x/G
            HYfaEqBWI8bcPfBwHv3g9F1sAk86W86IR6pB0mOwD/twW9/J7InW91xEz2Q9KhMR
            oWVWwF8IZzNWVb6Sjl6EXIaB+ssJXOtfWXyBD83w8Q==
            =TH/P
            -----END PGP MESSAGE-----
        fp: 53696D1AB6954C043FCBA478A23998F0CBF2A552      ◁── Fingerprint
    unencrypted_suffix: _unencrypted
    version: 3.6.1
```

Note that the file has been separated into two primary sections.

1 Keys from the original file are retained. Values are now encrypted.
2 SOPS related metadata including enough information to enable the encrypted values to be decrypted.

The contents can be easily updated as necessary, using the `helm secrets edit` command. To denote you are now using Helm Secrets to manage the content of our values file in a secure manner, update the value of the `greeting.message` property to read `Hello from Helm Secrets!`:

```
helm secrets edit helm_vars/values-kubernetes-secrets.yaml
```

Update the contents of the file:

```
greeting:
    message: Hello from Helm Secrets!
```

Now upgrade the chart with the updated encrypted values file using Helm Secrets:

```
helm secrets upgrade greeting-demo . -i -f
➥helm_vars/values-kubernetes-secrets.yaml
```

Revision 2 should be displayed, indicating a successful release. However, if you attempt to query the endpoint exposed by the application, it will not reflect the updated values, since only the underlying secret was modified and a solution similar to the reloader introduced in chapter 2 is not in use.

Delete the running pod, which will allow the updated value to be injected into the newly created Pod:

```
kubectl delete pod -l=app.kubernetes.io/instance=greeting-demo
```

Once the newly created Pod is running, query the application endpoint to confirm the response displays the property contained within your encrypted values file:

```
curl $(minikube ip):$(kubectl get svc --namespace
➥kubernetes-secrets-helm \
  greeting-demo -o jsonpath="{.spec.ports[*].nodePort}")/hello
```

One benefit of using Helm Secrets is that it provides an introduction to SOPS, a tool that can be used to protect sensitive key–value files for secure storage outside the Helm ecosystem. The management of sensitive assets does not end once the values have been encrypted. In the next section, we will discuss how rotating secrets can be used to improve your overall security posture beyond day one.

3.5   *Rotating secrets*

Individuals and organizations go to great lengths to protect sensitive information that could potentially enable access to critical systems. However, regardless of the strength of any secure value or the tools used to protect access to them, there is always the potential for compromise. The key is minimizing or reducing the potential.

With that in mind, one of the methods that can be used to reduce the attack vector is implementing some form of secret rotation. Rotation can occur in two primary areas:

- The actual value being secured
- The keys or values used to generate the encrypted asset

Rotating sensitive assets is a concept most of us should be familiar with—for example, resetting passwords on a regular basis. This practice, however, has been known to fall short in the context of managed assets, since systems make use of the asset instead of a human. Fortunately, each of the tools that has been introduced thus far to secure sensitive assets at rest (Ansible Vault, Sealed Secrets, and Helm Secrets) support some form of rotation.

3.5.1   *Ansible Vault secret key rotation*

Encrypted files generated by Ansible Vault can be rekeyed to allow a different password to be used to secure and access the stored asset using the rekey subcommand of ansible-vault. Using the `greeting-secret_ansible.yaml` file that was encrypted in listing 3.11, use the `ansible-vault rekey` subcommand to start the rekeying process, enter the existing password, and then enter a new password when prompted:

```
ansible-vault rekey greeting-secret_ansible.yaml

Vault password:
New Vault password:
Confirm New Vault password:
Rekey successful
```

The contents of the `greeting-secret_ansible.yaml` file has been updated.

3.5.2 *Sealed Secrets key rotation*

Whenever the Sealed Secret controller starts, it checks whether an existing public/private key pair is available (with the following label: `sealedsecrets.bitnami.com/sealed-secrets-key=active`). Otherwise, a new key pair will be generated. Sealing keys themselves are renewed automatically (a new secret is created) every 30 days, and the controller will consider any secret with the `sealedsecrets.bitnami.com/sealed-secrets-key=active` label to be a potential key used for decryption.

However, rotation can be initiated at any time, whether due to a compromise or other reasons, by either setting the `--key-cutoff-time` flag or using the `SEALED_SECRETS_KEY_CUTOFF_TIME` environment variable on the controller deployment. Using either method, the value must be in RFC1123 format. Force the Sealed Secrets controller to regenerate a new key pair by executing the following command to add an environment variable on the `sealed-secrets-controller` deployment:

```
kubectl -n kube-system set env deployment/sealed-secrets-controller \
  SEALED_SECRETS_KEY_CUTOFF_TIME="$(date -R)"
```

A new rollout of the `sealed-secrets-controller` will be initiated. Confirm the new key pair was generated:

```
kubectl -n kube-system get secrets \
  -l=sealedsecrets.bitnami.com/sealed-secrets-key=active

NAME                       TYPE                DATA   AGE
sealed-secrets-key6kdnd    kubernetes.io/tls   2      25m26s
sealed-secrets-keyqdrb5    kubernetes.io/tls   2      47s
```

With the new private key available to the controller, secrets associated with existing `SealedSecrets` can be reencrypted, or new secrets can be encrypted using the kubeseal CLI.

> **NOTE** Existing keys are not removed whenever a new key is added, as it is added to the list of active keys. Old keys can be removed manually only after the new key has been created.

3.5.3   *SOPS secret key rotation*

SOPS, the secrets management tool underlying Helm Secrets, also supports key rotation. There are two mechanisms for which rotation can be implemented within SOPS:

- The GPG key itself
- The data key used at encryption time

The most straightforward option is rotating the data key used to encrypt the file. To accomplish this task with your existing Helm values file located within the `helm_vars` folder, use the SOPS tool itself, passing the `-r` flag along with the location of the file to rotate:

```
sops -r --in-place helm_vars/values-kubernetes-secrets.yaml
```

You can confirm SOPS has updated the file by verifying the `lastmodified` property underneath the `sops` section.

In addition to the data key being rotated, the master GPG key can also be updated. To do so, create a new GPG key or reference an existing GPG, and pass the associated fingerprint of the key by using the `--add-pgp` flag:

```
sops -r --in-place --add-pgp <FINGERPRINT> \
  helm_vars/values-kubernetes-secrets.yaml
```

To remove the old key, execute this command, but replace `--add-pgp` with `--rm-pgp`, and use the fingerprint of the key you wish to remove. In any event, be sure to update the contents of the `helm_vars/.sops.yaml` file with the fingerprint of the key you would like Helm Secrets to use to manage the secure assets.

Regardless of the secrets management tool being used, once rotation has been completed, it is important that any systems or applications dependent on the secure asset are updated appropriately to reduce the potential of downtime or error due to misconfiguration.

Summary

- Expressing Kubernetes resources declaratively allows them to be captured and stored in version control systems.
- Tools such as Ansible and Helm have support for storing sensitive resources at rest securely.
- Operators automate actions in Kubernetes environments and can be used to encrypt sensitive values from within the cluster.
- SOPS is a general-purpose tool for encrypting various file formats and includes integration with KMS providers.
- Secret key rotation replaces existing encryption keys by generating new cryptographic keys, which reduces the risk of a compromise.

Encrypting data at rest

4

This chapter covers

- Data encryption at rest for Kubernetes cluster storage
- Enabling the KMS provider for data encryption

In chapter 3, you learned how to protect secrets when storing them in Git, but this is just one place secrets can be stored. In this chapter, we'll discuss storing them inside the Kubernetes cluster.

We'll demonstrate that secrets are not encrypted by default by directly querying the etcd database. Then we'll walk through the process of encrypting data at rest as well as enabling it in Kubernetes to encrypt secrets (figure 4.1).

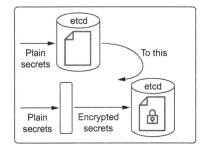

Figure 4.1   From plain text secrets to encrypted secrets

Finally, we will make the process secure using a key management service (KMS) to manage encryption keys, as shown in figure 4.2.

4.1 *Encrypting secrets in Kubernetes*

Imagine you have an application that needs to connect to a database server; obviously, a username and password are required to access it. These configuration values are secrets, and they need to be stored correctly, so if the system (or the cluster) is compromised, they are kept secret and the attacker will not be able to exploit them to access any part of your application. The solution is encrypting these secrets, so if they are compromised, the attacker would only get a chunk of bytes instead of the real values.

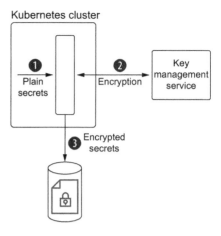

Figure 4.2   Key management service for managing keys

4.1.1 *Data at rest vs. data in motion*

We detailed the characteristics of *data at rest*—persisted data that is infrequently changed—extensively in chapter 3. On the other hand, *data in transit*, or *data in motion*, is data that is moving from one location to another, usually through the network. You can protect data in transit by using the mutual TLS protocol during communication between parties (figure 4.3), but this is outside the scope of this book; we will instead focus on how to protect data at rest. Before you address the problem of not encrypting data at rest, you'll need to create a plain text secret and get it by directly querying the etcd server, as an attacker might do.

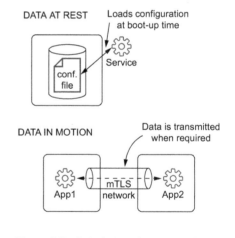

Figure 4.3   Data in transit needs to be encrypted at the communication level

4.1.2 *Plain secrets*

Let's create a secret using the kubectl tool by querying the etcd server using the etcdctl CLI.

CREATING THE SECRET

In a terminal window, move to the default Kubernetes namespace, and create a new secret with two key–value entries:

```
kubectl config set-context --current --namespace=default
```

```
kubectl create secret generic db-secret --from-literal=username=devuser
➥--from-literal=password=devpassword
```

We can list the created secret using `kubectl` tool:

```
kubectl get secrets
```

```
NAME                    TYPE                            DATA    AGE
db-secret               Opaque                          2       47s
```

INSTALLING ETCDCTL

`etcdctl` is a command-line client for interacting with the `etcd` server used for querying keys stored in the database, among other operations. This tool can be helpful for understanding how data is stored in the `etcd` database.

The installation process of the tool may differ, depending on the OS you are using; for more detailed instructions, see the official installation guide of the `etcd` version we use in this book to query the database (https://github.com/etcd-io/etcd/releases/tag/v3.4.14).

ACCESSING ETCD

The `etcd` server is running in the `kube-system` namespace under the 2379 port. Since you are using minikube, you can use the port forwarding feature to access the `etcd` server directly from your local machine. In a terminal window, run the following command to expose `etcd` in the `localhost` host:

```
kubectl port-forward -n kube-system etcd-minikube 2379:2379
```

> **IMPORTANT** If you run the previous commands you will get the following error: `Error from server (NotFound): pods "etcd-minikube" not found`. Run the following command to get the name of your environment:

```
kubectl get pods -n kube-system
```

```
NAME                                    READY   STATUS      RESTARTS    AGE
coredns-66bff467f8-mh55d                1/1     Running     1           5m22s
etcd-vault-book                         1/1     Running     1           5m36s
kube-apiserver-vault-book               1/1     Running     0           3m21s
kube-controller-manager-vault-book      1/1     Running     1           5m36s
kube-proxy-1bhd6                        1/1     Running     1           5m22s
kube-scheduler-vault-book               1/1     Running     1           5m36s
storage-provisioner                     1/1     Running     1           5m36s
```

In this case, the `etcd` Pod name is `etcd-vault-book`.

The second step to access the `etcd` server is copying the `etcd` certificates from the running Pod to the local machine. Open a new terminal window, and copy the certificates using the `kubectl` tool:

```
kubectl cp kube-system/etcd-minikube:/var/lib/minikube/certs/etcd/peer.key
➥/tmp/peer.key
kubectl cp kube-system/etcd-minikube:/var/lib/minikube/certs/etcd/peer.crt
➥/tmp/peer.crt
```

IMPORTANT   etcd-minikube is a directory that matches the etcd Pod name. Modify it according to your environment.

Finally, you can configure etcdctl to connect to the etcd server and query for the secret created in the previous step. etcd organizes its content in key–value format; for the specific case of secret objects, the content is stored in keys in the following format:

`/registry/secrets/<namespace>/<secret_name>.`

Execute the following commands in a terminal window as shown.

Listing 4.1   Configures `etcdctl`

```
export \                 ⟵─────────────────────┐  Configures etcdctl using
  ETCDCTL_API=3 \                               │  environment variables
  ETCDCTL_INSECURE_SKIP_TLS_VERIFY=true    \
  ETCDCTL_CERT=/tmp/peer.crt \
  ETCDCTL_KEY=/tmp/peer.key
                                            ┌  Query the etcd database
etcdctl get /registry/secrets/default/db-secret  ⟵┘  to get the secret.
```

The output should be similar to the one shown in the following listing. Notice that, although the output is not perfectly clear, it is not difficult to see the secret content.

Listing 4.2 `etcdctl` **output**

```
/registry/secrets/default/db-secret
k8s

v1Secret?
N
    db-secretdefault"*$df9e87f7-4eed-4f5b-985a-7888919198472???z
password
        devpassword           ⟵┐  Secrets are not encrypted
usernamedevuserOpaque"          │  but stored in plain text.
```

You can stop the port forwarding, as you do not need it for now, by aborting the process (ctrl-C on the first terminal)

You should understand now that if the etcd server is compromised, nothing will block an attacker from getting all secrets in plain text. In the following section, you will explore the first solution for storing encrypted secrets.

4.1.3   *Encrypting secrets*

To use encryption data at rest, you'll need to introduce a new Kubernetes object named EncryptionConfiguration. In this object, you will specify which Kubernetes object you want to encrypt; it can be a secret object, but it's actually possible to encrypt any other Kubernetes object. You will also need to specify the secrets provider, which is a pluggable system where you specify the encryption algorithm and encryption keys to be used.

At the time of writing, the following providers are supported:

- *identity*—No encryption enabled; the resources are written as is.
- *aescbc*—AES-CBC with PKCS#7 padding algorithm; it is the best option for encryption at rest.
- *secretbox*—XSalsa20 and Poly1305 algorithm; it is a new standard, but it might not be suitable in environments with high levels of review.
- *aesgcm*—AES-GCM with a random nonce algorithm; it is only recommended if you implement an automatic key rotation.
- *kms*—Uses an envelope encryption schema; key encryption keys are managed by the configured KMS. This is the most secure method, and you will explore it later in this chapter.

To examine how encryption data at rest works in Kubernetes, repeat the exercise from the previous section, except with Kubernetes configured to encrypt secrets.

ENABLING DATA ENCRYPTION AT REST

It is important to understand that data encryption at rest happens on the `kube-api-server` running in a master Node. If it is enabled, every time a Kubernetes object is sent to the Kubernetes cluster, the `kube-apiserver` delegates to the encryption configuration part to encrypt the objects before they are sent to the etcd database to be stored. Obviously, when a secret needs to be consumed, it is decrypted automatically, so from the point of view of a developer, nothing special is required; they work as usual (figure 4.4).

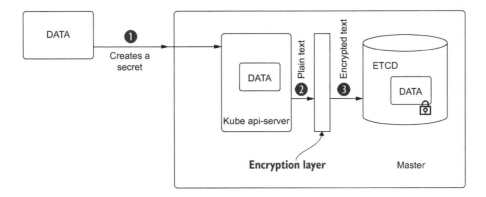

Figure 4.4 The encryption layer encrypts secrets automatically before sending them to etcd.

Now generate an `EncryptionConfiguration` object to ensure any Kubernetes Secret is encrypted using the `aescbc` algorithm and with a random encryption key, as shown in the following listing.

Listing 4.3   `EncryptionConfiguration`

```
apiVersion: apiserver.config.k8s.io/v1
kind: EncryptionConfiguration
resources:
  - resources:
    - secrets              ⟵┐  Secrets content is encrypted, but
    providers:               │  any Kubernetes resource is valid.
    - aescbc:                                                    Encryption key for
      keys:                                                      encrypting data
        - name: key1
          secret: b6sjdRWAPhtacXo8mOlcfgVYWXzwuls3T3NQOo4TBhk=  ⟵┐
    - identity: {}
```

TIP To generate a random key in Base64, you can use a tool such as `openssl` or `head`:

```
openssl rand -base64 32

head -c 32 /dev/urandom | base64 -i -
```

As you might remember, encryption occurs during the `kube-apiserver` process, which implies you need to materialize the EncryptionConfiguration file into master Nodes where it is running. The process of accessing a master Node differs for each Kubernetes platform; in minikube it is achieved by running the `minikube ssh` command to obtain an SSH session on the master Node. Once inside the master Node, run the `sudo -i` command to execute the following commands as a superuser.

Listing 4.4   **SSH'd minikube**

```
minikube ssh
sudo -i
```

TIP If you get an error like `Error getting config`, then you need to specify the minikube profile with the -p flag. You can list current active profiles with the `minikube profile list`:

```
minikube profile list
```

Profile	VM Driver	Runtime	IP	Port	Version	Status
istio	virtualbox	docker	192.168.99.116	8443	v1.18.6	Stopped
kube	virtualbox	docker	192.168.99.117	8443	v1.18.6	Started

```
minikube ssh -p kube.
```

And then inside the SSHed instance, run the `sudo` command.

Listing 4.5   **Update to superuser**

```
sudo -i
```

At this point, you are inside the minikube VM `kube-apiserver` is running. Let's create a new file at `/var/lib/minikube/certs/encryptionconfig.yaml` with the content shown in the following listing.

Listing 4.6 encryptionconfig.yaml

```
echo "
apiVersion: apiserver.config.k8s.io/v1
kind: EncryptionConfiguration
resources:
  - resources:
    - secrets
    providers:
    - aescbc:          ⟵——| Encryption provider                    The tee command
        keys:                                               creates echoed content
        - name: key1                                           for the given file.
          secret: b6sjdRWAPhtacXo8mO1cfgVYWXzwuls3T3NQOo4TBhk=
    - identity: {}
"  | tee /var/lib/minikube/certs/encryptionconfig.yaml      ⟵——————
```

The file is created in the master Node. Now we can quit the SSH terminal by typing exit twice.

```
exit
```

```
exit
```

Now you are back on your computer, but you still need to finish the last step before secrets are encrypted: updating the `kube-apiserver` to pick up the EncryptionConfig-uration file created in the previous step. To configure the `kube-apiserver` process, you need to set the `--encryption-provider-config` argument value to the `EncryptionConfiguration` path. The easiest way to do this in `minikube` is stopping the instance and starting it again using the argument `--extra-config`.

> **TIP** If you are not using minikube, the following link gives information about setting this configuration property in a Kubernetes `kube-apiserver`: https://kubernetes.io/docs/reference/command-line-tools-reference/kube-apiserver/.

```
minikube stop
minikube start --vm-driver=virtualbox
➥--extra-config=apiserver.encryption-provider-config=/var/lib/minikube/
➥certs/encryptionconfig.yaml
```

4.1.4 Creating the secret

In a terminal window, move to the `default` Kubernetes namespace, and create a new secret named `db-secret-encrypted` with two key–value entries.

```
kubectl config set-context --current --namespace=default
```

```
kubectl create secret generic db-secret-encrypted
➥--from-literal=username=devuser --from-literal=password=devpassword
```

At this point, the secret is created the same way as before, but let's explore how the data is stored inside `etcd`.

ACCESSING ETCD

Let's repeat exactly the same process in the accessing `etcd` section to get the content of the secret `db-secret-encrypted` and validate that now it is encrypted instead of in plain text.

In one terminal window, expose the `etcd` server in localhost:

```
kubectl port-forward -n kube-system etcd-minikube 2379:2379
```

In another terminal, repeat the process of copying the `etcd` certificates, and configure the `etcdctl` using environment variables:

```
kubectl cp kube-system/etcd-minikube:/var/lib/minikube/certs/etcd/peer.key
⮑ /tmp/peer.key
kubectl cp kube-system/etcd-minikube:/var/lib/minikube/certs/etcd/peer.crt
⮑ /tmp/peer.crt

export \
  ETCDCTL_API=3 \
  ETCDCTL_INSECURE_SKIP_TLS_VERIFY=true  \
  ETCDCTL_CERT=/tmp/peer.crt \
  ETCDCTL_KEY=/tmp/peer.key
```

You can now query `etcd` to get the value of the `db-secret-encrypted` key to validate it is encrypted and its values are impossible to decipher:

```
etcdctl get /registry/secrets/default/db-secret-encrypted
```

The output should be similar to the following:

```
/registry/secrets/default/db-secret-encrypted
cm?9>?*?-????????~?6I????=@????e????.??
                         8Y
t??p ?b?                 ??V????w??6????l??v??Ey?q.?^?Z?
⮑ ?n?xh??$???d??1??y??Q??q??LJ?}????????I?w??%;
```

Unlike in the previous section, the secrets are encrypted in `kube-apiserver` and then sent to be stored in the `etcd` server. You can stop port forwarding, as you do not need to for now, by aborting the process (ctrl-C on the first terminal).

You can now see that an attacker could get access to the `etcd` server or to a backup of `etcd` (please protect against this), but secrets are encrypted using the keys configured in the `EncryptionConfiguration` object. But is that enough?

SECURITY OF THE KEYS

Using `EncryptionConfiguration`, you've increased the hurdles attackers need to overcome to access the plain text secrets, but you still have some weaknesses. These weaknesses stem from the encryption keys being stored in plain text on the file system in the master Node. If the attacker gains access to the master machine, they can access the EncryptionConfiguration file, grab the keys, query the encrypted secrets, and decrypt them with the keys stolen from the master Node.

One of the main issues here is that the keys that encrypt data live alongside the data itself (figure 4.5). Any attacker who has access to your master Node can potentially access secrets and the keys to decrypt them. In other words, you've not improved the security much if a master Node is compromised.

To avoid this vector attack, encryption keys and data should be stored in separate machines. In this way an attacker needs to compromise multiple systems to gain access to the secrets, as shown in the figure 4.6.

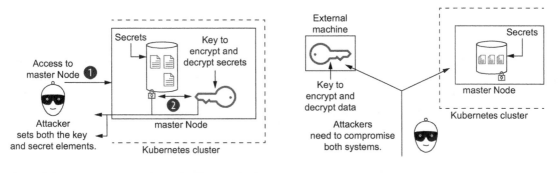

Figure 4.5   A compromised cluster implies that both data and keys to decrypt data are exposed.

Figure 4.6   Splitting data and keys into different machines makes the system safer.

In addition to this issue, there are other drawbacks to take into consideration when using the previous approach:

- The keys need to be generated manually using external tooling.
- The key management process is done manually.
- The key rotation is a manual process that requires an update to the Encryption-Configuration file with the implication of a restart on the `kube-apiserver` process.

Clearly, you've improved your security model by encrypting secrets, and it might be enough, depending on your use case and the level of security you expect, but there is still room for improvement. In the following section, we'll dig into how to use a KMS in Kubernetes to store encryption keys and encrypted data in different machines.

4.2   *Key management server*

The previous application secrets were encrypted, but the keys used to encrypt them were not protected. Any unwanted access would result in their loss and give the attacker a chance to decrypt application secrets. Now you will improve the previous application to protect these keys when using Kubernetes.

To increase the security of keys used to encrypt data you need a KMS to be deployed outside the Kubernetes cluster. In this way, keys are managed outside the cluster, while secrets are stored inside the cluster (`etcd`).

This new approach makes it difficult for a possible attacker to get your secrets, as two systems must be compromised. First of all, the attacker needs to access `etcd` or a disk backup to take the secrets, and assuming they get them, the secrets will just be a bunch of encrypted bytes. Next, the attacker will need to get the keys to decrypt them, but the big difference with the previous section is that now the keys are not in the same machine, nor are they stored in plain text. A second system needs to be compromised, as the attacker needs to gain access to the KMS and get the keys used at encryption time to decrypt the secrets. Of course, it is still possible, but you've added another layer of protection that needs to be broken.

As you want to keep your secrets protected and resilient to a possible attack, you need to move away from storing keys and encrypted data in the same machine to have a clear differentiation between the locations where keys and encrypted data are stored. A KMS is a server that centralizes the management of encryption keys and provides some capabilities for handling cryptographic operations on data in-transit. This makes it the perfect tool for having keys and data storage completely separated.

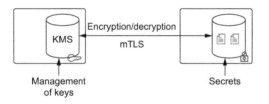

Figure 4.7   **Keys used to encrypt and decrypt are managed in the KMS.**

4.2.1   *Kubernetes and KMS provider*

You've seen in the enabling encryption data at rest section that Kubernetes can use encryption at rest to encrypt secrets and different kinds of providers are supported for encrypting data—one of which being the KMS provider. This provider is recommended when using an external KMS.

An important feature of the KMS encryption provider is its use of an envelope encryption schema to encrypt all data. It is important to understand exactly how this schema works and why it is adopted to store data in `etcd`.

ENVELOPE ENCRYPTION

To use an envelope encryption schema, you need three pieces of data: the data to encrypt (the secret), a data encryption key (DEK), and a key encryption key (KEK). Every time new data needs to be encrypted, a *new* data encryption key is generated and used to encrypt the data. As you can see, each piece of data (or secret) is encrypted by a new encryption key (DEK) and is created on the fly.

In addition to the data encryption key, the envelope encryption schema also has a key encryption key. This key is used to encrypt the data encryption key (DEK). In contrast, the KEK is just generated once, and it is stored in a third-party system like a KMS.

At this point, there are two chunks of encrypted bytes: data encrypted with DEK and DEK encrypted with KEK. Figure 4.8 shows both chunks and how they are encrypted.

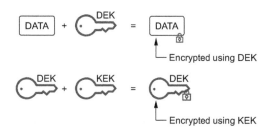
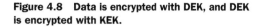

These two parts are appended together and stored as a single piece of data side by side. One of the big advantages of this approach is that each data has its own encryption key, meaning if the data encryption key is compromised (e.g., by using brute force) the attacker would only able to decrypt that secret but not the rest of the secrets. Figure 4.9 shows the whole process.

Figure 4.8   Data is encrypted with DEK, and DEK is encrypted with KEK.

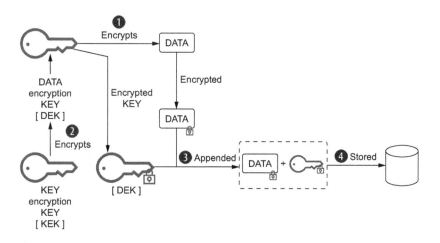

Figure 4.9   Envelope encryption schema

To decrypt a secret, use the reverse process. First of all, split the data again with two chunks of data (an encrypted secret and encrypted DEK); DEK is decrypted using KEK, and finally the secret is decrypted using the decrypted DEK, as shown in figure 4.10.

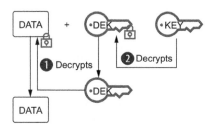

Figure 4.10   Decrypting the envelope encryption schema

KUBERNETES AND ENVELOPE ENCRYPTION

The Kubernetes KMS encryption provider uses envelop encryption in the following way: Every time data needs to be encrypted, a new data encryption key (DEK) is generated using the AES-CBC with PKCS7# padding algorithm. Then the DEK is encrypted using a key encryption key (KEK) managed by the remote KMS. Figure 4.11 shows this process.

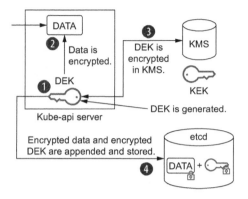

Figure 4.11   Kubernetes and the envelope encryption schema

HASHICORP VAULT AS A KMS

Using the KMS provider is the most secure way to encrypt and decrypt secrets, but you need a KMS implementation that manages the key encryption keys and encrypts the data encryption keys. But how does the Kubernetes cluster communicate with the remote KMS? To communicate with a remote server, the KMS provider uses the gRPC protocol to communicate with a Kubernetes KMS plugin deployed in the Kubernetes master Nodes. This plugin acts as a bridge between the kube-apiserver and the KMS, adapting the encryption and decryption kube-apiserver flow to the protocol required by the remote KMS. Figure 4.12 shows this protocol.

There are many Kubernetes KMS plugins already supported out of the box, including IBM Key Protect, SmartKey, AWS KMS, Azure Key Vault, Google Cloud KMS, and HashiCorp Vault, to name a few. Since the book is written to be cloud-provider agnostic, you will use HashiCorp Vault as a remote KMS, but keep in mind that the process would be similar to the one explained here for any other KMS implementation.

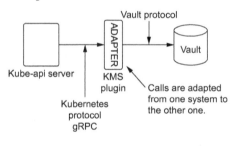

Figure 4.12   KMS provider/plugin system

For now, don't worry about what HashiCorp Vault is, as we will explore this in depth in the following chapter, as it offers many secret-specific key features. But for this specific chapter, think about HashiCorp Vault as a deployable service that offers an endpoint to encrypt and decrypt data in transit without storing it. All the key management occurs internally in the Vault service, so from the point of view of a user, the data is sent to the service, and it is returned ciphered or deciphered, depending on the use case. In the next section, we'll start moving the keys from the master Node to an external KMS.

> **TIP**   The KMS plugin system is designed to be extensible, so you could implement a new plugin for a specific KMS implementation. Usually, this should

not be required, since most of the KMS providers offer integration to Kubernetes, but keep in mind nothing blocks you from implementing a Kubernetes KMS plugin by yourself.

INSTALLING HASHICORP VAULT

We have repeated over and over again that secrets and encryption keys should be deployed in different machines, meaning the KMS must run separately from Kubernetes master Nodes. This is the way you should always proceed in a real scenario, but for this academic use case in which we are using minikube running inside a VM, and for the sake of simplicity, you will install Hashi-Corp Vault inside the VM but outside the Kubernetes cluster. Figure 4.13 illustrates the configuration.

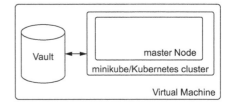

Figure 4.13   HashiCorp Vault as a KMS

> **IMPORTANT**   At the end of this section, we will provide you a single command that executes a script that automates all the steps explained in the following sections. Although the process is automated, we will explain the whole process, so you can repeat it in any other environment.

To install HashiCorp Vault, you need to download and install it into the VM and register it as a service in `systemd`, so it is started automatically every time you start the VM. The steps are shown in the following listing.

Listing 4.7   Installation script

```
curl -sfLo vault.zip https://releases.hashicorp.com/vault/1.1.2/
➥vault_1.1.2_linux_amd64.zip              ◁─┐ Download and
unzip vault.zip                               │ install Vault.
sudo mv vault /usr/bin/
sudo chmod +x /usr/bin/vault              ◁─┤ Set up a profile.
cat <<EOF | sudo tee /etc/profile.d/vault.sh
export VAULT_ADDR=http://127.0.0.1:8200
EOF                                          ┐ Create a user
source /etc/profile.d/vault.sh            ◁─┘ to run Vault.
sudo addgroup vault
sudo adduser -G vault -S -s /bin/false -D vault   ◁─┐ Create a Vault
sudo mkdir -p /etc/vault/{config,data}              │ configuration.

cat <<EOF | sudo tee /etc/vault/config/config.hcl
disable_mlock = "true"
backend "file" {
  path = "/etc/vault/data"
}
listener "tcp" {
  address      = "0.0.0.0:8200"
  tls_disable = "true"
}
EOF
```

```
sudo chown -R vault:vault /etc/vault                              Set up systemd
cat <<"EOF" | sudo tee /etc/systemd/system/vault.service          to start Vault.
[Unit]
Description="HashiCorp Vault - A tool for managing secrets"
Documentation=https://www.vaultproject.io/docs/
Requires=network-online.target
After=network-online.target
[Service]
User=vault
Group=vault
ExecStart=/usr/bin/vault server -config=/etc/vault/config
ExecReload=/bin/kill --signal HUP $MAINPID
ExecStartPost=-/bin/sh -c "/bin/sleep 5 && /bin/vault operator unseal
-address=http://127.0.0.1:8200 $(/bin/cat /etc/vault/init.json |
/bin/jq -r .unseal_keys_hex[0])"
KillMode=process
KillSignal=SIGINT
Restart=on-failure
RestartSec=5
TimeoutStopSec=30
StartLimitBurst=3

[Install]
WantedBy=multi-user.target
EOF

sudo systemctl start vault
```

> **WARNING**   For this example, the listening address has been set to 0.0.0.0, so any host can access the Vault server. This is OK for nonproduction environments or educational purposes, but in real environments, you could configure it appropriately.

CONFIGURING THE TRANSIT SECRET ENGINE

Vault needs to be unsealed, so it can be accessed externally, and the transit secret engine will be enabled, so Vault can be used to encrypt and decrypt data in transit. Don't worry if you still don't understand why these steps are required, as we will cover them in greater detail in the following chapter.

For this specific example, you will be configuring Vault to be accessed by a user providing the vault-kms-k8s-plugin-token value as a token and creating an encryption key named my-key:

```
vault operator init -format=json -key-shares=1 -key-threshold=1 |     Initialize and
sudo tee /etc/vault/init.json                                          unseal Vault.
vault operator unseal "$(cat /etc/vault/init.json |                  Log in to Vault using
jq -r .unseal_keys_hex[0])"                                           the root token.
vault login "$(cat /etc/vault/init.json | jq -r .root_token)"
vault token create -id=vault-kms-k8s-plugin-token                    Create a special token
vault secrets enable transit          Create the                     to access the transit
vault write -f transit/keys/my-key    encryption key.                secret engine.

                                                                     Enable the transit
                                                                     secret engine.
```

INSTALLING THE VAULT KMS PROVIDER

After Vault is up and running, you need to install and set up the Vault KMS provider/ plugin. There are four important things to configure for the KMS provider:

1. The encryption key name (`my-key`)
2. The address where the Vault server is running (`127.0.0.1`)
3. The token that is required to access to Vault (`vault-kms-k8s-plugin-token`)
4. The socket file for the Vault KMS provider (`/var/lib/minikube/certs/vault-k8s-kms-plugin.sock`)

Remember that the KMS provider is a gRPC server that acts as a bridge between `kube-apiserver` and the KMS. The steps are shown in the following listing.

Listing 4.8 Install `kms vault script`

```
curl -sfLo vault-k8s-kms-plugin https://github.com/lordofthejars/
kubernetes-vault-kms-plugin/releases/download/book/
vault-k8s-kms-plugin-amd64
unzip vault-k8s-kms-plugin.zip
sudo mv vault-k8s-kms-plugin /bin/vault-k8s-kms-plugin
sudo chmod +x /bin/vault-k8s-kms-plugin

sudo mkdir -p /etc/vault-k8s-kms-plugin
cat <<EOF | sudo tee /etc/vault-k8s-kms-plugin/config.yaml
keyNames:
- my-key
transitPath: /transit
addr: http://127.0.0.1:8200
token: vault-kms-k8s-plugin-token
EOF

sudo chown -R vault:vault /etc/vault-k8s-kms-plugin
cat <<EOF | sudo tee /etc/systemd/system/vault-k8s-kms-plugin.service
[Unit]
Description="KMS transit plugin"
Requires=vault.service
After=vault.service
[Service]
User=root
Group=root
ExecStart=/usr/bin/vault-k8s-kms-plugin -socketFile=/var/lib/minikube/
certs/vault-k8s-kms-plugin.sock -vaultConfig=/etc/vault-k8s-kms-plugin/
config.yaml
ExecReload=/bin/kill --signal HUP $MAINPID
KillMode=process
KillSignal=SIGINT
Restart=on-failure
RestartSec=5
TimeoutStopSec=30
StartLimitBurst=3
[Install]
WantedBy=multi-user.target
EOF

sudo systemctl start vault-k8s-kms-plugin
```

The Vault KMS plugin is downloaded.

The plugin is configured with the parameters we configured in Vault in the previous section.

Set up systemd to start the Vault KMS plugin.

Set the socketfile where the Vault KMS plugin is started.

CONFIGURING THE KUBERNETES KMS PROVIDER

In the previous example, enabling encryption data at rest, you created an Encryption-Configuration file to enable encryption data at rest in the Kubernetes cluster. Now you need to create an EncryptionConfiguration file to configure the Vault KMS provider instead of an `aescbc` provider. Figure 4.14 shows how the Kubernetes-api server interacts with the Kubernetes KMS plugin.

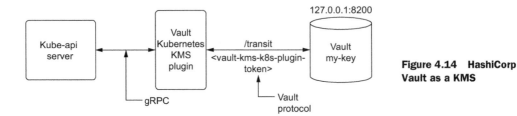

Figure 4.14   HashiCorp Vault as a KMS

The important parameter to set is the `endpoint` because that's the location the provider/plugin is communicating with. In this case, it was configured in the previous step with the `socketFile` parameter set to `/var/lib/minikube/certs/vault-k8s-kms-plugin.sock`.

```
cat <<EOF | sudo tee /var/lib/minikube/certs/encryption-config.yaml
kind: EncryptionConfiguration
apiVersion: apiserver.config.k8s.io/v1
resources:
- resources:
  - secrets
  providers:                    KMS is used
  - kms:                        as the provider.
      name: vault
      endpoint: unix:///var/lib/minikube/certs/vault-k8s-kms-plugin.sock
      cachesize: 100
  - identity: {}                        Set the socketFile specified
EOF                                     in the previous step.
```

Figure 4.15 shows the difference between the EncryptionConfiguration file when KMS is used and when it is not.

Figure 4.15   EncryptionConfiguration vs. KMS EncryptionConfiguration

RESTART KUBE-APISERVER

The last step is restarting the `kube-apiserver`, so the new configuration takes effect and envelope encryption happens using Vault as a remote KMS. In the past, you would need to restart the whole minikube instance, but in this case, you will use a different approach by just restarting the `kubelet` process.

```
sudo sed -i '/- kube-apiserver/ a \ \ \ \ - --encryption-provider-config=/  ◄┐
➥var/lib/minikube/certs/encryption-config.yaml' /etc/kubernetes/
➥manifests/kube-apiserver.yaml          ◄─┐ The kubelet          kube-apiserver is
sudo systemctl daemon-reload                │ is restarted.       configured to use the
sudo systemctl stop kubelet                                       EncryptionConfiguration
docker stop $(docker ps -aq)                                      file created to use KMS.
sudo systemctl start kubelet
```

PUTTING EVERYTHING TOGETHER

As previously noted, a script is provided to you to execute all the previous steps automatically. Moreover, we suggest you now use a new minikube instance, so you have a clean minikube instance with Vault installed inside the VM.

Create a minikube instance under the `vault` profile, SSH into the VM where it is running the Kubernetes cluster, and run the script that executes all the previously explained steps. Execute the following commands:

```
                    │ Stop the previous                    Start a new minikube instance
                    ┘ minikube instance.                     under the vault profile.
minikube stop  ◄─┘
minikube start -p vault --memory=8192 --vm-driver=virtualbox  ◄─┐
➥--kubernetes-version='v1.18.6'
minikube ssh "$(curl https://raw.githubusercontent.com/lordofthejars/  ◄─┐
➥vault-kubernetes-tutorial/master/scripts/install_vault_kms.sh -s)"
➥-p vault
                                                 Execute the script to
                                              configure the KMS provider.
```

4.2.2 *Creating the secret*

In a terminal window, create a new secret named `kms-db-secret-encrypted` with two key–value entries:

```
kubectl create secret generic kms-db-secret-encrypted
➥--from-literal=username=devuser --from-literal=password=devpassword
```

At this point, the secret is created the same way as before, but the secret is encrypted using the envelope encryption schema. Let's explore how the data is stored inside `etcd`.

ACCESSING ETCD

Repeat exactly the same process you followed in accessing `etcd` to get the content of the secret `kms-db-secret-encrypted`, and validate that it is stored encrypted instead of in plain text. In one terminal window, expose the `etcd` server in localhost:

```
kubectl port-forward -n kube-system etcd-vault 2379:2379
```

In another terminal, repeat the process of copying the `etcd` certificates, and configure the `etcdctl` using environment variables:

```
kubectl cp kube-system/etcd-vault:/var/lib/minikube/certs/etcd/peer.key
⮕/tmp/peer.key
kubectl cp kube-system/etcd-vault:/var/lib/minikube/certs/etcd/peer.crt
⮕/tmp/peer.crt

export \
  ETCDCTL_API=3 \
  ETCDCTL_INSECURE_SKIP_TLS_VERIFY=true  \
  ETCDCTL_CERT=/tmp/peer.crt \
  ETCDCTL_KEY=/tmp/peer.key
```

You can now query etcd to get the value of the kms-db-secret-encrypted key to validate that it is encrypted and its values are impossible to decipher.

```
etcdctl get /registry/secrets/default/kms-db-secret-encrypted
```

The output should be similar to that in the following listing.

Listing 4.9   Encrypted KMS secret

```
/registry/secrets/default/kms-db-secret-encrypted
cm?9>?*?-????????~?6I????=@????e????.??
                              8Y
t??p ?b?                    ??V????w??6???l??v??Ey?q.?^?Z?
⮕?n?xh??$???d??1??y??Q??q??LJ?}????????I?w??%;
```

Unlike in the previous section, the secrets are encrypted in kube-apiserver using envelope encryption schema and then sent to be stored in the etcd server. You can stop port forwarding, as you do not need to for now, by aborting the process (ctrl-C on the first terminal). You can also stop the current minikube instance and start the default one that only contains a running Kubernetes instance:

```
minikube stop -p vault
```

```
minikube start
```

Summary

- Secrets are not encrypted in etcd by default; hence you need to find a way to encrypt them to prevent any attacker with access to etcd from reading them.
- The EncryptionConfiguration Kubernetes object is key in configuring Kubernetes to encrypt resources (secrets), but if a remote KMS is not used, both encrypted data and encryption keys are stored in the same machine.
- To allow data and keys to be stored in different machines, Kubernetes supports the use of a remote KMS.

HashiCorp Vault and Kubernetes

This chapter covers

- Enabling HashiCorp Vault for use by end user applications deployed to Kubernetes
- Integrating Kubernetes authentication to simplify access to Vault resources
- Accessing secrets stored in HashiCorp Vault by applications deployed to Kubernetes

Chapter 4 introduced HashiCorp Vault as a KMS that could be used to provide encryption for secrets and other resources stored in `etcd`—the key/value datastore for Kubernetes—so these values could not be readily accessed because they were stored at rest.

This chapter focuses on the importance of using a secrets management tool, like HashiCorp Vault, to securely store and manage sensitive assets for applications deployed to Kubernetes as well as demonstrating how both applications and Vault can be configured to provide seamless integration with one another. By using a tool like Vault, application teams can offload some of the responsibilities involved in managing sensitive resources to a purpose-built tool, while still being able to integrate with their applications.

5.1 *Managing application secrets using HashiCorp Vault*

As you've seen thus far, sensitive assets can be used by either the core infrastructure components of Kubernetes or by applications deployed to the platform. Chapter 4 focused primarily on the infrastructure portion and how to properly secure the primary database of Kubernetes, `etcd`, by encrypting the values using HashiCorp Vault. While Vault can aid in keeping the platform secure, it is more commonly used to store and protect properties for use in applications.

When securing the values for storage within `etcd`, as described in chapter 4, Vault was used as an intermediary to perform the cryptographic functions needed to encrypt and decrypt data in transit using Vault's transit secrets. For applications deployed to Kubernetes, they themselves are not designed to act as a secrets store and would look to another tool that is better designed for this purpose. This is where Vault can be used as a solution.

Imagine you wanted to use Vault to store the secret locations where field agents are deployed around the world. While a database could be used in this scenario, we will demonstrate how to store arbitrary data in a secure fashion using a Vault instance deployed to Kubernetes and access the values within an application deployed to Kubernetes (figure 5.1).

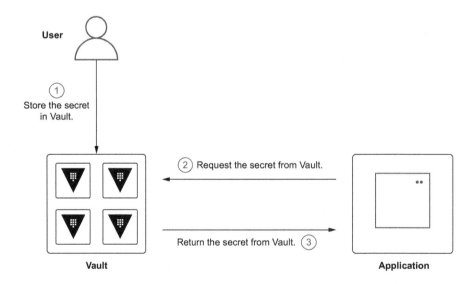

Figure 5.1   Secrets storage within Vault and an application requesting access to retrieve the stored values

5.1.1   *Deploying Vault to Kubernetes*

In chapter 4, you installed HashiCorp Vault within the minikube VM to provide a clear separation between the Kubernetes infrastructure components (particularly etcd) and the KMS. Since etcd is so crucial to the functionality of the Kubernetes cluster, you should ensure there are no dependencies upon one another for proper operation (aka the *chicken or the egg* dilemma).

Since there is less of a hard dependency between applications and the KMS (and vice versa), and to be able to take advantage of many of the benefits of Kubernetes itself (e.g., scheduling and application health monitoring), Vault will be deployed to Kubernetes for the purpose of acting as a KMS for applications. There are several methods you can use to deploy Vault to Kubernetes, but the most straightforward method is using Helm. A chart available from HashiCorp (https://github.com/hashicorp/vault-helm) supports the majority of deployment options needed for either a development instance or to support a production-ready cluster.

To get started, use the terminal from any directory to first add the Hashicorp repository to Helm containing the Vault chart:

```
helm repo add hashicorp https://helm.releases.hashicorp.com

"hashicorp" has been added to your
```

Then retrieve the latest updates from the remote repositories, which will pull down the content to your machine:

```
helm repo update

Hang tight while we grab the latest from your chart repositories...
...Successfully got an update from the "hashicorp" chart repository
Update Complete. ? Happy Helming!?
```

VAULT HA STORAGE USING INTEGRATED RAFTHA (HIGH AVAILABILITY) STORAGE

The next consideration whenever Vault is deployed is how you will handle the storage of its metadata. When Vault was deployed outside of Kubernetes within the minikube VM, the file system storage type was used. This configuration will persist to the local filesystem and is an easy way to get Vault running. However, when using a production-style deployment, the file system storage type is not desirable, as it only supports a single instance.

Another benefit of deploying Vault on Kubernetes, aside from the aforementioned benefits and to align with the desire for a more production style deployment, is the ability to achieve high availability (HA) easily. However, going beyond a single instance requires the use of a different storage type other than file system. While Vault supports a number of external storage backends, ranging from relational and NoSQL databases to cloud object storage, a simple option that is highly available and does not have any external dependency is integrated storage using Raft (figure 5.2).

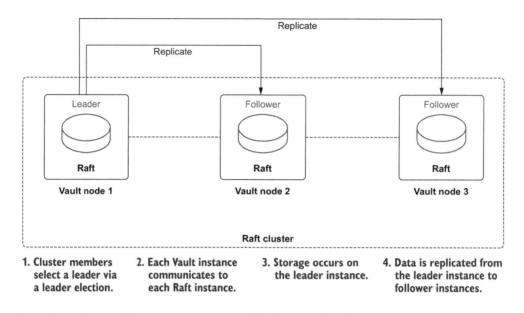

1. Cluster members select a leader via a leader election.
2. Each Vault instance communicates to each Raft instance.
3. Storage occurs on the leader instance.
4. Data is replicated from the leader instance to follower instances.

Figure 5.2   Leader election and the replication of data using Raft storage

Raft is a distributed *consensus algorithm*, in which multiple members form a cluster after an election occurs. A leader is determined based on the outcome of the election, when they have the responsibility of determining the the shared state of the cluster and replicating the state to each of the followers. The minimum number in any cluster is 3 ($N/2+1$, where N is the number of total nodes) to ensure there is a minimum number of nodes if a failure occurs. Raft is a common protocol and is used by other solutions in the cloud-native space, including etcd, when it operates in a highly available configuration.

With an understanding of the storage requirement's needed to support a highly available deployment of Vault, install the Vault Helm chart by setting the server.ha.enabled=true and server.ha.raft.enabled=true values, which will enable HA along with enabling Raft. In addition, since you are attempting to deploy a highly available deployment to a single minikube node, set the server.affinity value to ""; this will skip the default Pod affinity configurations, which would attempt to schedule each Vault Pod to a separate node and, thus, result in a scheduling failure. Execute the command in the following listing to install the chart.

Listing 5.1   Deploying vault using Helm

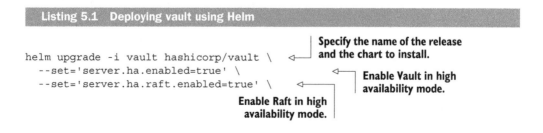

```
helm upgrade -i vault hashicorp/vault \
  --set='server.ha.enabled=true' \
  --set='server.ha.raft.enabled=true' \
```

Specify the name of the release and the chart to install.

Enable Vault in high availability mode.

Enable Raft in high availability mode.

```
--set='server.affinity=""' -n vault \           ◁── Disable Pod
--create-namespace   ◁── Create a namespace called vault │ affinity.
                         if it does not already exist.
```

Confirm that three instances of Vault are deployed to the vault namespace:

```
kubectl get pods -n vault
```

```
NAME                                    READY   STATUS    RESTARTS   AGE
vault-0                                 0/1     Running   0          76s
vault-1                                 0/1     Running   0          76s
vault-2                                 0/1     Running   0          76s
vault-agent-injector-76d54d8b45-dvzww   1/1     Running   0          76s
```

In addition to the three expected Vault instances, another Pod prefixed with vault-agent-injector is also deployed and serves the purpose of dynamically injecting secrets into Pods. The Vault Agent Injector will be covered in detail later in the chapter. If any of the Vault or Vault Injector Pods are not currently in a Running state or none of the Pods appear, use the kubectl get events -n vault command to investigate the cause of such issues.

With Vault deployed, the first step is to initialize Vault. Since there are multiple instances of Vault, one of them should be designated as the initial leader—vault-0 in this instance.

First check the status of Vault, which should denote it has yet to be initialized:

```
kubectl -n vault exec -it vault-0 -- vault operator init -status
```

```
Vault is not initialized
```

Now initialize the Vault, so you can begin interacting with it, as follows.

Listing 5.2   Initializing the vault

```
kubectl -n vault exec -it vault-0 -- vault operator init           ◁───┐
```

> The output will display each of the keys that can be used
> to unseal the Vault along with the initial root token.

When Vault is initialized, it will be put into *sealed* mode, meaning it knows how to access the storage layer but cannot decrypt any of the content. When Vault is in a sealed state, it is akin to a bank vault, where the assets are secure, but no actions can take place. To be able to interact with Vault, it must be unsealed.

Unsealing is the process of obtaining access to the master key. However, this key is only one portion of how data in Vault is encrypted. When data is stored in Vault, it is encrypted using an *encryption key*. This key is stored along with the data in Vault and encrypted using another key, known as the *master key*. However, it does not stop there. The master key is also stored with the data in Vault and encrypted one more time by the *unseal key*. The unseal key is then distributed into multiple shards using an algorithm known as Shamir's Secret Sharing. To reconstruct the *seal key*, a certain number of shards must be provided individually, which will enable access to the combined key and, ultimately, to the data stored within Vault (figure 5.3).

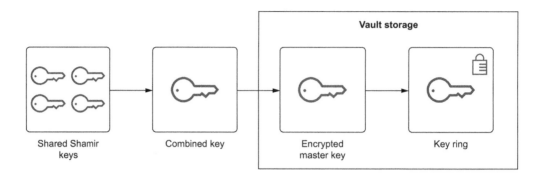

Figure 5.3   The steps involved in unsealing Vault

When Vault was initialized, five unsealed keys were provided, representing the shards that will be used to construct the combined key. By default, three keys are needed to reconstruct the combined key. Begin the process of unsealing the vault for the vault-0 instance.

Execute the following command to begin the unsealing process. When prompted, enter the value of the key next to Unseal Key 1 at the prompt from the vault operator init command executed in the following listing.

```
kubectl -n vault exec -it vault-0 -- vault operator unseal

Unseal Key (will be hidden):
```

Listing 5.3   Progression of unsealing the vault

```
Key                 Value
---                 -----
Seal Type           shamir
Initialized         true
Sealed              true
Total Shares        5
Threshold           3              ┐ Unseal
Unseal Progress     1/3      ◁────┘ progress
Unseal Nonce        fbb3714f-27cb-e362-ba40-03db093aea23
Version             1.7.2
Storage Type        raft
HA Enabled          true
```

The unsealing process is underway, as the Unseal Progress row shown in listing 5.3 indicates one of the keys has been entered. Execute the same kubectl -n vault exec -it vault-0—vault operator unseal two more times, providing the values next to Unseal Key 2, Unseal Key 3, and so on when prompted.

Keep providing keys until you see an output similar to that in the following listing.

Listing 5.4   An unsealed Vault instance

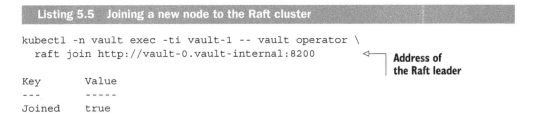

```
Key                    Value
---                    -----
Seal Type              shamir
Initialized            true
Sealed                 false      ⊲─┤ Sealed status
Total Shares           5
Threshold              3
Version                1.7.2
Storage Type           raft
Cluster Name           vault-cluster-c5e28066            ⊲─┤ Cluster name
Cluster ID             0a3170f4-b486-7358-cba7-381349056f3e
HA Enabled             true       ⊲─┐ HA Mode
HA Cluster             n/a          │ status
HA Mode                standby
Active Node Address    <none>
Raft Committed Index   24
```

The vault-0 instance is now unsealed. However, since Vault is running in HA mode, the other two members must be joined to the newly created cluster and undergo the unsealing process.

First join the vault-1 instance to the Raft cluster, as follows.

Listing 5.5   Joining a new node to the Raft cluster

```
kubectl -n vault exec -ti vault-1 -- vault operator \
  raft join http://vault-0.vault-internal:8200     ⊲─┐ Address of
                                                      │ the Raft leader
Key        Value
---        -----
Joined     true
```

Next execute the following command three times, providing a different unseal key, as accomplished with vault-0:

```
kubectl -n vault exec -it vault-1 -- vault operator unseal

Unseal Key (will be hidden):
```

Once these steps have been completed on the vault-1 instance, perform the vault operator join and vault operator unseal commands on the vault-2 instance.

To confirm that the highly available Vault cluster is ready, log in to the vault-0 instance using the Initial Root Token provided by the vault operator init command as follows:

```
kubectl -n vault exec -it vault-0 -- vault login

Token (will be hidden):
Success! You are now authenticated. The token information displayed below
is already stored in the token helper. You do NOT need to run "vault login"
again. Future Vault requests will automatically use this token.

Key                  Value
---                  -----
token                s.cm8HyaIxR2MPseDxTvOU7ugD
token_accessor       Fx23YMxqiYabU8u5Ptt2qpcH
token_duration       ?
token_renewable      false
token_policies       ["root"]
identity_policies    []
policies             ["root"]
```

Now that you have logged in with the root token, confirm all members have successfully joined to the Vault cluster by listing all Raft members:

```
kubectl -n vault exec -ti vault-0 -- vault operator raft list-peers
```

Node	Address	State	Voter
8b58cb62-7da7-5e8d-298b-95d4e8203ea5	vault-0.vault-internal:8201	leader	true
4cef7124-d40a-bba8-4dac-4830936ceea3	vault-1.vault-internal:8201	follower	true
d1a8d5fd-82be-feb7-a3e7-ca298d81d050	vault-2.vault-internal:8201	follower	true

Notice how vault-0 is listed as the leader with the other two members being followers, as indicated by the State column. If three Raft instances do not appear, confirm
that each member was successfully joined in listing 5.5. At this point, the highly available Vault has been deployed to the minikube instance.

SECRETS ENGINES

We spoke earlier about the types of storage backends that can be used as durable storage for Vault information. The actual storage, generation, and encryption of data
within Vault itself is facilitated by one of the supported secrets engines. Secrets
engines can perform simple operations, like storing or reading data. However, more
complex secrets engines may call out to external resources to generate assets on
demand. The transit secrets engine, as described in chapter 4, aided in the encryption
and decryption of values stored in etcd, but for applications looking to retrieve values
stored in Vault, like the one you are looking to implement in this chapter, the Key/
Value, or kv, secrets engine can be used.

The kv engine does exactly what it sounds like it would: it enables the storage of
key–value pairs within Vault. This secrets engine has evolved over time, and there are,
as of this writing, two versions that can be used.

- kv*version 1*—Nonversioned storage of key–value pairs. Updated values overwrite
  existing values. There is a smaller storage footprint, since there is no requirement to store additional metadata that supports versioning.

- kv*version 2*—Support for versioned key–value pairs. It provides enhanced support for avoiding unintentionally overwriting data. There is an additional storage requirement for the metadata used to track versioning.

Either kv version could be used in this case, but given that most implementations make use of version 2, it is the one that will be used. Secrets engines are enabled on a given *path*, or location within Vault. For your application, you will use the agents path.

Before enabling the kv engine, list all of the enabled secrets engines:

```
kubectl -n vault exec -it vault-0 -- vault secrets list

Path        Type       Accessor          Description
----        ----       --------          -----------
cubbyhole/  cubbyhole  cubbyhole_4cc71c5d  per-token private secret storage
identity/   identity   identity_9f9aa91a   identity store
sys/        system     system_8f066be3     system endpoints used for control,
                                           policy and
```

Now enable the kv-v2 secrets engine on the agents path to enable the storing of key–value pair secrets, as follows.

Listing 5.6 Enabling the kv secrets engine

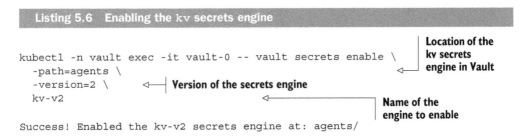

```
kubectl -n vault exec -it vault-0 -- vault secrets enable \        Location of the
  -path=agents \                                                   kv secrets
  -version=2 \        ←— Version of the secrets engine             engine in Vault
  kv-v2                                                            Name of the
                                                                   engine to enable

Success! Enabled the kv-v2 secrets engine at: agents/
```

With the engine enabled on the agents path, you can now store a few values. Each agent will have several attributes associated with their key:

- name
- email
- location

Create a new entry for agent bill:

```
kubectl -n vault exec -it vault-0 -- vault kv put agents/bill \
  name="Bill Smith" \
  email="bill@acme.org" \
  location="New York, USA"

Key             Value
---             -----
created_time    2021-05-29T17:20:48.24905171Z
deletion_time   n/a
destroyed       false
version         1
```

Retrieving the value stored in Vault is just as simple:

```
kubectl -n vault exec -it vault-0 -- vault kv get agents/bill

====== Metadata ======
Key                Value
---                -----
created_time       2021-05-29T17:20:48.24905171Z
deletion_time      n/a
destroyed          false
version            1

====== Data ======
Key        Value
---        -----
email      bill@acme.org
location   New York, USA
name       Bill Smith
```

Now that you have confirmed you were able to add and retrieve a secret successfully, add a few more agents:

```
kubectl -n vault exec -it vault-0 -- vault kv put agents/jane \
  name="Jane Doe" \
  email="jane@acme.org" \
  location="London, United Kingdom"
kubectl -n vault exec -it vault-0 -- vault kv put agents/maria \
  name="Maria Hernandez" \
  email="maria@acme.org" \
  location="Mexico City, Mexico"
kubectl -n vault exec -it vault-0 -- vault kv put agents/james \
  name="James Johnson" \
  email="james@acme.org" \
  location="Tokyo, Japan"
```

At this point, there should be four secrets stored in Vault.

APPLICATION ACCESS AND SECURITY

The root token currently being used to interact with Vault has unrestricted access to all of Vault's capabilities and is not recommended to be used within applications interacting with the Vault server. Instead, applying the principle of least privilege, a separate method for the application to authenticate against Vault should be used. Vault supports multiple auth methods for a consumer to identify itself, including username and password, TLS certificates, and the aforementioned token, just to name a few.

An auth method can be associated with one or more *policies*, which define the privileges against different paths in Vault. Each policy is associated with *capabilities*, which provide fine-grained control against a particular path (figure 5.4).

The following is the set of capabilities available in Vault:

- `create`—Allows the creation of data against a given path
- `read`—Allows the reading of data at a given path
- `delete`—Allows the deletion of data against a given path
- `list`—Allows the listing of values against a given path

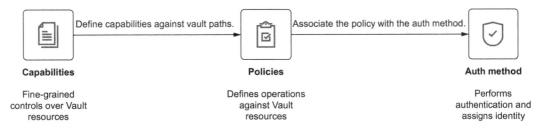

Figure 5.4   The relationships between capabilities, policies, and auth methods

Policies are written either in JSON or HashiCorp Configuration Language (HCL [compatible with JSON]) format and are submitted to the Vault server using the CLI at creation time.

Create a new file called `agents-policy.hcl`, which will define the policy that provides access to `read` and `list` the values within the `agents` path, as follows.

Listing 5.7   Creating a policy to govern access to Vault content

```
path "agents/data/*" {
  capabilities = ["list", "read"]        List of capabilities
}                                        associated at a given path
path "agents/metadata/*" {
  capabilities = ["list", "read"]
}
```

IMPORTANT   Versioned content, as in kv version 2, stores content prefixed with `data/`, which was omitted in kv version 1 and must be accounted for when designing policies.

Create a new policy called `agents_reader` by copying the .hcl policy file created in listing 5.7 to the Vault Pod and creating the policy:

```
cat agents-policy.hcl | \
  kubectl -n vault exec -it vault-0 -- vault policy write agents_reader -

Unable to use a TTY - input is not a terminal or the right kind of file
Success! Uploaded policy: agents_reader
```

Now create a new token that can be used by the Agents application and only provides access to the `agents` path, and assign it to a variable called `AGENTS_APP_TOKEN`, as shown.

Listing 5.8   Creating a token for the Agents application

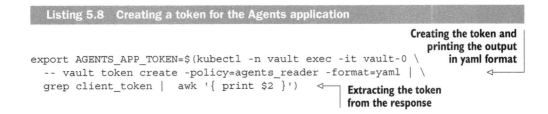

```
export AGENTS_APP_TOKEN=$(kubectl -n vault exec -it vault-0 \
  -- vault token create -policy=agents_reader -format=yaml | \
  grep client_token | awk '{ print $2 }')
```

Creating the token and printing the output in yaml format

Extracting the token from the response

You can view information about the token by looking up its details:

```
kubectl -n vault exec -it vault-0 -- vault token lookup $AGENTS_APP_TOKEN
```

```
Key                      Value
---                      -----
accessor                 9N8JDsdVrGfspYILad3DxZUq
creation_time            1622320692
creation_ttl             768h
display_name             token
entity_id                n/a
expire_time              2021-06-30T20:38:12.973925141Z
explicit_max_ttl         0s
id                       s.1ErBLPR3QTrNks8HhLNQcpjv          ◁─── The id of the token that
issue_time               2021-05-29T20:38:12.973933315Z          can be used to interact
meta                     <nil>                                    with the agents path
num_uses                 0
orphan                   false
path                     auth/token/create
policies                 [agents_reader default]
renewable                true
ttl                      767h51m20s
type
```

If the command returned an error or no values at all, confirm the value of the $AGENTS_APP_TOKEN value that was assigned in listing 5.8.

By default, the *time to live* (TTL), or the period of time in which the token is valid, is set for 32 days. In many enterprise organizations, limiting the length in time for which a token is valid increases the security posture and reduces the threat vector in the event a token becomes compromised. To explicitly set the TTL of a token, the -ttl flag can be added to the vault token create command to customize the duration a token is valid.

Confirm the token can only view resources in the agents path, as described by the agents_reader policy. First, back up the current root token to another location within the Vault Pod, so you can restore access later on:

```
kubectl -n vault exec -it vault-0 -- \
  cp /home/vault/.vault-token \
  /home/vault/.vault-token.root
```

Now log in with the new token created in listing 5.8:

```
echo $AGENTS_APP_TOKEN | kubectl -n vault exec -it vault-0 -- vault login -
```

```
Unable to use a TTY - input is not a terminal or the right kind of file
Success! You are now authenticated. The token information displayed below
is already stored in the token helper. You do NOT need to run "vault login"
again. Future Vault requests will automatically use this token.
```

```
Key                      Value
---                      -----
token                    s.1ErBLPR3QTrNks8HhLNQcpjv
token_accessor           9N8JDsdVrGfspYILad3DxZUq
```

```
token_duration        767h26m48s
token_renewable       true
token_policies        ["agents_reader" "default"]
identity_policies     []
policies              ["agents_reader" "default"]
```

Logging in displays key information about traits associated with the token, including the time it is valid and the permissions that it contains. Confirm the keys within the agents path can be listed:

```
kubectl -n vault exec -it vault-0 -- vault kv list /agents

Keys
---
bill
james
jane
maria
```

If an error occurs, confirm the policy was created properly, starting with listing 5.7.

If the keys were listed properly, attempt to access a resource, such as listing enabled secrets engines for which the token should not have access:

```
kubectl -n vault exec -it vault-0 -- vault secrets list

Error listing secrets engines: Error making API request.

URL: GET http://127.0.0.1:8200/v1/sys/mounts
Code: 403. Errors:

* 1 error occurred:
        * permission denied
```

With the restricted level of permissions confirmed, restore the root token by copying the backup token to the default location Vault expects, so you can once again execute elevated permissions:

```
kubectl -n vault exec -it vault-0 -- \
  cp /home/vault/.vault-token.root \
  /home/vault/.vault-token
```

Confirm an elevated request can be executed, so subsequent steps can be implemented:

```
kubectl -n vault exec -it vault-0 -- vault secrets list
```

5.1.2 *Deploying an application to access Vault*

Using a token that can be used to access the agents path within Vault, deploy an application that demonstrates accessing values within Vault. The source code is available on GitHub (http://mng.bz/WMXa), but we will not cover the application itself from a programming perspective in this chapter.

The first step is creating a Kubernetes Secret called `agents-vault-token`, which will contain our token that will be injected as an environment variable within the application, so it can communicate with Vault:

```
kubectl create secret generic agents-vault-token \
  --from-literal=token=$(echo -n $AGENTS_APP_TOKEN | tr -d '\r\n')

secret/agents-vault-token created
```

Create a file called `serviceaccount.yml` to define a Kubernetes service account called `agents` to associate with the application, as shown in the following listing. It is always recommended for each workload to be executed under a separate Service Account to delegate only the necessary permissions required. This will be demonstrated in further detail in listing 5.14.

Listing 5.9   serviceaccount.yml

```
---
apiVersion: v1
kind: ServiceAccount
metadata:
  name: agents
```

Create the `agents` service account referencing the manifest created in the following:

```
kubectl -n vault apply -f serviceaccount.yml

serviceaccount/agents created
```

Create a file called `deployment_token_auth.yml` containing the manifest for the application that will use token-based authentication with the token defined within the `agents-vault-token` secret created earlier, as follows.

Listing 5.10   deployment_token_auth.yml

```
---
apiVersion: apps/v1
kind: Deployment
metadata:
  name: agents
spec:
  replicas: 1
  selector:
    matchLabels:
      app: agents
  strategy:
    rollingUpdate:
      maxSurge: 25%
      maxUnavailable: 25%
    type: RollingUpdate
  template:
    metadata:
```

```
    labels:
      app: agents
  spec:
    containers:
      - env:
          - name: QUARKUS_VAULT_AUTHENTICATION_CLIENT_TOKEN
            valueFrom:
              secretKeyRef:            ◁─────────┐  Token stored within a Kubernetes secret
                key: token                       │  injected as an environment variable
                name: agents-vault-token
        image: quay.io/ablock/agents
        imagePullPolicy: Always
        name: agents
        ports:
          - containerPort: 8080
            protocol: TCP
    restartPolicy: Always
    serviceAccountName: agents
```

Apply the Deployment to the cluster to create the application:

```
kubectl -n vault apply -f deployment_token_auth.yml
```

```
deployment.apps/agents
```

With the deployment created, confirm the application is running:

```
kubectl -n vault get pods -l=app=agents
```

```
NAME                      READY   STATUS    RESTARTS   AGE
agents-595b85fc6-6fdbj    1/1     Running   0          66s
```

The Vault token is exposed to the application via the QUARKUS_VAULT_AUTHENTICATION_
CLIENT_TOKEN environment variable. The application framework then facilitates the
backend communication to the Vault server.

Now test out the application to confirm values can be received. The application
exposes a restful service at the /agents endpoint on port 8080 that can be used to
query for agents stored in Vault.

Attempt to locate the record for the agent bill by first locating the name of the
running agents Pod and then invoking the service at the /agents/bill endpoint.

```
AGENTS_POD=$(kubectl get pods -l=app=agents \
  -o jsonpath={.items[0].metadata.name})
kubectl -n vault exec -it $AGENTS_POD -- \
  curl http://localhost:8080/agents/bill
```

```
{"email":"bill@acme.org","location":"New York, USA","name":"Bill Smith"}
```

Since you were able to retrieve a valid result, now attempt to retrieve a nonexistent
value, which should return an empty result:

```
kubectl -n vault exec -it $AGENTS_POD -- \
  curl http://localhost:8080/agents/bad
```

Feel free to query for the other agents that were stored in Vault to fully exercise the application. In the next section, you will explore how to avoid using Vault tokens to authenticate to Vault.

5.2   *Kubernetes auth method*

Section 5.1.2 explored how an application can make use of Vault tokens, using the token auth method to interact with the Vault server to access stored values. While using tokens to access Vault is fairly straightforward, it requires the additional step of managing the life cycle of the token, which can, in the end, result in a reduction of the overall security posture.

Vault, as described in 5.1, supports a diverse set of auth methods. Since you are operating within a Kubernetes environment, you can take advantage of a different method—the *Kubernetes auth method*—to simplify how applications interact with Vault. Using this method will prevent you from needing to oversee the additional task of managing tokens to access Vault.

The Kubernetes auth method does not do away with the concept of tokens (quite the opposite), but instead of managing separate tokens that originate in Vault, it makes use of the JSON Web Tokens (JWTs) associated with Kubernetes Service Accounts. Running applications on Kubernetes interact with Vault using the Service Account token mounted within the Pod (/var/run/secrets/kubernetes.io/ serviceaccount/token). *Roles* are then created within Vault, which map Kubernetes service accounts and Vault policies that define the level of access granted. A diagram of the components involved in the Kubernetes Auth Method is shown in figure 5.5.

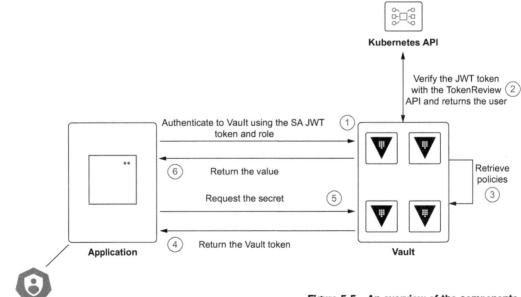

Figure 5.5   An overview of the components involved in the Kubernetes auth method

5.2.1 Configuring Kubernetes auth

Your first step is enabling the Kubernetes auth method within Vault:

```
kubectl -n vault exec -it vault-0 -- vault auth enable kubernetes

Success! Enabled kubernetes auth method at: kubernetes/
```

Since Vault will be interacting with the Kubernetes Service Account, it must be able to verify who the submitted token is associated with and if it is still valid. Fortunately, Kubernetes exposes the TokenReview API for just this purpose and essentially performs a reverse lookup of JWT tokens. By authenticating against the TokenReview API with a given JWT token of a ServiceAccount, details about the account will be returned, including, but not limited to, the username.

For Vault to interact with the Kubernetes TokenReview API to inspect tokens provided by applications, it must be given permissions to make such requests. Create a new service account called `vault-tokenreview` in a file called `vault-tokenreview-serviceaccount.yml` that will be used to by the Kubernetes auth method, as shown in the following listing.

Listing 5.11   vault-tokenreview-serviceaccount.yml

```
---
apiVersion: v1
kind: ServiceAccount
metadata:
  name: vault-tokenreview        ◄───┐ Name of the service account that will be
                                      └── used by the Kubernetes auth method
```

Now create the `vault-tokenreview` service account using the manifest created in listing 5.11:

```
kubectl -n vault apply -f vault-tokenreview-serviceaccount.yml

serviceaccount/vault-tokenreview
```

With the `vault-tokenreview` service account now created, it must be granted permissions to make requests against the Token Review API. There is an included Kubernetes `ClusterRole` that provides this level of access, called `system:auth-delegator`. Create a new `ClusterRoleBinding` called `vault-tokenreview-binding` in a file called `vault-tokenreview-binding.yml`, containing the following.

Listing 5.12   vault-tokenreview-binding.yml

```
apiVersion: rbac.authorization.k8s.io/v1
kind: ClusterRoleBinding
metadata:
  name: vault-tokenreview-binding
roleRef:
  apiGroup: rbac.authorization.k8s.io
  kind: ClusterRole
```

```
   name: system:auth-delegator
subjects:
  - kind: ServiceAccount
    name: vault-tokenreview
    namespace: vault
```

Create the `ClusterRoleBinding` from the manifest contained in the vault-
tokenreview-binding.yml file:

```
kubectl -n vault apply -f vault-tokenreview-binding.yml
```

```
clusterrolebinding.rbac.authorization.k8s.io/vault-tokenreview-binding created
```

Since the JWT of the `vault-tokenreview` service account is needed by Vault to communicate to Kubernetes, execute the following set of commands to first find the name
of the Kubernetes secret that contains the JWT token and then the Base64 decoded
token value stored within the secret.

> **Listing 5.13   Setting Vault `TokenReview` variables**

```
SA_SECRET_NAME=$(kubectl -n vault get serviceaccount vault-tokenreview \
  -o jsonpath={.secrets[0].name})
VAULT_TOKENREVIEW_SA_TOKEN=$(kubectl -n vault get secret $SA_SECRET_NAME \
  -o jsonpath='{.data.token}' | base64 -d)
```

Obtains the JWT token for the vault-tokenreview ServiceAccount

Locates the name of the secret associated with the vault-tokenreview ServiceAccount

Next specify the configuration of the Kubernetes cluster by providing the location of
the Kubernetes API, the certificate of the certificate authority, and the JWT of the service account obtained in listing 5.13:

```
kubectl -n vault exec -it vault-0 -- vault write auth/kubernetes/config \
  kubernetes_host="https://kubernetes.default.svc" \
  kubernetes_ca_cert="@/var/run/secrets/kubernetes.io/\
  serviceaccount/ca.crt" \token_reviewer_jwt=$VAULT_TOKENREVIEW_SA_TOKEN
```

```
Success! Data written to: auth/kubernetes/config
```

Now that Vault is capable of authenticating requests, applications that want to obtain
resources from within Vault must have a role associated with them to gain access to
values stored within Vault. A *role* consists of the name and namespace of the Service
Account submitting the request along with a set of Vault policies. Recall from listing
5.10, the Agents application is running using a Service Account called `agents`. While
there was little distinction between which Service Account was used to run the application previously, it is needed at this point to facilitate the integration with Vault using
the Kubernetes auth method. Execute the following to create a new role within Vault
called `agents`.

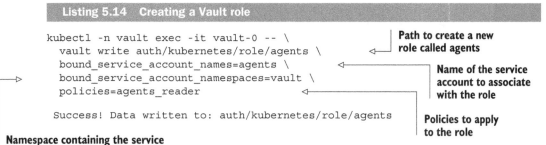

Listing 5.14   Creating a Vault role

The creation of the role within Vault allows the Agents application to make use of the Kubernetes auth method to retrieve values from Vault.

5.2.2   Testing and validating Kubernetes auth

To test and validate the integration of Kubernetes auth within the Agents application, first remove any existing artifacts that may still exist from the prior token-auth-method-based approach, as they will no longer be needed:

```
kubectl -n vault delete deployment agents
kubectl -n vault delete secrets agents-vault-token
```

> **NOTE**   Feel free to ignore any errors related to resources not being found. This step ensures you have a fresh environment that implements the Kubernetes auth method.

In the prior deployment of the Agents application, the QUARKUS_VAULT_AUTHENTICATION_CLIENT_TOKEN contained the value of the token used to authenticate against Vault. When migrating to the Kubernetes auth method, the QUARKUS_VAULT_AUTHENTICATION_KUBERNETES_ROLE will be used instead and reference the agents role created in Vault in listing 5.14.

Create a file called deployment_kubernetes_auth.yml containing the following Deployment definition.

Listing 5.15   deployment_kubernetes_auth.yml

```
---
apiVersion: apps/v1
kind: Deployment
metadata:
  name: agents
spec:
  replicas: 1
  selector:
    matchLabels:
      app: agents
  strategy:
    rollingUpdate:
      maxSurge: 25%
```

```
        maxUnavailable: 25%
      type: RollingUpdate
  template:
    metadata:
      labels:
        app: agents
    spec:
      containers:
        - env:
            - name: QUARKUS_VAULT_AUTHENTICATION_KUBERNETES_ROLE
              value: "agents"
          image: quay.io/ablock/agents
          imagePullPolicy: Always
          name: agents
          ports:
            - containerPort: 8080
              protocol: TCP
      restartPolicy: Always
      serviceAccountName: agents
```

Now create the deployment from the manifest created in listing 5.15:

```
kubectl -n vault apply -f deployment_kubernetes_auth.yml

deployment.apps/agents
```

Once the application has started, query for agent `maria` to confirm the value stored in Vault can be successfully retrieved, thus validating the Kubernetes auth method has been successfully integrated.

```
kubectl -n vault exec -it $(kubectl get pods -l=app=agents \
  -o jsonpath={.items[0].metadata.name}) -- \
  curl http://localhost:8080/agents/maria

{"email":"maria@acme.org","location":"Mexico City,
Mexico","name":"Maria Hernandez"}
```

A successful response demonstrates how the Kubernetes auth method can be used to retrieve secrets from Vault, without explicitly providing the application a Vault token to authenticate. If a successful result was not returned, confirm the steps described in this section.

5.3   *The Vault Agent Injector*

The Kubernetes Auth Method simplified how applications deployed on Kubernetes can access values stored within Vault. One of the challenges presented by using either the token or Kubernetes auth methods, as described in section 5.2.1, is that the application needs to be Vault aware. In many cases, especially in legacy applications or those provided by third-party vendors, it may not be possible to modify the source code to configure this type of integration.

To overcome these challenges, several approaches emerged, using patterns in the Kubernetes ecosystem to address how values stored within Vault are made available to applications. Each leaned on a key characteristic of a Pod in Kubernetes, through which volumes could be shared between containers using an `emptyDir` volume type. A separate container could then be packaged within the Pod with the responsibility of facilitating the interaction with Vault and providing the secret values to the application through the shared volume.

Two patterns in Kubernetes were adopted to support this approach:

- *init container*—A container, or set of containers, that executes before the application containers are started. In the context of Vault, assets are retrieved from Vault and placed in a shared volume that is pre-populated for the application to consume.
- *sidecar*–Containers that run alongside the application container. In the context of Vault, they continue to interact with Vault and refresh the content of the shared volume with assets from Vault.

To avoid the burden of requiring end users to develop and maintain their own set of containers for interacting with Vault as well as providing a mechanism for automatically injecting Vault-aware containers into Pods, the Vault Agent Injector from HashiCorp was created. The *Vault Agent Injector* runs as a Pod in Kubernetes and monitors for applications seeking to becoming Vault aware, based on annotations declared within their Pod. Once the injector has been installed to a cluster, when any other Pod is created, an admission webhook is sent to the Vault Agent Injector with the details of the Pod. If specific annotations and, in particular, `vault.hashicorp.com/agent-inject: true` are present within the Pod, the definition of Pod itself is modified to automatically inject an `initContainer` and/or `sidecar` container. This process leverages the Kubernetes `MutatingWebhookConfiguration` feature, which allows the modification of Kubernetes resources before they are persisted to `etcd` (figure 5.6).

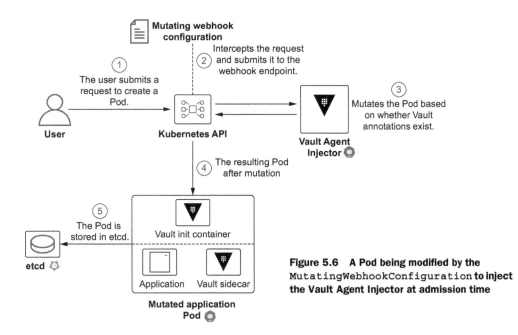

Figure 5.6   A Pod being modified by the `MutatingWebhookConfiguration` to inject the Vault Agent Injector at admission time

5.3.1   *Configurations to support Kubernetes Vault Agent injection*

To demonstrate how an application can have values stored in Vault injected with minimal changes to the application itself, you'll once again use the Agents application as the target. First define a new secret within Vault called `config`, containing properties related to the application. Through the Vault Agent Injector, the values provided within the secret will be added to a file within the application Pod.

First define the `config` secret in Vault by executing the command as follows.

Listing 5.16   Creating a key–value secret

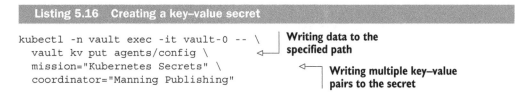

```
kubectl -n vault exec -it vault-0 -- \          Writing data to the
  vault kv put agents/config \                  specified path
  mission="Kubernetes Secrets" \
  coordinator="Manning Publishing"              Writing multiple key–value
                                                pairs to the secret
```

With the new value added, the next step is modifying the Deployment for the Agents application by defining several annotations needed to not only support automatic container injection but also to customize how the values presented in the Pod.

Create a new file called `deployment_vault_agent.yml`, as shown.

Listing 5.17   deployment_vault_agent.yml

```
apiVersion: apps/v1
kind: Deployment
metadata:
  name: agents
spec:
  replicas: 1
  selector:
    matchLabels:
      app: agents
  strategy:
    rollingUpdate:
      maxSurge: 25%
      maxUnavailable: 25%
    type: RollingUpdate
  template:                                        Enables Vault
    metadata:                                      Agent injection
      annotations:                                                    The name of the role
        vault.hashicorp.com/agent-inject: "true"                      associated with the
        vault.hashicorp.com/role: "agents"                            Kubernetes auth method
        vault.hashicorp.com/agent-inject-secret-config.properties:
        "agents/config"                                    The name of the Vault secret as the
        vault.hashicorp.com/agent-inject-template-         value and the resulting filename
        config.properties: |                               within the application Pod
          {{- with secret "agents/config" }}
          {{- range $k, $v := .Data.data }}        A template to describe how the
          {{ $k }}: {{ $v }}                       secret content will be rendered
          {{- end }}
          {{- end }}
```

```
    labels:
      app: agents
  spec:
    containers:
      - image: quay.io/ablock/agents
        imagePullPolicy: Always
        name: agents
        ports:
          - containerPort: 8080
            protocol: TCP
    restartPolicy: Always
    serviceAccountName: agents
```

The Vault Agent Injector builds upon the Kubernetes auth method, so a portion of the configurations applied in section 5.1 will be reused.

The `vault.hashicorp.com/role` denotes the name of the role associated with the service account running the Pod as well as the policies for granting access to content within Vault. The code line beginning with `vault.hashicorp.com/agent-inject-secret-` is used to define the file that will ultimately be created within the application Pod. The value of this annotation refers to the name of the secret within Vault. The secret `config` within the `agents` path was created in listing 5.16. The remainder of the annotation key refers to the name of the file that will be created in the Pod. So an annotation with the key `vault.hashicorp.com/agent-inject-secret-config.properties` results in a file named `config.properties` within the Pod.

Finally, the code line beginning with `vault.hashicorp.com/agent-inject-template-` refers to a template in the Consul language and defines how the content of the secret is rendered. Like the line beginning with `vault.hashicorp.com/agent-inject-secret-`, the remaining portion references the name of the file that will be created. The template defined here merely loops through all the keys and values contained within the secret.

If an existing agents deployment is present in the cluster, delete it to ensure any of the existing integrations with Vault, as described in sections 5.1.2 and 5.2, are not used moving forward:

```
kubectl -n vault delete deployment agents
```

```
deployment.apps/agents
```

Now execute the following command to create the agents deployment, which will make use of the Kubernetes Vault Agent Injector:

```
kubectl -n vault apply -f deployment_vault_agent.yml
```

```
deployment.apps/agents
```

If you observe the state of the `agents` Pod, you will notice several differences with this deployment.

```
kubectl -n vault get pod -l=app=agents
```

```
NAME                     READY   STATUS    RESTARTS   AGE
agents-795fcd5565-6f6cg  2/2     Running   0          79s
```

First notice, under the READY column, there are now two containers. The additional container is the sidecar responsible for keeping the contents of the secrets sourced from Vault up to date. In addition, before either the sidecar or agents container started, an init container called vault-agent-init also present in the Pod preseeded the an emptyDir volume mounted at /vault/secrets with the contents of the Vault secret. (This path can be modified via an annotation.) Since the init container must successfully complete before starting the primary containers, and since both containers within the Pod are currently running, you can rest assured the secret values have been retrieved from Vault. Let's verify by viewing the contents of the file located at /vault/secrets/config.properties within the agents container.

Listing 5.18   Viewing the file created by the vault secrets injector

```
kubectl -n vault exec -it $(kubectl get pods -l=app=agents \
  -o jsonpath={.items[0].metadata.name}) \                   ◁┐ Obtaining the name
  -c agents -- cat /vault/secrets/config.properties ◁─┐      │ of the running
                                                      │      │ agents Pod
coordinator: Manning Publishing         Printing the contents of
mission: Kubernetes Secrets                the file created by the
                                           Vault Agent Injector
```

Feel free to update the contents of the config secret within Vault. The sidecar container bundled within the Pod will routinely check the status of the secret and update the contents of the file within the application container. By using the Kubernetes Vault Agent Injector, Vault secrets can be provided automatically to application without any changes to the application, abstracting the use of Vault entirely, while providing the benefits of referencing sensitive values stored in HashiCorp Vault.

Summary

- HashiCorp Vault can be installed quickly and easily to a Kubernetes environment using a Helm chart.
- Unsealing a HashiCorp Vault instance is the process of obtaining the plain text root key to enable access to the underlying data.
- The Kubernetes auth method uses a Kubernetes service account to authenticate with HashiCorp Vault.
- The Kubernetes TokenReview API provides a method for extracting user details from a JWT token.
- The HashiCorp Vault Agent Injector mutates the definition of a Pod, allowing it to obtain secrets stored in Vault.

Accessing cloud
secrets stores

6

This chapter covers

- Using the Container Storage Interface (CSI) and the Secrets Store CSI Driver to inject secrets as volumes from cloud secrets stores
- Populating cloud secrets into Kubernetes clusters as Kubernetes Secrets
- Using auto rotation of secrets in the Secret Storage CSI Driver to improve security posture
- Consuming sensitive information from cloud secrets stores

Chapter 5 introduced HashiCorp Vault, which can be used for securely storing and managing sensitive assets for applications deployed to Kubernetes and demonstrated how both applications and Vault can be configured to provide seamless integration with one another. This chapter expands the idea introduced in the previous chapter of using an external secrets management tool to store secrets and injecting them inside the Pod, either as a volume or as an environment variable.

But in this chapter we'll focus on cloud secrets stores, like Google Secret Manager, Azure Key Vault, and AWS Secrets Manager.

First you'll learn about the Container Storage Interface (CSI) and the Secrets Store CSI Driver, using them to inject secrets stored in HashiCorp Vault. Then you'll learn about injecting Kubernetes Secrets using the Secrets Store CSI Driver as well as secret auto rotation. Finally, we'll discuss the integration between the CSI driver and Google Secret Manager, Azure Key Vault, and AWS Secrets Manager, so secrets can be injected directly from the secrets store to the Pod.

6.1   The Container Storage Interface and Secrets Store CSI Driver

As you have seen thus far, the etcd database stores the Kubernetes Secrets either unencrypted (by default) or encrypted, as shown in chapter 4. But what if you don't want to store your secrets in the etcd and instead would like to store and manage them outside of the Kubernetes cluster? One option, shown in chapter 5, is using HashiCorp Vault and HashiCorp Vault Agent to store secrets and inject them into a Pod.

HashiCorp Vault is an option, but nowadays cloud providers also offer their key vaults; for example, Google offers Google Secret Manager, and Amazon offers AWS Secrets Manager. What would happen if you wanted to use them to store secrets instead of etcd or Hashicorp Vault? Could you use the same approach previously but inject secrets as volume or environment variables from an external cloud store instead of etcd?

The answer is yes! But before we show you how to do it, we need to introduce the CSI initiative—a standard for exposing arbitrary block and file storage systems to containerized workloads like Kubernetes.

6.1.1   Container Storage Interface

As you've seen in chapter 2, a Kubernetes volume is a directory containing some data access to the containers running inside Pods. The physical storage of the volume is determined by the volume type used, and the volume is mapped during Pod initialization, executing the following steps:

1 The API server receives a command to create a new Pod in the Kubernetes cluster.
2 The scheduler finds a node that meets the desired criteria and sends the Pod definition to the node.
3 The node kubelet reads the Pod definition, sees that you want to attach a volume to the Pod container, and creates the volume via the volume plugin. This volume plugin is responsible for connecting to the configured persistence storage.

Figure 6.1 summarizes all these steps.

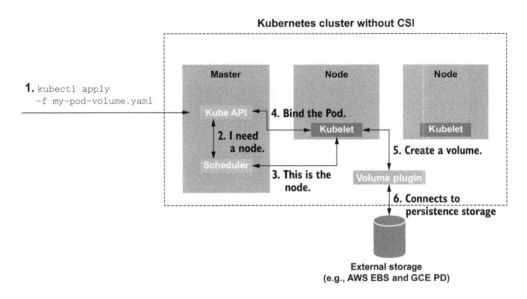

Figure 6.1   Process of creating a Volume from Pod perspective

As you can see, the *volume plugins* belong to the Kubernetes core. However, this approach has the following drawbacks:

- Volume plugin development is coupled to the Kubernetes development and release cycle. Any new supported volume (and volume plugin) requires a new version of Kubernetes.
- Any correction in a volume plugin (e.g., a fix bug or improvement) requires a new release of Kubernetes.
- Since volume plugins are inside Kubernetes, the source code is open; this is not a problem, until you need to make the plugin private.

CSI is an initiative that can be used to unify the storage interface of container orchestrator (CO) systems, like Kubernetes, Mesos, Docker Swarm, and so on, combined with storage vendors, like Ceph, Azure Disk, GCE persistent disk, and so on.

The first implication of CSI is that any implementation is guaranteed to work with all COs. The second implication is the location of the CSI elements; they are outside the CO core (i.e., the Kubernetes core), making them free to develop and release independently of the CO. Figure 6.2 shows a brief overview of the CSI.

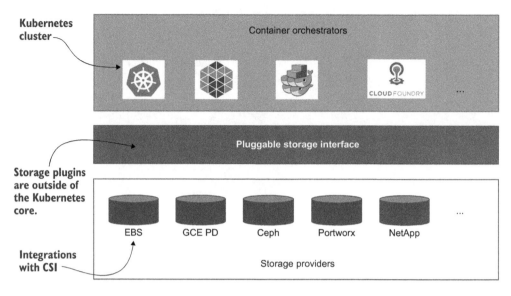

Figure 6.2   CSI schema

The CSI driver is the bridge between container clusters and the persistent storage implementing the operations required by the CSI specification for the specific storage. CSI drivers provide the following functionality:

- Creating persistent external storage
- Configuring persistent external storage
- Managing all input/output (I/O) between cluster and storage
- Providing advanced disk features, such as snapshots and cloning

CSI drivers include AliCloud Disk, AWS Elastic Block Storage, Azure Disk Storage, CephFS, DigitalOcean Block Storage, and GCE Persistent Disk.

6.1.2   *Container Storage Interface and Kubernetes*

CSI gained general availability (GA) status at version 1.13 of Kubernetes and can be used with Kubernetes volumes components (e.g., persistent volumes, persistent volumes claims, and storage classes). Kubernetes has some components that don't belong to the core that interact with the external pluggable container storage. This interaction occurs via Google Remote Procedure Calls (gRPCs) on domain sockets.

A Kubernetes cluster with CSI installed has the following components:

- *Kubernetes core*—This is the core of Kubernetes, where most of the elements introduced in this book live.
- *CSI external components*—This is a set of Linux containers, which contains common logic to trigger appropriate Kubernetes events to the CSI driver. Although these containers aren't mandatory, they help reduce the amount of boilerplate code required to implement the CSI driver.

- *Third-party external components*—These are vendor-specific implementations to communicate with the persistent storage solution.

Each of these components has subcomponents, and the most important ones can be seen in figure 6.3.

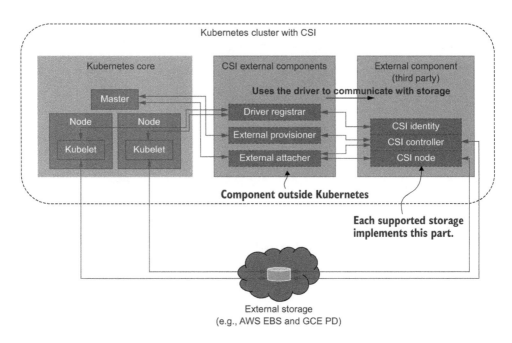

Figure 6.3 Kubernetes cluster with CSI

For the scope of this book, this is all you need to know about CSI specification and its integration with Kubernetes. A deep understanding of the system would be required to implement a specific CSI driver for a persistent storage system. Thanks to this separation of concerns, you can now write and deploy plugins, exposing new storage systems in Kubernetes without having to touch the Kubernetes core, so no further release of Kubernetes is required.

6.1.3 CSI and secrets

CSI is designed to create a standard manner of exposing all the different storage systems to Kubernetes and container workloads. With this standard in place, all you have to do is deploy the plugin (CSI driver) on your cluster. Can this be extended to other kinds of systems, such as secrets stores?

The Secrets Store CSI Driver is no different from any other CSI driver, allowing Kubernetes to attach a secret placed in an external secrets store into Pods as a volume. After the Volume is attached, the secret is available in the container's file system.

One of the elements that makes the Secrets Store CSI Driver extensible is the Secrets Store CSI provider. Instead of connecting to a secrets store directly, the driver has a new level of abstraction in the form of a provider, so depending on the secrets store used, the only element you need to install is the specific provider.

At the time of writing, the following secrets stores are supported:

- AWS Secrets Manager Systems Manager Parameter Store (AWS Provider)
- Azure Key Vault (Azure Provider)
- Google Secret Manager (GCP Provider)
- HashiCorp Vault (Vault Provider)

Figure 6.4 shows an overview of the Secrets Store CSI architecture.

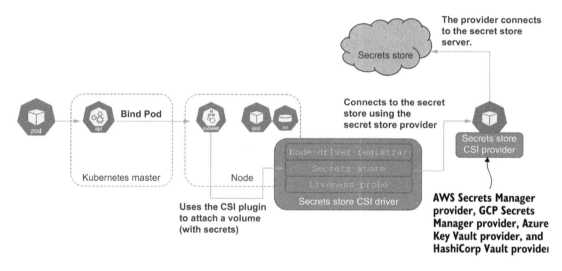

Figure 6.4   Kubernetes cluster with CSI

Before you use CSI and the Secrets Store CSI Driver, you will need to create a Kubernetes cluster and install CSI and the Secrets Store CSI Driver. We detail this process in the following sections.

6.1.4   *Installing prerequisites*

Start a new minikube instance by running the following command in a terminal window.

Listing 6.1   Start minikube

```
minikube start -p csi --kubernetes-version='v1.21.0'
    --vm-driver='virtualbox' --memory=8196          Creates a Kubernetes cluster
                                                     under the CSI profile
```

6.1.5 Installing the Secrets Store CSI Driver

The latest version of the Secrets Store CSI Driver at this time is `0.1.0`; although you might think it's an immature project, the truth is that it has been under development for a long time. Run the commands shown in the following listing to install Secrets Store CSI.

Listing 6.2 Install the Secrets Store CSI Driver

```
kubectl apply -f https://raw.githubusercontent.com/
➥kubernetes-sigs/secrets-store-csi-driver/v0.1.0/        Configures RBAC for
➥deploy/rbac-secretproviderclass.yaml                    the secret provider
kubectl apply -f https://raw.githubusercontent.com/
➥kubernetes-sigs/secrets-store-csi-driver/v0.1.0/        Configures
➥deploy/csidriver.yaml                                   the CSI driver
kubectl apply -f https://raw.githubusercontent.com/
➥kubernetes-sigs/secrets-store-csi-driver/v0.1.0/deploy/  Registers Secrets
➥secrets-store.csi.x-k8s.io_secretproviderclasses.yaml   Store CRDs
kubectl apply -f https://raw.githubusercontent.com/kubernetes-sigs/
➥secrets-store-csi-driver/v0.1.0/deploy/
➥secrets-store.csi.x-k8s.io_secretproviderclasspodstatuses.yaml
kubectl apply -f https://raw.githubusercontent.com/kubernetes-sigs/
➥secrets-store-csi-driver/v0.1.0/deploy/
➥secrets-store-csi-driver.yaml                Installs the Secrets
                                              Store CSI Driver
```

Since we'll be using the mapping between secrets-store content as Kubernetes Secrets and autorotation of secrets later, some additional RBAC permissions are required to enable it, as shown.

Listing 6.3 Installing RBAC

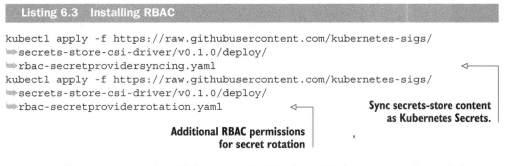

```
kubectl apply -f https://raw.githubusercontent.com/kubernetes-sigs/
➥secrets-store-csi-driver/v0.1.0/deploy/
➥rbac-secretprovidersyncing.yaml
kubectl apply -f https://raw.githubusercontent.com/kubernetes-sigs/
➥secrets-store-csi-driver/v0.1.0/deploy/
➥rbac-secretproviderrotation.yaml                    Sync secrets-store content
                                                     as Kubernetes Secrets.
              Additional RBAC permissions
              for secret rotation
```

NOTE If you are running Kubernetes in Windows Nodes (notice that minikube runs inside a Linux VM, so you don't need to run the command), you'll need to run the following command too:

```
kubectl apply -f https://raw.githubusercontent.com/kubernetes-sigs/
➥secrets-store-csi-driver/v0.1.0/deploy/
➥secrets-store-csi-driver-windows.yaml          Use this command if you are
                                                running Windows Nodes.
```

To validate the installation of the Secrets Store CSI Driver, run the commands shown in the following listing to validate that Pods are running correctly.

```
kubectl get pods --namespace=kube-system        ⊲──┐ Get Pods from the
                                                     kube-system namespace
```

You should see the Secrets Store CSI Driver Pods running on each agent node:

```
csi-secrets-store-8xlcn        3/3     Running   0        4m
```

Now that you've installed the Secrets Store CSI Driver into the Kubernetes cluster, it's time to select a Secrets Store CSI provider and deploy it. In the first example, you'll use HashiCorp Vault, as it's an agnostic secrets store, and you've already used it in the previous chapter.

The most significant deviation from your previous use of HashiCorp Vault is how a secret will be injected into the Pod. In one of the examples in chapter 5, you saw the HashiCorp Vault agent in charge of performing the injection; figure 6.5 contains a recap of how HashiCorp Vault Agent works. However, in this chapter, no agent will be used, and the Secrets Store CSI Driver will inject the secrets.

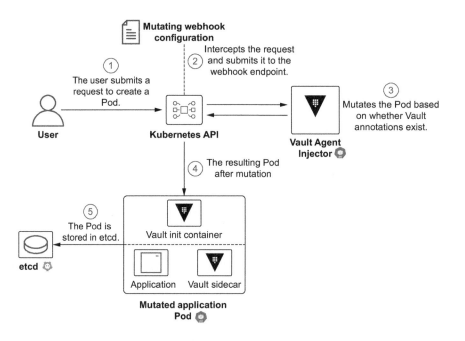

Figure 6.5   A Pod being modified by the `MutatingWebhookConfiguration` to inject the Vault Agent Injector at admission time

6.1.6   Consuming HashiCorp Vault secrets via the Secrets Store CSI Driver and the HashiCorp Vault provider

In this section, you will use HashiCorp Vault as a secrets store and consume the secrets using the Secrets Store CSI Driver and the HashiCorp Vault provider. Figure 6.6 shows an overview of what you will implement in this section.

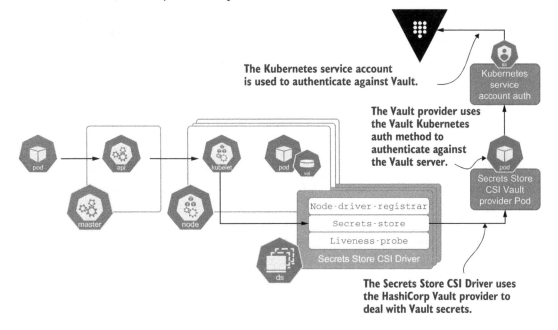

The Kubernetes service account is used to authenticate against Vault.

The Vault provider uses the Vault Kubernetes auth method to authenticate against the Vault server.

The Secrets Store CSI Driver uses the HashiCorp Vault provider to deal with Vault secrets.

Figure 6.6   The Secrets Store CSI Driver with the HashiCorp Vault provider

The first thing you'll need is a HashiCorp Vault instance running in the Kubernetes cluster. You've already deployed a HashiCorp Vault instance in Kubernetes in chapter 5; now you'll do it again in the current cluster. To get started, first add the HashiCorp repository to Helm as follows.

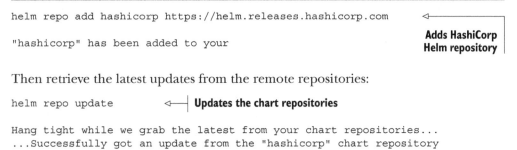

Listing 6.5   Adding Helm chart

```
helm repo add hashicorp https://helm.releases.hashicorp.com        ⟵

"hashicorp" has been added to your
```
Adds HashiCorp Helm repository

Then retrieve the latest updates from the remote repositories:

```
helm repo update        ⟵⎯  Updates the chart repositories

Hang tight while we grab the latest from your chart repositories...
...Successfully got an update from the "hashicorp" chart repository
Update Complete. ? Happy Helming!?
```

Execute the command in the following listing to install the chart in development mode with Vault CSI provider enabled.

Listing 6.6   Deploying HashiCorp Vault with a Secrets Store CSI provider

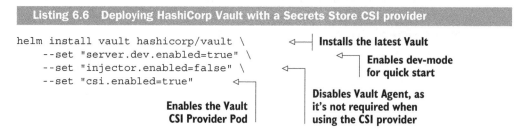

```
helm install vault hashicorp/vault \          Installs the latest Vault
    --set "server.dev.enabled=true" \         Enables dev-mode
    --set "injector.enabled=false" \          for quick start
    --set "csi.enabled=true"
```

Disables Vault Agent, as it's not required when using the CSI provider

Enables the Vault CSI Provider Pod

Run the command shown in the following listing to wait until HashiCorp Vault deployment is up and running.

Listing 6.7   Waiting until HashiCorp Vault is ready

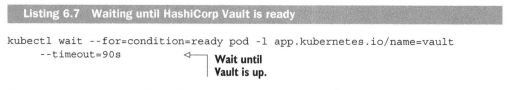

```
kubectl wait --for=condition=ready pod -l app.kubernetes.io/name=vault
    --timeout=90s          Wait until
                           Vault is up.
```

CREATING A SECRET INSIDE HASHICORP VAULT

Now create a key–value secret inside Vault by opening an interactive shell session on the Vault Pod.

Listing 6.8   Opening an interactive shell

```
kubectl exec -it vault-0 -- /bin/sh          Opens an interactive shell
                                             against the Vault container
```

From this point forward, the commands issued will be executed on the Vault container. Now create the secret at the secret/pass path with a `my_secret_password` value.

Listing 6.9   Creating a secret

```
vault kv put secret/pass password="my_secret_password"      Creates a new secret in
                                                            the Vault secrets store
Key             Value
---             -----
created_time    2021-08-03T04:59:49.920719431Z
deletion_time   n/a
destroyed       false
version         1
```

CONFIGURING KUBERNETES AUTHENTICATION

The primary authentication method for Vault when using the Vault CSI Provider is the service account attached to the Pod. For this reason, you need to enable the Kubernetes authentication method and configure it, so it can be used by the Vault CSI Driver. Still inside the Vault container, run the commands shown in the following listing.

Listing 6.10   Enabling and configuring the Kubernetes auth method

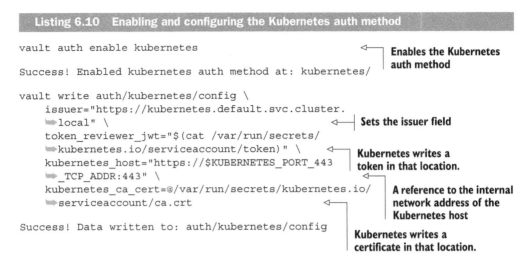

```
vault auth enable kubernetes                          ⊲—┐ Enables the Kubernetes
                                                          auth method
Success! Enabled kubernetes auth method at: kubernetes/

vault write auth/kubernetes/config \
    issuer="https://kubernetes.default.svc.cluster.
    ➥local" \                                        ⊲—┤ Sets the issuer field
    token_reviewer_jwt="$(cat /var/run/secrets/
    ➥kubernetes.io/serviceaccount/token)" \         ⊲—┐ Kubernetes writes a
    kubernetes_host="https://$KUBERNETES_PORT_443     │ token in that location.
    ➥_TCP_ADDR:443" \                                ⊲—┐
    kubernetes_ca_cert=@/var/run/secrets/kubernetes.io/  A reference to the internal
    ➥serviceaccount/ca.crt                          ⊲—┐ network address of the
                                                          Kubernetes host
Success! Data written to: auth/kubernetes/config
                                                       Kubernetes writes a
                                                       certificate in that location.
```

Reading secrets using the Secrets Store CSI Driver requires read permissions for all mounts and access to the secret itself. Create a policy named `csi-internal-app`.

Listing 6.11   Applying the Vault policy

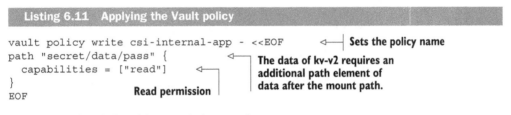

```
vault policy write csi-internal-app - <<EOF          ⊲—┤ Sets the policy name
path "secret/data/pass" {                            ⊲—┐ The data of kv-v2 requires an
    capabilities = ["read"]                      ⊲—┐    additional path element of
}                                                        data after the mount path.
EOF                              Read permission
```
```
Success! Uploaded policy: csi-internal-app
```

Finally, create a Kubernetes authentication role named `my-app` that binds this policy with a Kubernetes service account named `app-sa` as in the following listing. The role is used in the Vault CSI provider configuration (you'll see this in the following section), and the service account is used to run the Pod.

Listing 6.12   Creating the Kubernetes authentication role

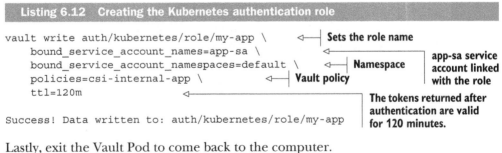

```
vault write auth/kubernetes/role/my-app \        ⊲—┤ Sets the role name
    bound_service_account_names=app-sa \                      app-sa service
    bound_service_account_namespaces=default \   ⊲—┤ Namespace  account linked
    policies=csi-internal-app \         ⊲—┤ Vault policy        with the role
    ttl=120m                    ⊲
                                                   The tokens returned after
Success! Data written to: auth/kubernetes/role/my-app  authentication are valid
                                                   for 120 minutes.
```

Lastly, exit the Vault Pod to come back to the computer.

Listing 6.13   Exiting the shell session

```
exit
```

DEFINE A SECRETPROVIDERCLASS RESOURCE

The `SecretProviderClass` Kubernetes custom resource describes the configuration parameters given to the Secrets Store CSI Driver. The Vault CSI provider requires the following parameters:

- The address of the Vault server
- The name of the Vault Kubernetes authentication role
- The secrets to inject into the Pod

The `SecretProviderClass` definition to connect to Vault installation is shown in the following listing.

Listing 6.14   vault-spc.yaml

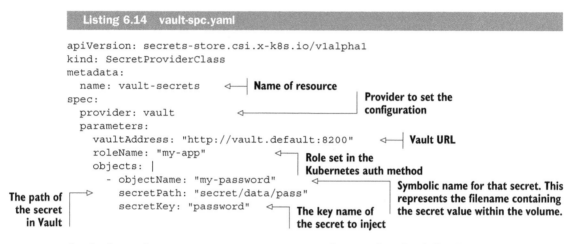

Apply the vault-secrets `SecretProviderClass` by running the following command.

Listing 6.15   Applying the Vault secrets `SecretProviderClass`

```
kubectl apply -f vault-spc.yaml -n default        Registers the service
                                                  provider class
```

DEPLOYING A POD WITH A SECRET MOUNTED

With everything in place, it's time to create a service account with the name app-sa (the same name configured in the section "Configuring Kubernetes authentication" section) and one Pod creating a volume from the secrets store created by CSI as shown in the following listing. The volume configuration now contains a csi section, where you will set the CSI driver to use—in this case, secrets store one (secrets-store.csi.k8s.io) as well as the previously created SecretProviderClass name (vault-secrets).

Listing 6.16   vault-app-pod.yaml

```
kind: ServiceAccount
apiVersion: v1
metadata:                   Service account set in
  name: app-sa              Kubernetes auth method
---
```

```
kind: Pod
apiVersion: v1
metadata:
  name: greeting-demo
  labels:
    app: greeting
spec:
  serviceAccountName: app-sa         ◁──┐  Service account
  containers:                              used to run the Pod
  - image: quay.io/lordofthejars/greetings-jvm:1.0.0
    name: greeting-demo
    volumeMounts:                    ◁──┐  Volume mount section
    - name: secrets-store-inline
      mountPath: "/mnt/secrets-vault"  ◁──┐  Path where secrets
      readOnly: true                        are mounted
  volumes:
    - name: secrets-store-inline     ◁──┐  Starts csi
      csi:                                  section        Sets the secrets
        driver: secrets-store.csi.k8s.io  ◁──              store driver
        readOnly: true
        volumeAttributes:                              References
          secretProviderClass: "vault-secrets"  ◁──   SecretProviderClass
```

Figure 6.7 shows the relationship between all these elements.

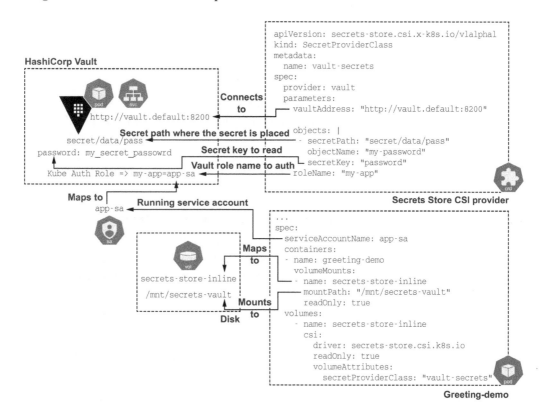

Figure 6.7   The relationship between the secret provider, Pod, and Vault

Deploy the Pod by running the following command.

Listing 6.17   Applying the Pod with CSI volume

```
kubectl apply -f vault-app-pod.yaml -n default
```
◁─┐ **Deploys the service account**
   and the application

When the Pod is deployed, it will contain a volume with all the Vault secrets mounted as files. Then wait until the Pod is running, as shown.

Listing 6.18   Waiting until the greeting Pod is running

```
kubectl wait --for=condition=ready pod -l app=greeting --timeout=90s
```
◁──┐

Waiting until the
application is ready

Finally, validate that the secret is mounted in /mnt/secrets-vault, as specified in volumesMount section, and the file containing the secret is my-password, as set in the objectName field. Run the command shown in the following listing.

Listing 6.19   Reading the injected secret

```
kubectl exec greeting-demo -- cat /mnt/secrets-vault/my-password

my_secret_password%
```
◁─┐ **The value displayed matches the**
   password value for the secret.

To recap, you've seen how to install CSI and the Secrets Store CSI Driver and created a SecretProviderClass resource to configure the Secrets Store CSI Driver to use HashiCorp Vault as secret storage. You should now understand how the Secrets Store CSI Driver works, and you've seen that the secret is mounted as a volume to disk. But in some cases, you may need to mount these secrets as Kubernetes Secrets. Let's explore how this is done.

6.2   *Synchronizing CSI secrets as Kubernetes Secrets*

Synchronization is especially useful when the application (usually legacy application) needs to read secrets either as an environment variable or directly using the Kubernetes API server. The Secrets Store CSI Driver mounts the secrets to disk using Kubernetes Volumes, but mirroring these secrets to Kubernetes Secrets is supported too by using the optional secretObjects field in the SecretProviderClass custom resource (figure 6.8).

> **IMPORTANT**   The volume mount is still required and must be defined to sync with Kubernetes Secrets.

You will expand the previous HashiCorp Vault example by also mapping the secret as a Kubernetes Secret.

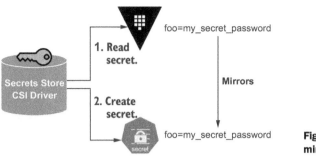

Figure 6.8   The Secrets Store CSI Driver mirrors secrets as Kubernetes Secrets.

6.2.1 Preparing the namespace

Before mapping the secrets as Kubernetes Secrets, you may delete the `Secret-ProviderClass` resource and undeploy the `greeting-demo` Pod to have a clean environment. In a terminal window, run the following commands.

Listing 6.20   Cleaning up the environment

```
kubectl delete -f vault-app-pod.yaml -n default     ◁───┤ Undeploy the Pod.

kubectl delete -f vault-spc.yaml -n default     ◁───┐
                                                     │ Delete the
                                                     │ SecretProviderClass
                                                     │ resource.
```

With the example undeployed, you can start the synchronization example.

6.2.2 Defining a SecretProviderClass resource with secretObjects

To mount the secrets from secret storage using the Secrets Store CSI Driver, modify the `SecretProviderClass` resource, adding the `secretObjects` field. This field is used to define how to map a secret from a secrets store to a Kubernetes Secret.

In the following snippet, you will see how the value of a secret placed at the secrets store with the name `foo` is mapped into a key named `bar` of an `opaque` Kubernetes Secret with the name `foosecret`:

```
apiVersion: secrets-store.csi.x-k8s.io/v1alpha1
kind: SecretProviderClass
metadata:
  name: my-provider
spec:
  provider: vault
  secretObjects:
  - data:
    - key: bar
      objectName: foo
    secretName: foosecret
    type: Opaque
```

The key name used to look up a secret value in the secret resource

The name of the mounted content to sync

The name of the Kubernetes secret object

The type of secret

Figure 6.9 shows the relationship between the secret storage, the `SercretProvider-Class` definition, and the Kubernetes Secret.

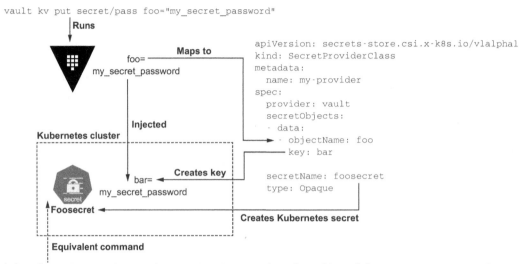

```
vault kv put secret/pass foo="my_secret_password"
```

Figure 6.9   **Secret store, SecretProviderClass, and Kubernetes Secrets**

About supported secret types

At the time of writing this book the following secret types are supported:

- Opaque
- kubernetes.io/basic-auth
- bootstrap.kubernetes.io/token
- kubernetes.io/dockerconfigjson
- kubernetes.io/dockercfg
- kubernetes.io/ssh-auth
- kubernetes.io/service-account-token
- kubernetes.io/tls

Open the `vault-spc.yaml` created previously, and add the `secretObjects` section to make the data stored in the HashiCorp Vault a Kubernetes Secret.

Listing 6.21   vault-spc.yaml

```
apiVersion: secrets-store.csi.x-k8s.io/vlalpha1
kind: SecretProviderClass
```

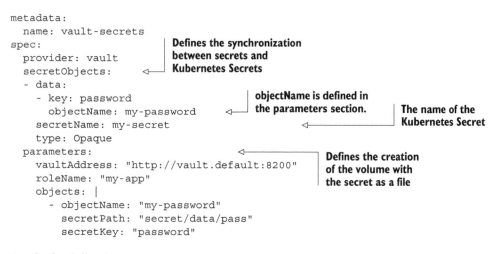

```
metadata:
  name: vault-secrets
spec:
  provider: vault
  secretObjects:
  - data:
    - key: password
      objectName: my-password
    secretName: my-secret
    type: Opaque
  parameters:
    vaultAddress: "http://vault.default:8200"
    roleName: "my-app"
    objects: |
      - objectName: "my-password"
        secretPath: "secret/data/pass"
        secretKey: "password"
```

Defines the synchronization between secrets and Kubernetes Secrets

objectName is defined in the parameters section.

The name of the Kubernetes Secret

Defines the creation of the volume with the secret as a file

Apply the following resource.

Listing 6.22 Applying the `SecretProviderClass`

```
kubectl apply -f vault-spc.yaml
```

Deploys the SecretProviderClass

With `SecretProviderClass` deployed, it's time to deploy the Pod.

DEPLOY A POD WITH A SECRET MOUNTED AND SECRET OBJECTS

The secrets will only sync once you start a Pod mounting the secrets. List the current secrets in the default namespace before deploying the Pod.

Listing 6.23 Listing secrets

```
kubectl get secrets -n default
```

Listing secrets

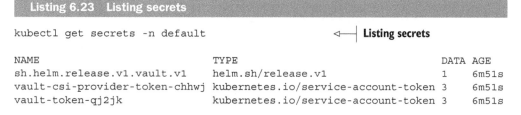

```
NAME                                TYPE                                  DATA AGE
sh.helm.release.v1.vault.v1         helm.sh/release.v1                    1    6m51s
vault-csi-provider-token-chhwj      kubernetes.io/service-account-token   3    6m51s
vault-token-qj2jk                   kubernetes.io/service-account-token   3    6m51s
```

With everything in place, it's time to redeploy the Pod defined in the previous section.

Listing 6.24 Applying the Pod with a CSI volume

```
kubectl apply -f vault-app-pod.yaml -n default
```

Deploying a Pod using the CSI driver

Wait until the Pod is running.

Listing 6.25 Waiting until the greeting Pod is running

```
kubectl wait --for=condition=ready pod -l app=greeting --timeout=90s
```

Waiting until it is deployed

List the secret after the Pod has been deployed to confirm the secret is now created.

Listing 6.26   Listing secrets

```
kubectl get secrets -n default
```
> A secret is created with the name set in the secretName field.

```
NAME                                TYPE                                    DATA AGE
my-secret                           Opaque                                  1    28s  ◁┘
sh.helm.release.v1.vault.v1         helm.sh/release.v1                      1    9m19s
vault-csi-provider-token-chhwj      kubernetes.io/service-account-token     3    9m19s
vault-token-qj2jk                   kubernetes.io/service-account-token     3    9m19s
```

Describe the secret to validate it is created correctly.

Listing 6.27   Describing the secret

```
kubectl describe secret my-secret
```
> The name set in the secretName field

```
Name:         my-secret       ◁┘
Namespace:    default
Labels:       secrets-store.csi.k8s.io/managed=true  ◁┘
```
> The label to set the secret is managed by the Secrets Store CSI

```
Annotations:  <none>
```
> The type, as defined in the type field

```
Type:  Opaque      ◁┘

Data
====
password:  18 bytes      ◁┘
```
> The secret key name, as defined in the key field

The equivalent `kubectl` command to create a secret like the one created by Secrets Store CSI would be

```
kubectl create secret generic my-secret
➥--from-literal password=my_secret_password -n default
```

Finally, delete the Pod to validate it is automatically deleted, since no Pods are consuming the secret.

Listing 6.28   Deleting the Pod

```
kubectl delete -f vault-app-pod.yaml -n default   ◁┤ Delete the Pod.
```

List the secrets again, and you'll see the `my-secret` secret is removed, as no Pod is using it.

Listing 6.29   Listing secrets

```
kubectl get secrets -n default
```

```
NAME                                TYPE                                    DATA AGE
sh.helm.release.v1.vault.v1         helm.sh/release.v1                      1    11m
vault-csi-provider-token-chhwj      kubernetes.io/service-account-token     3    11m
vault-token-qj2jk                   kubernetes.io/service-account-token     3    11m
```

TIP Once the secret is created, you may set it as an environment variable with any Kubernetes Secret:

```
env:
- name: MY_SECRET
  valueFrom:
    secretKeyRef:
      name: my-secret
      key: password
```

Remember you are creating Kubernetes Secrets, and as such, they need to be managed as shown in chapters 3 and 4 (i.e., encrypting them in the Git repository and enabling KMS to store them in Kubernetes encrypted rather than encoded). So far, you've seen how to mount secrets from secrets stores as Kubernetes volumes and Kubernetes Secrets using the Secrets Store CSI Driver. But what happens when the secret is updated in the secrets store? The Secrets Store CSI Driver supports secret autorotation.

6.3 *Autorotating secrets to improve security posture*

Imagine you receive an attack to your system, and some of your secret data is compromised; one of the first things you should do is to regenerate secrets to new values (rotation of the secrets). The Secrets Store CSI Driver can detect an update of a secret in the external secrets store after the Pod is running and populate this change in the corresponding volume content and into the Kubernetes Secrets object if they are used as shown in figure 6.10.

Autorotating secrets is the process of automatically changing secrets data periodically. There are two big wins from changing secret data: The first is that it

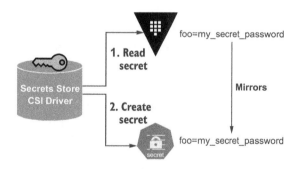

Figure 6.10   The Secrets Store CSI Driver mirrors secrets as Kubernetes Secrets

makes it more difficult for an attacker to get a value and able to decrypt it with a possible stolen key. The second is that if there is a secret data leak, you'll need to rotate the secrets as quickly as possible to avoid major problems.

It's important to keep in mind the Secrets Store CSI Driver only updates the location the secret is stored (volume or Kubernetes Secret), but the application consuming these secrets needs to implement some logic to react to these changes and read the new secret value. For example, when mounting the secret as a volume, the application will need to watch for changes. If the secret is injected as an environment variable, then the Pod needs to be restarted to get the latest secret as an environment variable.

> **TIP** Projects like Reloader (https://github.com/stakater/Reloader) help you push out rolling upgrades on Pods automatically when a change on the associated ConfigMap or Secret is detected.

6.3.1   Preparing the namespace

You may undeploy the `greeting-demo` Pod (although it shouldn't be necessary) before using the autorotation feature to have a brand new Pod, for example. If you have not deleted the Pod previously, run the following command in a terminal window.

Listing 6.30   Cleaning up the environment

```
kubectl delete -f vault-app-pod.yaml -n default     ⬅──┤ Undeploy the Pod.
```

The autorotation feature is disabled by default when the Secrets Store CSI Driver is installed. To enable this feature, the Secrets Store CSI Driver Pod should start with the `--enable-secret-rotation` flag set to `true` and the rotation poll interval (i.e., the frequency of checking if a secret has changed) set using the `rotation-poll-interval` flag. To enable autorotation, stop the previous deployment by running the following command in a terminal.

Listing 6.31   Undeploying the Secrets Store CSI Driver

```
kubectl delete -f https://raw.githubusercontent.com/kubernetes-sigs/
↪secrets-store-csi-driver/v0.1.0/deploy/secrets-store-csi-driver.yaml
```

Next modify the deployment file of the Secrets Store CSI Driver to configure `--enable-secret-rotation` and `rotation-poll-interval` flags. In this example, set the `rotation-poll-interval` time to `1 minute`, which means every minute, the driver will query the secrets store, checking if the value has been changed or not.

Listing 6.32   install-csi-polling.yaml

```
kind: DaemonSet          ⬅──┐ DaemonSet deploys the driver
apiVersion: apps/v1         │ in all Kubernetes nodes.
metadata:
  name: csi-secrets-store
  namespace: kube-system
spec:
  selector:
    matchLabels:
      app: csi-secrets-store
  template:
    metadata:
      labels:
        app: csi-secrets-store
      annotations:
        kubectl.kubernetes.io/default-logs-container: secrets-store
```

```
spec:
  serviceAccountName: secrets-store-csi-driver
  containers:
    - name: node-driver-registrar
      image: k8s.gcr.io/sig-storage/csi-node-driver-registrar:v2.2.0
      args:
        - --v=5
        - --csi-address=/csi/csi.sock
        - --kubelet-registration-path=/var/lib/kubelet/plugins/
          csi-secrets-store/csi.sock
      env:
        - name: KUBE_NODE_NAME
          valueFrom:
            fieldRef:
              apiVersion: v1
              fieldPath: spec.nodeName
      imagePullPolicy: IfNotPresent
      volumeMounts:
        - name: plugin-dir
          mountPath: /csi
        - name: registration-dir
          mountPath: /registration
      resources:
        limits:
          cpu: 100m
          memory: 100Mi
        requests:
          cpu: 10m
          memory: 20Mi
    - name: secrets-store
      image: k8s.gcr.io/csi-secrets-store/driver:v0.1.0
      args:
        - "--endpoint=$(CSI_ENDPOINT)"
        - "--nodeid=$(KUBE_NODE_NAME)"
        - "--provider-volume=/etc/kubernetes/secrets-store-csi-providers"
        - "--metrics-addr=:8095"
        - "--enable-secret-rotation=true"          ◁────  Enables secret
        - "--rotation-poll-interval=1m"                   rotation
        - "--filtered-watch-secret=true"
        - "--provider-health-check=false"
        - "--provider-health-check-interval=2m"
      env:
        - name: CSI_ENDPOINT
          value: unix:///csi/csi.sock
        - name: KUBE_NODE_NAME
          valueFrom:
            fieldRef:
              apiVersion: v1
              fieldPath: spec.nodeName
      imagePullPolicy: IfNotPresent
      securityContext:
        privileged: true
      ports:
        - containerPort: 9808
          name: healthz
```

Sets polling time to 1 minute

```
                    protocol: TCP
             livenessProbe:
                failureThreshold: 5
                httpGet:
                  path: /healthz
                  port: healthz
                initialDelaySeconds: 30
                timeoutSeconds: 10
                periodSeconds: 15
             volumeMounts:
               - name: plugin-dir
                 mountPath: /csi
               - name: mountpoint-dir
                 mountPath: /var/lib/kubelet/pods
                 mountPropagation: Bidirectional
               - name: providers-dir
                 mountPath: /etc/kubernetes/secrets-store-csi-providers
             resources:
               limits:
                 cpu: 200m
                 memory: 200Mi
               requests:
                 cpu: 50m
                 memory: 100Mi
         - name: liveness-probe
           image: k8s.gcr.io/sig-storage/livenessprobe:v2.3.0
           imagePullPolicy: IfNotPresent
           args:
           - --csi-address=/csi/csi.sock
           - --probe-timeout=3s
           - --http-endpoint=0.0.0.0:9808
           - -v=2
           volumeMounts:
             - name: plugin-dir
               mountPath: /csi
           resources:
             limits:
               cpu: 100m
               memory: 100Mi
             requests:
               cpu: 10m
               memory: 20Mi
       volumes:
         - name: mountpoint-dir
           hostPath:
             path: /var/lib/kubelet/pods
             type: DirectoryOrCreate
         - name: registration-dir
           hostPath:
             path: /var/lib/kubelet/plugins_registry/
             type: Directory
         - name: plugin-dir
           hostPath:
             path: /var/lib/kubelet/plugins/csi-secrets-store/
             type: DirectoryOrCreate
```

```
    - name: providers-dir
      hostPath:
        path: /etc/kubernetes/secrets-store-csi-providers
        type: DirectoryOrCreate
nodeSelector:
  kubernetes.io/os: linux
```

Finally, deploy the Secrets Store CSI Driver with the previous modification.

Listing 6.33   Deploying the Secrets Store CSI Driver with autorotation enabled

```
kubectl apply -f install-csi-polling.yaml
```
◁─┐ **Installing Secret Storage
     CSI with polling enabled**

Now wait until the Pod is running.

Listing 6.34   Waiting until the driver Pod is running

```
kubectl wait --for=condition=ready pod -l app=csi-secrets-store
➥--timeout=90s -n kube-system
```
◁─┐ **Waiting until the
     Pod is deployed**

6.3.2   *Deploying the Pod with a secret mounted*

Now redeploy the Pod defined in the previous section to inject the secret rotation example.

Listing 6.35   Applying the Pod with CSI volume

```
kubectl apply -f vault-app-pod.yaml -n default
```
◁─┐ **Deploying the Pod to the
     default namespace**

Wait until the Pod is running.

Listing 6.36   Waiting until the greeting Pod is running

```
kubectl wait --for=condition=ready pod -l app=greeting --timeout=90s
```
◁──┐

**Waiting until
the Pod is ready**

Finally, validate that the secret is mounted in /mnt/secrets-vault, as specified in the volumesMount section, and the file containing the secret is my-password, as set in the objectName field. Run the command shown in the following listing.

Listing 6.37   Reading the injected secret

```
kubectl exec greeting-demo -- cat /mnt/secrets-vault/my-password

my_secret_password%
```
◁─┐ **The current value
     of the secret**

6.3.3 *Updating the secret*

Now update the key with a new secret value inside Vault by opening an interactive shell session on the Vault Pod.

Listing 6.38   Opening an interactive shell

```
kubectl exec -it vault-0 -- /bin/sh        ◁─┐  Starting an interactive shell
                                              │  against the Vault container
```

From this point forward, the commands issued will be executed on the Vault container. Update the secret at the secret/pass path with the my_new_secret_password value.

Listing 6.39   Updating the secret

```
vault kv put secret/pass password=
➡"my_new_secret_password"        ◁─┐  The value
                                    │  is updated.
Key               Value
---               -----
created_time      2021-08-09T17:26:26.665179027Z
deletion_time     n/a
destroyed         false      ┐  The version is
version           2        ◁─┘  incremented by 1.
```

Type exit to quit the kubectl exec command. Wait at least one minute until the Secrets Store CSI Driver polls the secret, detects the change, and populates it to the Pod, and then run the command again to print the secret value.

Listing 6.40   Read the injected secret

```
kubectl exec greeting-demo -- cat /mnt/secrets-vault/my-password

my_new_secret_password%    ◁─┐  The new version of
                             │  the secret is printed.
```

Type exit to quit the kubectl exec command. Notice that the secret value has been injected without having to restart the Pod.

Now you should understand how the Secrets Store CSI Driver works; however, no cloud secrets stores were used in the example. We'll expand this example to cover store secrets in a public cloud secret storage in the following section.

6.4 *Consuming secrets from cloud secrets stores*

So far, you've used HashiCorp Vault as secret storage in this chapter and chapter 5. But if you're using a public cloud as a platform to deploy the Kubernetes cluster, you might want to use the secret storage service they provide in their infrastructure. For example, if you were using Azure Cloud Services, you might want to use Azure Key Vault as a secrets store. In this section, you'll see how to consume secrets from a cloud secret store using the Secrets Store CSI Driver.

The Secret Storage CSI Driver supports AWS Secrets Manager and the AWS Systems Manager Parameter Store; Azure Key Vault; and Google Secret Manager. You'll implement the same example as the previous section but consume the secrets from public cloud secrets stores instead of HashiCorp Vault. You'll start by integrating the secrets store CSI driver to Azure Key Vault.

> **IMPORTANT** The process of integrating a secret store and the Secrets Store CSI is the same in all cases:
> 1 Install and configure the secrets store.
> 2 Install the Secrets Store CSI Provider according to the secrets store used (e.g., Vault, AWS, or Azure).
> 3 Configure the `SecretProviderClass` with the secrets store configuration parameters.

The biggest difference between the two is the installation and configuration of the secrets store. In this section, we'll show you how to integrate cloud secrets stores with CSI, but we're assuming you have an account with the cloud providers to deploy the secrets store and a basic knowledge of how they work.

6.4.1 Azure Key Vault

Azure Key Vault is an Azure cloud service that provides a secure store for secrets (e.g., keys, passwords, and certificates). To run Azure Key Vaults you need an Azure account with at least the free services subscription, as Azure Key Vault cannot run outside of the Azure Cloud.

INSTALLING AND CONFIGURING AZURE KEY VAULT

To install Azure Key Vault, log in to your Azure subscription to create a service principal with policies to access the key vault.

Listing 6.41 Azure login

```
az login        ⟵┤ Log in to Azure.
```

Once logged in to Azure, you can create a service principal executing the command shown in the following listing.

Listing 6.42 Creating an Azure service principal

```
az ad sp create-for-rbac --skip-assignment --name alex   ⟵┐ Creates a service principal
                                                          ┘ with the name alex
```

The command returns a JSON document with some sensitive parameters you'll need to configure the CSI driver later on:

```
{                                                          ┐ This is the client ID
  "appId": "7d3498f8-633e-4c58-bbaa5-1b2a015017a7",   ⟵─┘ required by the CSI driver.
  "displayName": "alex",
  "name": "http://alex",
```

```
    "password": "2CAT7NvT9OzrLneTdi3..rYnU.M4_qGIMP",
    "tenant": "66ee79ad-f624-4a81-b14e-319d7dd9e699"
}
```
This is the client secret required by the CSI driver.

TIP   Creating a specific service principal for Azure Key Vault isn't mandatory, and you could instead use the default service principal.

Next you'll need to create the Azure Key Vault through the Azure portal. Visit https://portal.azure.com/, and log in with your account. In the portal, go to the top search bar, type `Key Vault`, and click the Azure Key Vault resource, as shown in figure 6.11.

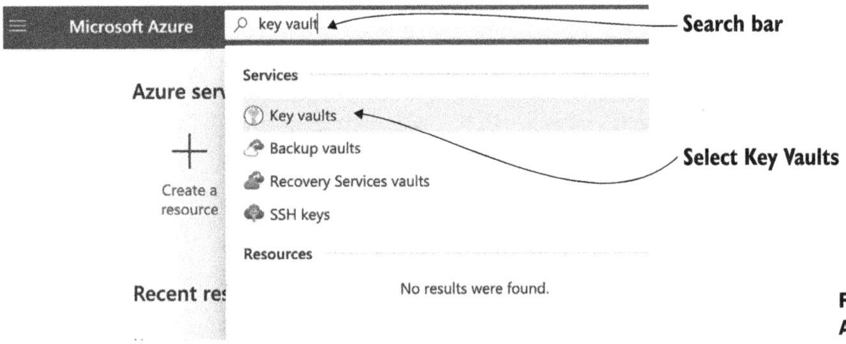

Figure 6.11 Azure portal

In the Key Vaults section, click the Create Key Vault button to start creating an Azure Key Vault instance (figure 6.12).

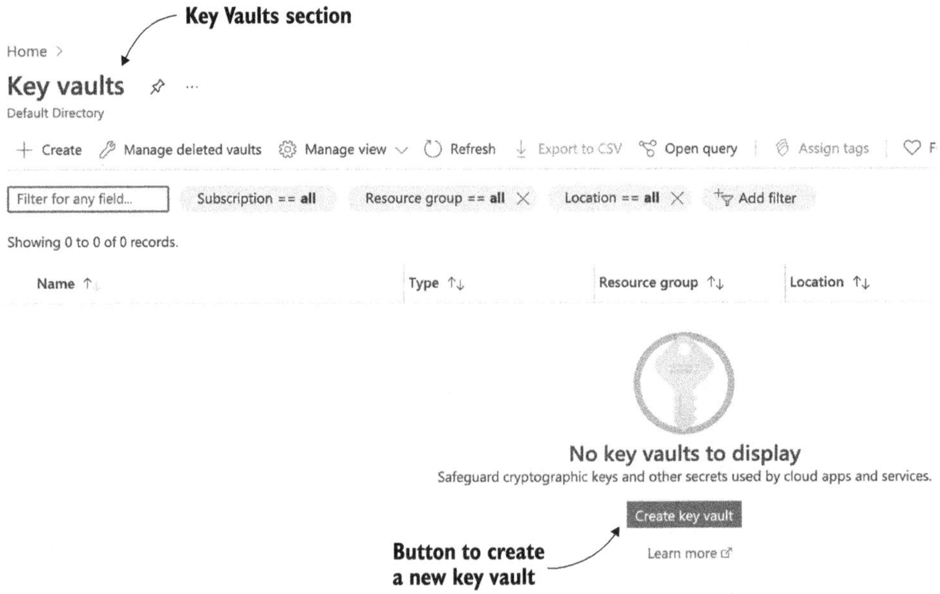

Figure 6.12   Azure Key Vault portal; cloud providers tweak their web interfaces on a ongoing basis.

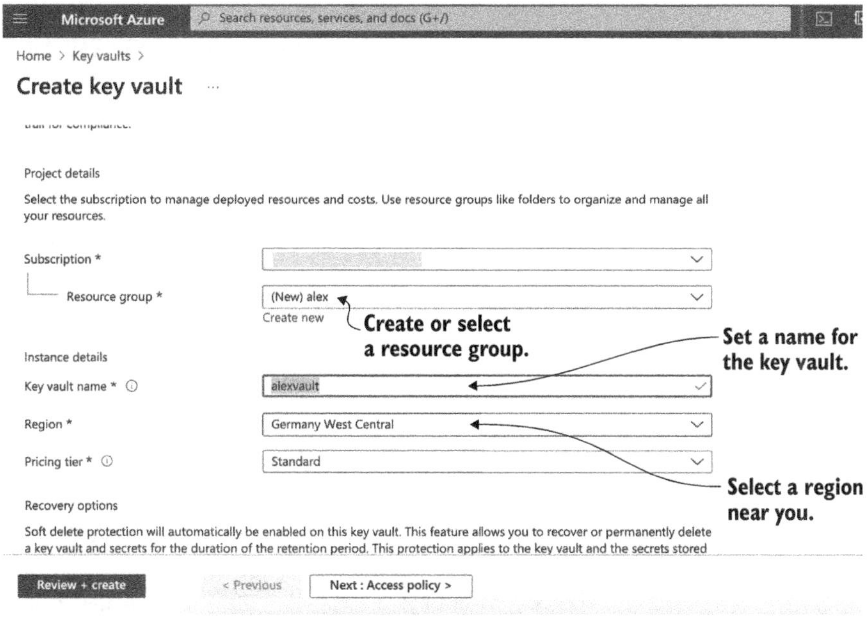

Figure 6.13 Creating the Azure Key Vault

Fill the Create Key Vault wizard with the parameters shown in figure 6.13.

The Key vault name in this example is alexvault, but it could be any other name, region, and pricing tier. Click Review + Create, review the values, and click Create.

The overview of the created key vault should now be shown (figure 6.14). At this point, click the JSON View link, which will show the same content, but in JSON format, and the tenant ID of the key vault.

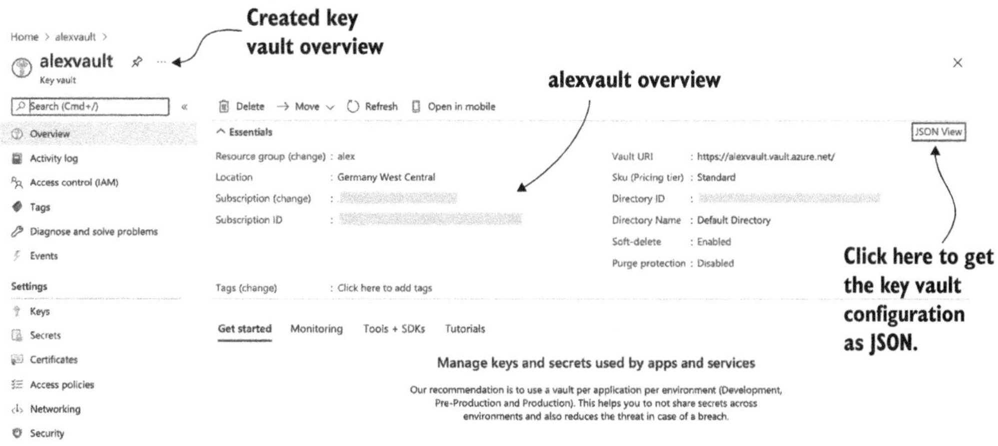

Figure 6.14 Overview of Azure Key Vault

You need to create the secret to be injected into the Pod. Click the Secrets section in the left menu, and click the Generate/Import button in the top-left menu, as shown in figure 6.15.

Figure 6.15   Creating the Azure Key Vault secret

Fill the name field with the password value and the value field with my_password; then click Create, as shown in figure 6.16.

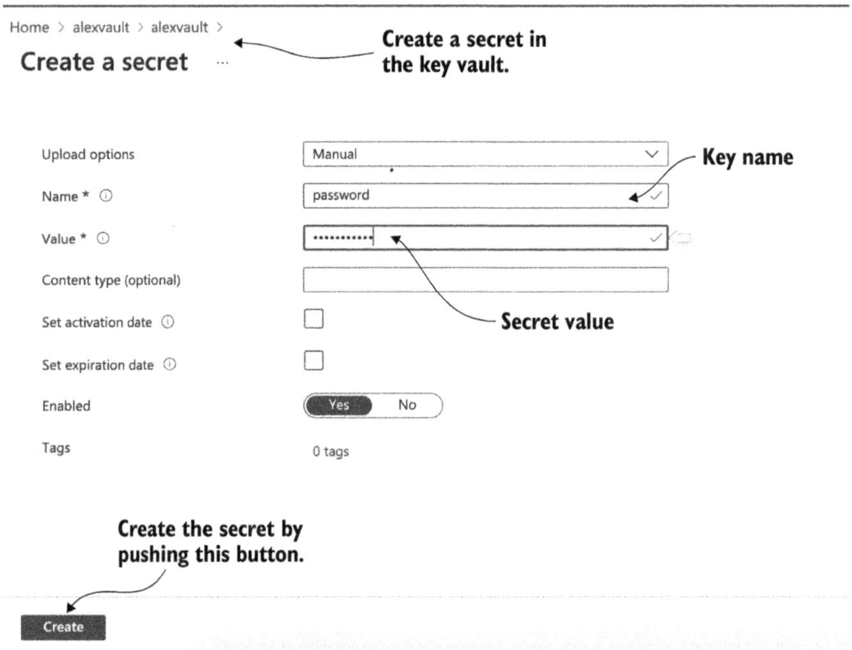

Figure 6.16   Creating the Azure Key Vault secret

> **NOTE**   A secret can be created using the az CLI tool by running `az keyvault secret set --vault-name "alexvault" --name "password" --value "my_password"`.

Finally, you need to assign the permissions from the previously created service principal to the key vault you just created. Return to the terminal window, and execute the following commands.

Listing 6.43   Assigning permissions

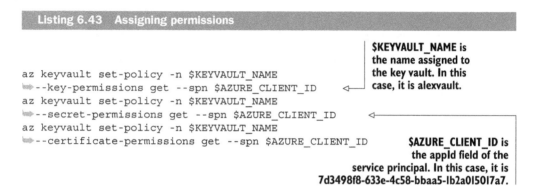

```
az keyvault set-policy -n $KEYVAULT_NAME
--key-permissions get --spn $AZURE_CLIENT_ID
az keyvault set-policy -n $KEYVAULT_NAME
--secret-permissions get --spn $AZURE_CLIENT_ID
az keyvault set-policy -n $KEYVAULT_NAME
--certificate-permissions get --spn $AZURE_CLIENT_ID
```

$KEYVAULT_NAME is the name assigned to the key vault. In this case, it is alexvault.

$AZURE_CLIENT_ID is the appId field of the service principal. In this case, it is 7d3498f8-633e-4c58-bbaa5-1b2a0l50l7a7.

You are now ready to return to Kubernetes! In the next section, you will learn how to configure it for consuming secrets from Azure Key Vault.

AZURE KEY VAULT CSI DRIVER

First install and configure the Azure Key Vault CSI Driver. You'll need to create a new Kubernetes namespace to deploy the Azure example.

Listing 6.44   Creating an Azure namespace

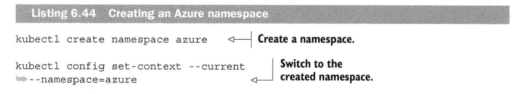

```
kubectl create namespace azure
```
Create a namespace.

```
kubectl config set-context --current
--namespace=azure
```
Switch to the created namespace.

Install the Azure Secrets Store CSI Provider to inject secrets from Azure Key Vault into Pods using the CSI interface.

Listing 6.45   Installing the Azure Secrets Store CSI provider

```
kubectl apply -f https://raw.githubusercontent.com/Azure/
secrets-store-csi-driver-provider-azure/v0.1.0/deployment/
provider-azure-installer.yaml -n azure
```

> **TIP**   For Windows Nodes, you need to apply the `provider-azure-installer-windows.yaml` file.

Check that the provider is running by executing the following command.

Listing 6.46 Checking the Azure Secrets Store CSI provider

```
kubectl get pods -n azure          ⟵┤ List Pods.

NAME                                    READY   STATUS    RESTARTS   AGE
csi-secrets-store-provider-azure-6fcdc  1/1     Running   1          161m
```

WARNING For AKS clusters, the provider needs to be installed in the kube-system namespace to establish connection with the Kube API Server.

Then you will set the service principal credentials as Kubernetes Secrets accessible by the Azure Secrets Store CSI Driver. The driver uses this secret to log in to the remote Azure Key Vault. The secret must contain clientid and clientsecret keys set to the service principal app ID and password fields, respectively. Figure 6.17 shows an overview of the authentication steps.

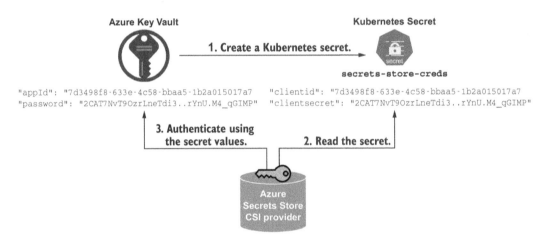

Figure 6.17 The authentication process of the Azure Secrets Store CSI provider

The following listing shows the creation of a Kubernetes Secret with the Azure credentials.

Listing 6.47 Creating a Kubernetes Secret

```
kubectl create secret generic secrets-store-creds --from-literal
⟿clientid=$AZURE_CLIENT_ID --from-literal
⟿clientsecret=$AZURE_CLIENT_SECRET -n azure          ⟵
```

> $AZURE_CLIENT_ID is the appId field of
> service principal. In this case, it is 7d3498f8-633e-4c58-bbaa5-1b2a015017a7.
> $AZURE_CLIENT_SECRET is the password field of service principle.
> In this case, it is 2CAT7NvT9OzrLneTdi3..rYnU.M4_qGIMP.

IMPORTANT Secrets must be created in the same namespace as the application Pod. Moreover, as with any Kubernetes Secret, it needs to be managed as discussed in chapters 3 and 4.

Moreover, you can label the secrets (like the one created just above) used in the `nodePublishSecretRef` section to limit the amount of memory used by the CSI driver.

Listing 6.48 Creating a Kubernetes Secret

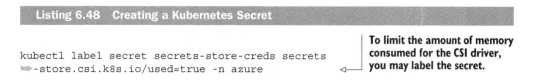

```
kubectl label secret secrets-store-creds secrets
➡-store.csi.k8s.io/used=true -n azure
```

To limit the amount of memory consumed for the CSI driver, you may label the secret.

Before creating a Pod with the secret, the last step is configuring the `SecretProvider-Class` with the Azure Key Vault name and the Azure Key Vault tenant ID.

Listing 6.49 azure-spc.yaml

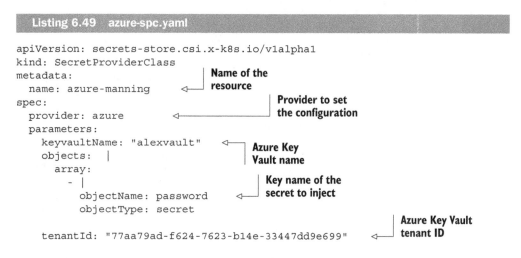

```
apiVersion: secrets-store.csi.x-k8s.io/v1alpha1
kind: SecretProviderClass
metadata:
  name: azure-manning          Name of the
                               resource
spec:
  provider: azure                    Provider to set
                                     the configuration
  parameters:
    keyvaultName: "alexvault"       Azure Key
    objects:  |                     Vault name
      array:
        - |                          Key name of the
          objectName: password       secret to inject
          objectType: secret
                                                 Azure Key Vault
    tenantId: "77aa79ad-f624-7623-b14e-33447dd9e699"    tenant ID
```

Apply the `azure-manningSecretProviderClass` by running the following command:

Listing 6.50 Applying the `azure-manningSecretProviderClass`

```
kubectl apply -f azure-spc.yaml -n azure
```

Registering the Azure
SercretProviderClass

DEPLOYING A POD WITH A SECRET MOUNTED

The configuration is similar to what you saw in the HashiCorp Vault example; you have the `csi` section, where you set the CSI driver to `secrets-store.csi.k8s.io`, as well as the `SecretProviderClass` name just created (`azure-manning`). But in this case, set the `nodePublishSecretRef` pointing out the previously created Kubernetes secret with the Azure service principal credentials (`secrets-store-creds`) to access the Azure Key Vault.

Listing 6.51   azure-app-pod.yaml

```
kind: Pod
apiVersion: v1
metadata:
  name: greeting-demo
  labels:
    app: greeting
spec:
  containers:
  - image: quay.io/lordofthejars/greetings-jvm:1.0.0
    name: greeting-demo
    volumeMounts:                        ⟵┤ Volume mount section
    - name: secrets-store-inline
      mountPath: "/mnt/secrets-azure"    ⟵┐ Path where secrets
      readOnly: true                       │ are mounted
  volumes:
    - name: secrets-store-inline
      csi:
        driver: secrets-store.csi.k8s.io
        readOnly: true                              ┐ References the
        volumeAttributes:                           │ SecretProviderClass
          secretProviderClass: "azure-manning"  ⟵──┘
        nodePublishSecretRef:                   ┐ Required when using the
          name: secrets-store-creds         ⟵──┘ service principal as a secret
```

Deploy the Pod by running the following command.

Listing 6.52   Applying the Pod with a CSI volume

```
kubectl apply -f azure-app-pod.yaml -n azure    ⟵┐ Deploy a Pod configured to use the
                                                  │ Azure Secrets Store CSI provider.
```

Now wait until the Pod is running.

Listing 6.53   Waiting until the greeting Pod is running

```
kubectl wait --for=condition=ready pod -l app=greeting --timeout=90s
    -n azure                                    ⟵┐ Wait until the
                                                  │ Pod is ready.
```

In the following snippet, a complete SecretProviderClass object is provided, so you see all possible options.

```
apiVersion: secrets-store.csi.x-k8s.io/v1alpha1
kind: SecretProviderClass
metadata:
  name: azure-kvname
spec:
  provider: azure                 ┐ Set to true to use the
  parameters:                     │ aad-pod-identity to access
    usePodIdentity: "false"   ⟵──┘ the key vault (false).
```

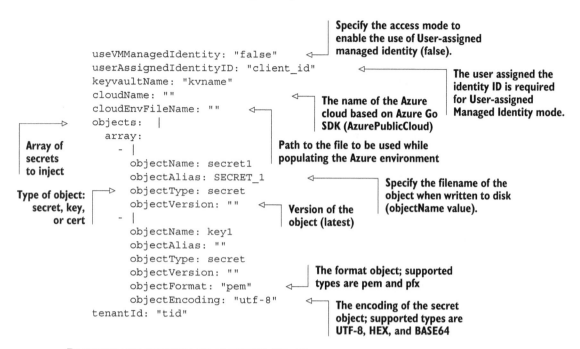

PROVIDING THE IDENTITY FOR ACCESSING KEY VAULT

In this section, we've given the identity access to Key Vault using a service principal. At the time of writing, this is the only way to connect to Azure Key Vault from a non-Azure environment. But if you are in an Azure environment (i.e., AKS), then these other authentication modes are supported:

- AAD pod identity
- User-assigned managed identity
- System-assigned managed identity

You know how to use Secrets Store CSI Driver to inject secrets stored in Azure Key Vault. As mentioned earlier, Secrets Store CSI Driver supports providers other than Azure. In the following section, you will review the same example—this time storing the secret in GCP Secret Manager.

6.4.2 GCP Secret Manager

GCP Secret Manager is a Google cloud service that provides a secure store for secrets (e.g., keys, passwords, and certificates). To run GCP Secret Manager, you need a GCP account with Secret Manager installed, as it cannot run outside of the Google cloud.

INSTALLING AND CONFIGURING GCP SECRET MANAGER

To install GCP Secret Manager, log in to GCP console (https://console.cloud.google .com/home) with your GCP account, and enable Secret Manager. In the search bar at the top of the page, search for *Secret Manager,* and click it on the search results, as shown in figure 6.18.

Figure 6.18   Searching for GCP Secret Manager

Then enable GCP Secret Manager by clicking on the Enable button (figure 6.19).

Figure 6.19   Enabling Secret Manager

With Secret Manager enabled, create a new secret to be injected into the Pod using CSI. Select the Secret Manager resource from the Security section in the left menu, and click the Create Secret button, as shown in figure 6.20.

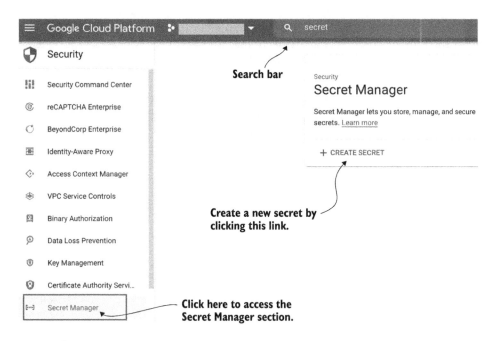

Figure 6.20 Creating the secret

Fill out the Create Secret form with Name as app-secret and Value as my_password, as shown in figure 6.21.

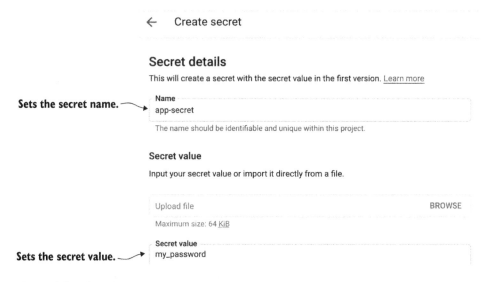

Figure 6.21 Creating the secret

A list of all created secrets is shown when you create a secret. Now click on the name of the created secret to inspect its details and get the resource name, as you will need it later on for the GCP Secrets Store CSI provider configuration (figure 6.22).

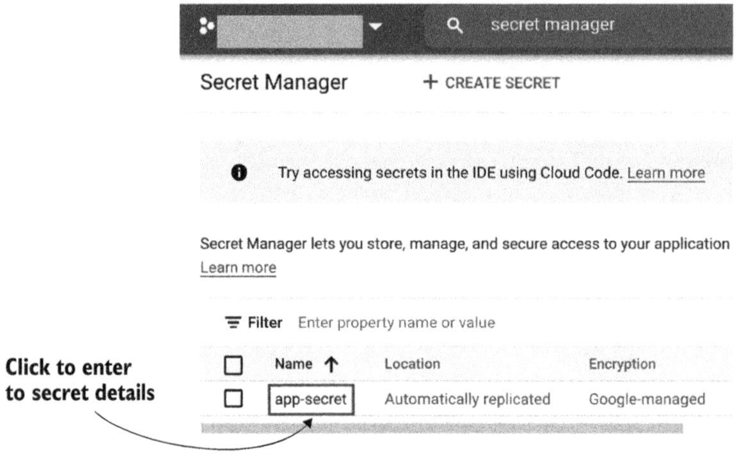

Figure 6.22
Selecting the created secret

Write down the Resource ID value (projects/466074950013/secrets/app-secret), since you will need it as a parameter when the SecretProviderClass is created. Figure 6.23 shows an example of the overview of a secret.

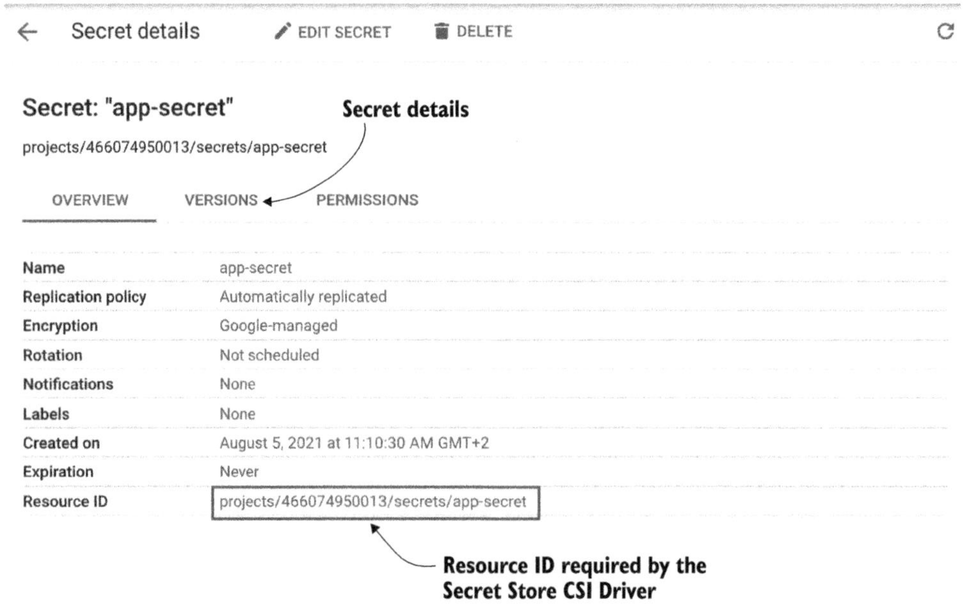

Figure 6.23 Overview of the created secret

The final step before leaving GCP console is exporting the GCP service account credential keys to authenticate against the Secret Manager instance. Typically this JSON file is downloaded automatically when the keys are added to the service account. If you don't have a key, you can add a new one by clicking the Service Accounts menu and then the Add Key button, as shown in figure 6.24.

Figure 6.24 Overview of the created secret

It's important to generate a key in JSON format and with enough permissions to access GCP Secret Manager. Finally go back to the secret overview page, click the Permissions tab and the Add button to add the previous service account as an account that can consume the secret. This process is shown in figure 6.25.

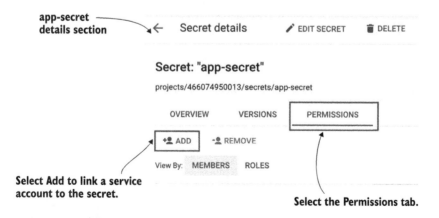

Figure 6.25 Give the service account permissions to access the secret

GCP SECRET MANAGER CSI DRIVER

Let's install and configure the GCP Secret Manager CSI Driver. First of all, create a new Kubernetes namespace to deploy the GCP example.

Listing 6.54   Create GCP namespace

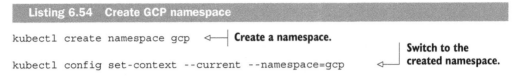

Install the GCP Secrets Store CSI Provider, as shown in listing 6.55, to inject secrets from GCP Secret Manager into Pods using the CSI interface.

Listing 6.55   Installing the GCP Secrets Store CSI provider

Check that the provider is running by executing the following command.

Listing 6.56   Checking the GCP Secrets Store CSI provider

```
kubectl get pods -n kube-system        ◁—— List the Pods in the kube-system namespace.

NAME                                      READY   STATUS    RESTARTS   AGE
coredns-558bd4d5db-4l9tk                  1/1     Running   4          5d20h
csi-secrets-store-8xlcn                   3/3     Running   11         5d3h
csi-secrets-store-provider-gcp-62jb5      1/1     Running   0          17s
```

> **WARNING** The provider is installed in the kube-system namespace to establish connection with the Kube API Server.

Then set the service account credentials as Kubernetes Secrets accessible by the GCP Secrets Store CSI Driver, as shown in listing 6.57. The driver uses this secret to log in to the remote GCP Secret Manager. The secret must have a key key.json with a value of an exported GCP service account credential.

Listing 6.57   Creating a Kubernetes Secret namespace

IMPORTANT   Secrets must be created in the same namespace as the application Pod. Moreover, as with any Kubernetes Secret, it needs to be managed as shown in chapters 3 and 4.

Before creating a Pod with the secret, the last step is configuring the `SecretProvider-Class` with the secret resource ID and the filename where the content of the secret is written.

Listing 6.58   gcp-spc.yaml

```
apiVersion: secrets-store.csi.x-k8s.io/v1alpha1
kind: SecretProviderClass
metadata:
  name: gcp-manning
spec:
  provider: gcp
  parameters:
    secrets: |
      - resourceName: projects/466074950013/secrets/
        app-secret/versions/latest
        fileName: app-secret
```

Refers to a secret version in the following format:
<Resource ID>//versions/

The filename where the secret content is written

Apply the gcp-manning `SecretProviderClass` by running the following command.

Listing 6.59   Applying the gcp-manning `SecretProviderClass`

```
kubectl apply -f gcp-spc.yaml -n gcp
```

Registers the GCP SecretProviderClass

DEPLOYING A POD WITH A SECRET MOUNTED

The configuration in this example is similar to what you saw in the HashiCorp Vault example; you have the `csi` section, where you set the CSI driver to `secrets-store.csi.k8s.io`, as well as the `SecretProviderClass` name created previously (`gcp-manning`). But in this case, set the `nodePublishSecretRef` pointing out the Kubernetes secret created previously with the GCP service account credentials (`secrets-store-creds`) to access the GCP Secret Manager.

Listing 6.60   gcp-app-pod.yaml

```
kind: Pod
apiVersion: v1
metadata:
  name: greeting-demo
  labels:
    app: greeting
spec:
  containers:
  - image: quay.io/lordofthejars/greetings-jvm:1.0.0
    name: greeting-demo
```

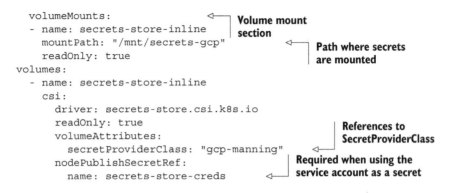

```
    volumeMounts:                        ⬐ Volume mount
    - name: secrets-store-inline         │ section
      mountPath: "/mnt/secrets-gcp"            ⬐ Path where secrets
      readOnly: true                           │ are mounted
  volumes:
  - name: secrets-store-inline
    csi:
      driver: secrets-store.csi.k8s.io
      readOnly: true                           ⬐ References to
      volumeAttributes:                        │ SecretProviderClass
        secretProviderClass: "gcp-manning"  ⬐
      nodePublishSecretRef:                  ⬐ Required when using the
        name: secrets-store-creds           │ service account as a secret
```

Deploy the Pod by running the following command.

Listing 6.61 Applying the Pod with the CSI volume

```
kubectl apply -f gcp-app-pod.yaml -n gcp   ⬐ Deploy a Pod configured to use the
                                           │ GCP Secrets Store CSI provider.
```

Wait until the Pod is running.

Listing 6.62 Waiting until the greeting Pod is running

```
kubectl wait --for=condition=ready pod -l app=greeting --timeout=90s  ⬐

                                                   Wait until the Pod is ready.
```

Finally, validate that the secret is mounted in /mnt/secrets-gcp, as specified in the volumesMount section, and the file containing the secret is named app-secret, as specified in fileName field. Run the command shown in the following listing.

Listing 6.63 Reading the injected secret

```
kubectl exec greeting-demo -- cat /mnt/secrets-gcp/app-secret

my_secret%   ⬐ The value displayed matches the previous
             │ set password value for the secret.
```

PROVIDING IDENTITY TO THE GCP SECRET MANAGER

In this section, you've provided the identity access to GCP Secret Manager using a service account. At the time of writing, this is the only way to connect to GCP Secret Manager from a non-GCP environment. The following authentication modes are also supported:

- Pod workload identity
- GCP provider identity

You now know how to use secrets store CSI drivers to inject secrets stored in GCP Secret Manager. In the following section, you will see the same example—this time for storing secrets in AWS Secrets Manager.

6.4.3 AWS Secrets Manager

AWS Secrets Manager is an AWS cloud service that provides a secure store for secrets (e.g., keys, passwords, certificates). To run AWS Secrets Manager, you need an AWS account with AWS Secrets Manager installed; it cannot run outside of the AWS cloud. Moreover, at time of writing, AWS Secrets Manager can run in an Amazon Elastic Kubernetes Service (EKS) 1.17+.

We won't explain the whole process of preparing an EKS cluster in this book. We'll also assume that an EKS cluster is up and configured and the `eksctl` CLI tool is installed on your machine.

CREATING A SECRET IN AWS SECRETS MANAGER

As you've done in the previous sections, you need to store a secret into the secrets store—in this case AWS Secrets Manager—to be consumed by the secrets store CSI driver. Use the aws CLI tool (http://mng.bz/ZpaR) to create a secret named AppSecret and with the value my_secret.

Listing 6.64 Creating the Secret

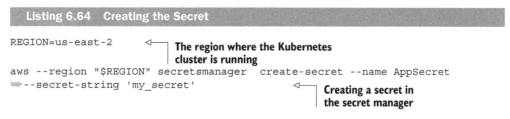

```
REGION=us-east-2          ◁── The region where the Kubernetes
                               cluster is running
aws --region "$REGION" secretsmanager  create-secret --name AppSecret
⮑--secret-string 'my_secret'           ◁── Creating a secret in
                                            the secret manager
```

Then create an IAM access policy to access the secret created in the previous step. This step is important, as you'll associate this access policy with the Kubernetes service account running the `greeting-demo` Pod in a similar way as in the HashiCorp Vault Kubernetes authentication mode.

Run the command shown in listing 6.65 to create an access policy with the name `greeting-deployment-policy` to access to the AppSecret secret. The policy name is important, as you'll need to make a link between the policy and the Kubernetes service account.

Listing 6.65 Creating the access policy

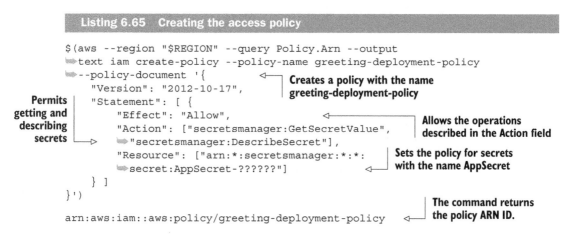

```
$(aws --region "$REGION" --query Policy.Arn --output
⮑text iam create-policy --policy-name greeting-deployment-policy
⮑--policy-document '{                 ◁── Creates a policy with the name
    "Version": "2012-10-17",              greeting-deployment-policy
    "Statement": [ {
        "Effect": "Allow",            ◁──────────── Allows the operations
        "Action": ["secretsmanager:GetSecretValue",  described in the Action field
        ⮑"secretsmanager:DescribeSecret"],
        "Resource": ["arn:*:secretsmanager:*:*:       Sets the policy for secrets
        ⮑secret:AppSecret-??????"]      ◁────────── with the name AppSecret
    } ]
}')

arn:aws:iam::aws:policy/greeting-deployment-policy  ◁── The command returns
                                                         the policy ARN ID.
```

Permits getting and describing secrets

You need an IAM OIDC provider for the cluster to create the association between the IAM access policy and the Kubernetes service account. If you don't already have one, create one by running the following command.

Listing 6.66   Creating an IAM OIDC provider

```
eksctl utils associate-iam-oidc-provider --region="$REGION"
  --cluster="$CLUSTERNAME" --approve        ← $CLUSTERNAME is the
                                              name of your cluster.
```

Finally create an IAM service account to be used by the Pod, and associate it with the IAM access policy (`arn:aws:iam::aws:policy/greeting-deployment-policy`) created previously. In this case, use `greeting-deployment-sa` as the service account name and the Kubernetes service account name.

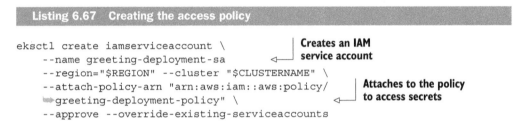

Listing 6.67   Creating the access policy

```
eksctl create iamserviceaccount \                Creates an IAM
  --name greeting-deployment-sa          ←──┘    service account
  --region="$REGION" --cluster "$CLUSTERNAME" \
  --attach-policy-arn "arn:aws:iam::aws:policy/   Attaches to the policy
  greeting-deployment-policy" \          ←──┘    to access secrets
  --approve --override-existing-serviceaccounts
```

The process is summarized in figure 6.26.

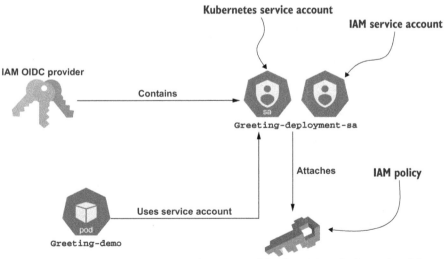

Figure 6.26   Pod-Volume connection

AWS SECRETS MANAGER CSI DRIVER

Now install and configure the AWS Secret Manager CSI Driver. First create a new Kubernetes namespace to deploy the AWS example.

Listing 6.68   Creating an AWS namespace

```
kubectl create namespace aws       ◁──┤ Create a namespace.

                                           ┐ Switch to the
kubectl config set-context --current --namespace=aws   ◁──┘ created namespace.
```

Install the AWS Secrets Store CSI Provider, as shown in listing 6.69, to inject secrets from AWS Secret Manager into Pods using the CSI interface.

Listing 6.69   Installing the AWS Secrets Store CSI Provider

```
kubectl apply -f https://raw.githubusercontent.com/aws/
➥secrets-store-csi-driver-provider-aws/main/deployment/      ┐ Installs the AWS Secrets
➥aws-provider-installer.yaml                           ◁──┘ Store CSI provider
```

Check that the provider is running by executing the following command:

Listing 6.70   Checking the GCP Secrets Store CSI provider

```
                                      ┐ List the Pods in the
kubectl get pods -n kube-system    ◁──┘ kube-system namespace.

NAME                                    READY   STATUS    RESTARTS   AGE
coredns-558bd4d5db-4l9tk                1/1     Running   4          5d20h
csi-secrets-store-8xlcn                 3/3     Running   11         5d3h
csi-secrets-store-provider-aws-34bj1    1/1     Running   0          17s
```

> **WARNING**   The provider is installed in the kube-system namespace to establish connectivity to the Kube API Server.

The last step before creating a Pod with a secret is configuring the SecretProvider-Class with the secret's name.

Listing 6.71   aws-spc.yaml

```
apiVersion: secrets-store.csi.x-k8s.io/v1alpha1
kind: SecretProviderClass
metadata:
  name: aws-manning
spec:
  provider: aws
  parameters:
    objects: |
                                     ┐ Sets the secret's name
        - objectName: "AppSecret"  ◁──┘ created earlier
          objectType: "secretsmanager"
```

Apply the aws-manningSecretProviderClass by running the following command.

Listing 6.72   Applying the aws-manning `SecretProviderClass`

```
kubectl apply -f aws-spc.yaml -n aws        ◁──┐  Registers AWS
                                                 SecretProviderClass
```

DEPLOYING A POD WITH A SECRET MOUNTED

The configuration in this example is similar to what you saw in the HashiCorp Vault example. You have the csi section, where you set the CSI driver to secrets-store .csi.k8s.io, as well as the SecretProviderClass name created previously (aws-manning). In this case, set the service account name to the service account created in the previous step (greeting-deployment-sa) to access the AWS Secrets Manager.

Listing 6.73   aws-app-pod.yaml

```
kind: Pod
apiVersion: v1
metadata:
  name: greeting-demo
  labels:
    app: greeting
spec:
  serviceAccountName: greeting-deployment-sa
  containers:
  - image: quay.io/lordofthejars/greetings-jvm:1.0.0
    name: greeting-demo
    volumeMounts:                ◁──┤  Volume mount section
    - name: secrets-store-inline
      mountPath: "/mnt/secrets-aws"    ◁──┐  Path where secrets
      readOnly: true                        are mounted
  volumes:
    - name: secrets-store-inline
      csi:
        driver: secrets-store.csi.k8s.io
        readOnly: true
        volumeAttributes:                       ┐  References the
          secretProviderClass: "aws-manning"  ◁──┘  SecretProviderClass
```

Deploy the Pod by running the following command.

Listing 6.74   Applying the Pod with the CSI volume

```
kubectl apply -f aws-app-pod.yaml -n aws    ◁──┐  Deploy a Pod configured to use
                                                 the AWS Secrets Store CSI provider.
```

Wait until the Pod is running.

Listing 6.75   Wait until the greeting Pod is running

```
kubectl wait --for=condition=ready pod -l app=greeting --timeout=90s    ◁──┐

                                                         Wait until the Pod is ready.
```

Finally, validate the secret is mounted in /mnt/secrets-aws, as specified in the volumesMount section, and the file containing the secret is named as set in object-Name. Run the command shown in the following listing.

Listing 6.76 Read the injected secret

```
kubectl exec greeting-demo -- cat /mnt/secrets-aws/AppSecret
```

```
my_secret%
```
◁—— **The value displayed matches the previously set password value for the secret set.**

OTHER CONFIGURATION PARAMETERS

AWS CSI provider has other configuration parameters not shown in the previous example; in the following snippet, you can see a SecretProviderClass example with all possible parameters.

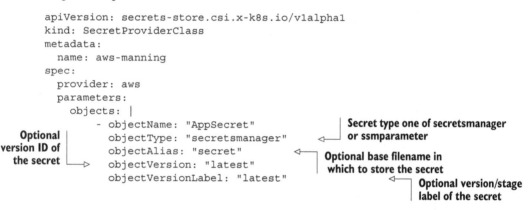

```
apiVersion: secrets-store.csi.x-k8s.io/v1alpha1
kind: SecretProviderClass
metadata:
  name: aws-manning
spec:
  provider: aws
  parameters:
    objects: |
      - objectName: "AppSecret"
        objectType: "secretsmanager"
        objectAlias: "secret"
        objectVersion: "latest"
        objectVersionLabel: "latest"
```

Optional version ID of the secret └——▷

Secret type one of secretsmanager or ssmparameter ◁——┘

Optional base filename in which to store the secret ◁——

Optional version/stage label of the secret ◁——

Global security considerations when using secrets store CSI drivers

As we mentioned in chapter 2, mounting secrets as volumes or injecting them as environment variables exposes you to some threats worth considering:

- When the secret is mounted on the filesystem, potential vulnerabilities—like directory traversal attack, unforbidden access to the node disk, or gaining access to the Pod—can become a problem, as the attacker may gain access to the secret data. You need to protect against these problems at the application level (e.g., for directory traversal) and Kubernetes level (e.g., for disabling kubectl exec).
- When the secret is injected through environment variables, potential vulnerabilities, like logging environment data at the application level or gaining access to the Pod, can become a problem, as the attacker may read the secret data.
- When syncing secrets to the Kubernetes Secrets store, remember to apply all the security considerations learned in chapter 4. You may have the secrets securely placed in the external secrets store but lose all these confidentialities when moved to Kubernetes secrets.

(continued)

There are different tools and projects that can help us detect security threats automatically and provide some guidance for solving the security issue. In our opinion, there are two tools that, combined together, can best help you detect and audit security misconfigurations as well as unusual behvior in your containers.

The first project is KubeLinter (https://docs.kubelinter.io/). The project is a static code analysis tool that analyzes Kubernetes YAML files and Helm charts, checking for security misconfigurations and best practices. Some of the issues it detects include running containers in privileged mode, exposing privileged ports, exposing SSH'd ports, unsetting resource requirements, and reading secrets from environment variables.

The second project is Falco (https://falco.org/). This project works at runtime, parsing Linux sytem calls from the Kernel and checking them against a list of rules to validate whether they are permitted. In the case of a violation of a rule, an alert is triggered, and some actions can be taken as a response. Falco comes with a set of rules; some of them include notifying read/writes to well-known directories, such as `/etc`, `/usr/bin`, and `/usr/sbin`; ownership and mode changes; and executing SSH binaries, such as `ssh`, `scp`, and `sftp`.

It's safe to say that now you know why CSI and secrets store CSI drivers are perfect abstractions for dealing with multiple secret managers.

Summary

- The Container Storage Interface is an initiative to unify the storage interface of container orchestrators.
- Secrets Store CSI is an implementation of the CSI spec to consume secrets from external data stores.
- Secrets Store CSI allows us to inject secrets into Pods from HashiCorp Vault, AWS Secret Manager, GCP Secret Manager, and Azure Key Vault.
- Although Secrets Store CSI supports key rotation, the application needs to support it by either watching disk changes or reloading the Pod.

Part 3

Continuous integration and continuous delivery

Part 3 provides an end-to-end overview for implementing Kubernetes-native continuous integration and delivery using a Kubernetes-native tool, such as Tekton and Argo CD, as well as how to manage sensitive assets throughout the whole pipeline.

Chapter 7 focuses on aspects of continuous integration, including how to build and publish container images securely without exposing the secrets of the application. Chapter 8 covers continuous delivery for deploying and releasing the application to Kubernetes automatically. Many of the concepts introduced throughout the book are exemplified in this concluding chapter, so you can deliver applications with sensitive assets to Kubernetes securely.

7
Kubernetes-native continuous integration and Secrets

This chapter covers

- Integrating the application for any change using continuous integration methodology
- Implementing continuous integration pipelines with Kubernetes-native Tekton
- Testing, building, and pushing a Linux container to an external registry with a Kubernetes-native CI pipeline

In the previous chapter you saw how to inject secrets from a secret store to containers, and in earlier chapters, you learned how to keep secrets secret in the different phases of the lifecycle of an application. Now it's time to bring these concepts together and start applying them.

We'll demonstrate how to implement a Kubernetes-native continuous integration pipeline to release an application or service continuously and automatically, yet keeping the secrets secret using Tekton. In this chapter, we want to achieve delivering quality applications rapidly to hit the market sooner and better, while managing the secrets correctly during the whole pipeline, so no secrets leak in this phase of the development.

7.1   *Introduction to continuous integration*

Developing software isn't an individual task but a team task with many people working together and concurrently to create an application. Integrating all the work done by each developer at the end of the process might not be the best strategy, as several problems may emerge, including a merge hell, components not integrating together correctly, and working parts breaking down. The best integration strategy is integrating as much and as soon as possible, so any error will be detected quickly and can be located and fixed more easily.

Continuous integration (or CI) is a set of practices that automates the integration of code changes from multiple developers into a single repository. The commits to the repository must occur frequently (usually several times per day), and it must trigger an automated process to verify the correctness of the new code.

The ultimate goal of CI is establishing a steady and automated way to build, package, and test applications, so any change to the source code can be integrated quickly, without waiting weeks, and validated after the commit. Therefore any break in the integration process is detected in the early stages.

For every commit, the code should run in the following stages:

- *Build*—The code is compiled and packaged. The output depends on the platform and language used to develop the application—in the case of Java, it can be a JAR or WAR file, and in Go, it will be a binary executable.
- *Test*—The application runs the first batch of tests. These tests aren't end-to-end tests or long tests but unit tests, some component tests, and a minimal subset of end-to-end tests validating the green path of core business functionalities.
- *Security Checks*—In this stage, the code is analyzed for vulnerabilities and bad practices, typically using static code analysis tools.
- *Release*—The delivery artifact is published in an artifact repository. It can be the JAR file, the Go executable, or a Linux container.

Figure 7.1 summarizes each step in a continuous integration pipeline.

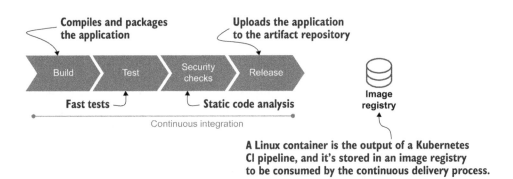

Figure 7.1   Common steps that composes a continuous integration pipeline

The benefits of continuous integration include the following:

- Integration bugs are detected in the early stages and are easy to fix, as the original code didn't change it much.
- Application is integrated continuously, so weeks or months are not required to integrate all the pieces.
- When a test failure is detected, it's easier to find the cause (as only small changes are done), and in the case of rolling back to a previous version, only a small number of features are lost.
- Since the application is integrated frequently, there is always a version ready for deploying (or releasing) to any of the environments (staging, preproduction, and production).

IMPORTANT   A CI pipeline must provide quick feedback, meaning it must not take more than 10 minutes, since the main goal of this pipeline is providing fast feedback to the developer and notifying them of any integration error as quickly as possible.

After this brief introduction to continuous integration, it's time to implement it in a Kubernetes-native way using Tekton.

7.2   *Tekton*

You'll implement a simple CI pipeline for a Java application using Tekton, a Kubernetes-native framework to create cloud-native CI pipelines. This pipeline will build the application, containerize it, and push the container to a container registry.

Tekton (https://tekton.dev/) is an open source, Kubernetes-native project for building continuous integration/continuous delivery (CI/CD) pipelines, which provide custom resource definitions (CRDs) that define the building blocks you can create and reuse in your pipelines. The Tekton CRDs can be grouped into two big blocks: one group that represents any element that define a pipeline and another group that represents the pipeline execution.

If this separation of elements seems confusing to you, consider the analogy of classes and instances in programming languages: the class object is the definition of a concept, while an instance of the class is the real object in memory, with specific parameters, and can be instantiated multiple times. The definition of a developer class and the creation of two instances of the class is shown in figure 7.2.

Figure 7.2   Class definition vs. class instance

Before installing Tekton, you need to create a Kubernetes cluster and deploy a Git server and a container registry.

7.2.1   *Installing prerequisites*

Start a new minikube instance by running the following command in a terminal window.

Listing 7.1   Start minikube

```
minikube start -p argo --kubernetes-version='v1.19.0' --vm-
    driver='virtualbox' --memory=8196
```
⟵ **Creates a Kubernetes cluster under the argo profile**

In this chapter, you'll need a Git repository with writing permissions to some repositories. To avoid relying on an external service (e.g., GitHub or GitLab), you will need to deploy a Git server (https://gitea.io/en-us/) into the Kubernetes cluster.

Listing 7.2   Deploying Gitea

```
kubectl apply -f https://gist.githubusercontent.com/
➥lordofthejars/1a4822dd16c2dbbafd7250bcb5880ca2/
➥raw/65ecee01462426252d124410ca0cc19afac382c3/
➥gitea-deployment.yaml
```
⟵ **Applying the Gitea deployment script**

Wait until Gitea deployment is up and running.

Listing 7.3   Waiting until Gitea is ready

```
kubectl wait --for=condition=ready pod -l app=gitea-demo --timeout=90s
```
⟵ **Waiting until Gitea is deployed**

A Git server is accessible within the Kubernetes cluster through the `gitea` DNS name. Register a new user to the system with the username `gitea` and password `gitea1234`, using the rights to push the source code used in the chapter.

Listing 7.4   Creating a Gitea user

```
kubectl exec svc/gitea > /dev/null
-- gitea admin create-user --username gitea
➥--password gitea1234 --email gitea@gitea.com
➥--must-change-password=false
```
⟵ **Executing the creation of a user in the Gitea container**

Finally, the source code used is migrated from GitHub to the internal Git server.

Listing 7.5   Migrating the application to Gitea

```
kubectl exec svc/gitea > /dev/null -- curl -i -X POST -H
➥"Content-Type:application/json" -d '{"clone_addr":
```

```
"https://github.com/lordofthejars/kubernetes-secrets
-source.git","private": false,"repo_name": "kubernetes
-secrets-source","uid": 1}'http://gitea:gitea1234@localhost:3000/
api/v1/repos/migrate
```
◄─┐ **Executing the migration of the Git**
   repository in the Gitea container

Moreover, a container registry is required to store the containers build during the CI phase. To avoid relying on an external service, deploy a container registry (https://docs.docker.com/registry/) into the Kubernetes cluster.

Listing 7.6   Installing a Docker registry

```
kubectl apply -f https://gist.githubusercontent.com/
lordofthejars/d386a28c07a54a6fd8717ce78a652b8b/raw/
a03b22afd549f8164dca2e38d6fab4fecfbc318a/
registry-deployment.yaml
```
◄──────────┐ **Applying a Docker registry**
            deployment script

Wait until the registry deployment is up and running.

Listing 7.7   Waiting until the registry is ready

```
kubectl wait --for=condition=ready pod -l
app=registry-demo --timeout=90s
```
◄─┐ **Waiting until the Docker**
   registry is deployed

Container images are pulled by Kubernetes nodes, which means DNS names used in Kubernetes services are not valid in the physical machines (in this example, in the minikube node). To make containers pushed to the registry pullable from nodes, you need to add a /etc/hosts entry with the DNS name and the Kubernetes service IP of registry service to the Kubernetes node. Get the registry service IP by running the following command.

Listing 7.8   Getting the registry IP

```
kubectl get service/registry -o jsonpath=
'{.spec.clusterIP}'
```
◄─┐ **Getting the**
   service IP

```
10.111.129.197
```

Then access the minikube machine, and add the following entry to /etc/hosts.

Listing 7.9   Registering the registry IP to the host

```
minikube ssh -p argo

sudo -i
echo "10.111.129.197 registry" >> /etc/hosts
```
◄─┐ **Substitute the IP with**
   the correct value.
```
exit
exit
```

You are now ready to install Tekton in the Kubernetes cluster.

7.2.2   *Installing Tekton*

Install Tekton 0.20.1 by applying the code in listing 7.10. This command will install all role-based access controls (RBAC), Custom Resource Definitions (CRD), Config-Maps, and Deployments to use Tekton.

Listing 7.10   Installing Tekton

```
kubectl apply --filename https://github.com/tektoncd/
⮡pipeline/releases/download/v0.20.1/release.yaml          ◄──┐  Applying the Tekton
                                                              │  deployment script
namespace/tekton-pipelines created
podsecuritypolicy.policy/tekton-pipelines created
clusterrole.rbac.authorization.k8s.io/
⮡tekton-pipelines-controller-cluster-access created
clusterrole.rbac.authorization.k8s.io/
⮡tekton-pipelines-controller-tenant-access created
clusterrole.rbac.authorization.k8s.io/
⮡tekton-pipelines-webhook-cluster-access created
role.rbac.authorization.k8s.io/tekton-pipelines-controller created
role.rbac.authorization.k8s.io/tekton-pipelines-webhook created
role.rbac.authorization.k8s.io/tekton-pipelines-leader-election created
serviceaccount/tekton-pipelines-controller created
serviceaccount/tekton-pipelines-webhook created
clusterrolebinding.rbac.authorization.k8s.io/
⮡tekton-pipelines-controller-cluster-access created
clusterrolebinding.rbac.authorization.k8s.io/
⮡tekton-pipelines-controller-tenant-access created
clusterrolebinding.rbac.authorization.k8s.io/
⮡tekton-pipelines-webhook-cluster-access created
rolebinding.rbac.authorization.k8s.io/tekton-pipelines-controller created
rolebinding.rbac.authorization.k8s.io/tekton-pipelines-webhook created
rolebinding.rbac.authorization.k8s.io/
⮡tekton-pipelines-controller-leaderelection created
rolebinding.rbac.authorization.k8s.io/
⮡tekton-pipelines-webhook-leaderelection created
customresourcedefinition.apiextensions.k8s.io/
⮡clustertasks.tekton.dev created
customresourcedefinition.apiextensions.k8s.io/conditions.tekton.dev created
customresourcedefinition.apiextensions.k8s.io/
⮡images.caching.internal.knative.dev created
customresourcedefinition.apiextensions.k8s.io/pipelines.tekton.dev created
customresourcedefinition.apiextensions.k8s.io/
⮡pipelineruns.tekton.dev created
customresourcedefinition.apiextensions.k8s.io/
⮡pipelineresources.tekton.dev created
customresourcedefinition.apiextensions.k8s.io/runs.tekton.dev created
customresourcedefinition.apiextensions.k8s.io/tasks.tekton.dev created
customresourcedefinition.apiextensions.k8s.io/taskruns.tekton.dev created
secret/webhook-certs created
validatingwebhookconfiguration.admissionregistration.k8s.io/
⮡validation.webhook.pipeline.tekton.dev created
```

```
mutatingwebhookconfiguration.admissionregistration.k8s.io/
↪webhook.pipeline.tekton.dev created
validatingwebhookconfiguration.admissionregistration.k8s.io/
↪config.webhook.pipeline.tekton.dev created
clusterrole.rbac.authorization.k8s.io/tekton-aggregate-edit created
clusterrole.rbac.authorization.k8s.io/tekton-aggregate-view created
configmap/config-artifact-bucket created
configmap/config-artifact-pvc created
configmap/config-defaults created
configmap/feature-flags created
configmap/config-leader-election created
configmap/config-logging created
configmap/config-observability created
configmap/config-registry-cert created
deployment.apps/tekton-pipelines-controller created
service/tekton-pipelines-controller created
horizontalpodautoscaler.autoscaling/tekton-pipelines-webhook created
poddisruptionbudget.policy/tekton-pipelines-webhook created
deployment.apps/tekton-pipelines-webhook created
service/tekton-pipelines-webhook created
```

TIP Tekton CLI is command-line utility used to interact with Tekton resources. Although it isn't mandatory to install, it is very helpful, especially for viewing what's happening in the pipeline. To install it, visit https://github.com/tektoncd/cli/releases/tag/v0.16.0, download the package for your platform, uncompress it, and copy the tkn file into a PATH directory, so it can be accessed anywhere.

The overall picture of what you've installed so far is shown in figure 7.3.

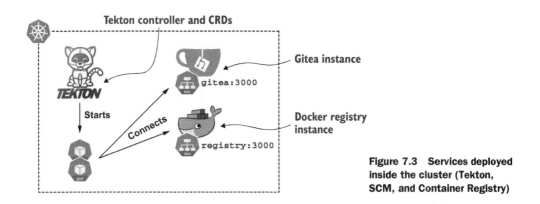

Figure 7.3 Services deployed inside the cluster (Tekton, SCM, and Container Registry)

At this point, you're ready to start learning and using Tekton in the Kubernetes cluster.

7.2.3 *Tekton pipelines*

In summary, Tekton provides two group of Kubernetes objects to define and execute pipelines. The first group is a collection of Kubernetes objects for defining the tasks and `steps` used to compose a CI pipeline. The most important objects are `Pipelines`, which are composed of `Tasks`, which are composed of `Steps`, as shown in figure 7.4.

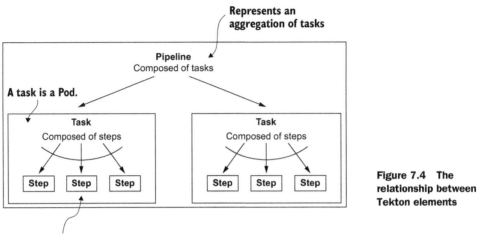

Figure 7.4   The relationship between Tekton elements

The second group is a collection of Kubernetes objects for instantiating `tasks` and `pipelines`. The most important objects are `PipelineRun`, `TaskRun`, and `Triggers`. `Triggers` are not covered in this book, as they are out of its scope, but suffice it to say that triggers enable the execution of a `pipeline` because of an external event (e.g., a commit to the source repository).

THE PIPELINERESOURCE

A `PipelineResource` is a Kubernetes object that defines a set of resources used as input and output parameters for a `task`. Examples of input resources include Git repositories and container images. Examples of output resources include container images and files.

To set the URL of the Git repository, create a `PipelineResource`, setting the type to `git` and the `url` parameter to the Git Repository location as shown in the following listing.

Listing 7.11   build-resources.yaml

```
apiVersion: tekton.dev/v1alpha1
kind: PipelineResource
metadata:
  name: git-source
spec:                          Sets the PipelineResource
  type: git        ◁——┘       to the git type
  params:                                   The Git resource has the url
    - name: url        ◁————————┘           configuration parameter.
      value: https://github.com/lordofthejars/kubernetes-secrets-source.git
```

The newly created `PipelineResource` is named git-source; you'll refer to it later.

STEPS

A `step` represents an operation in the `pipeline`; for example, some `steps` include compiling an application, running tests, and building a Linux container image. Each `step` is executed within a provided container image, and any step can mount volumes or use environment variables.

A `step` is defined in the `steps` section, in which you set the name of the `step`, the container image used in the `step`, and the command to execute inside that container. Furthermore, you can set the directory where the command is run by using the `workingDir` attribute. An example of building a Java application using Apache Maven is shown in the following listing.

Listing 7.12   build-app-task.yaml

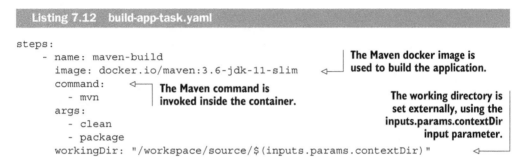

```
steps:
    - name: maven-build
      image: docker.io/maven:3.6-jdk-11-slim
      command:
        - mvn
      args:
        - clean
        - package
      workingDir: "/workspace/source/$(inputs.params.contextDir)"
```

The Maven docker image is used to build the application.

The Maven command is invoked inside the container.

The working directory is set externally, using the inputs.params.contextDir input parameter.

TASKS

A `task` is a Kubernetes object composed of a list of `steps` in order. Each `task` is executed in a Kubernetes Pod, where it runs a container in the Pod.

Since all containers within a Pod share resources (e.g., CPU, disk, and memory), and a `task` is composed of several `steps` (containers) running in the same Pod, anything written in the disk by one `step` is accessible inside any step of the `task`. Figure 7.5 shows how all these elements are interconnected.

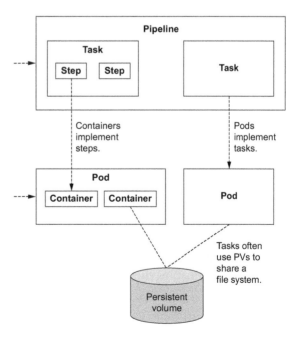

Figure 7.5 Tekton `Task`, Pod, and container relationships

A task is configured in the spec section, where you set the list of steps to execute and optional configuration parameters, like input parameters, the input and output resources required by the task, and volumes. An example of a task registering the step defined in the previous section, defining the input parameter for the working-Dir attribute and defining an input resource of Git type to clone a repository before any step is executed is shown in the following listing.

Listing 7.13   build-app-task.yaml

```
apiVersion: tekton.dev/v1beta1
kind: Task
metadata:
  name: build-app          A list of input params are registered. In this
spec:                      case, the contextDir param is required by the
  params:             ◁──┘ maven-build step to set the working directory.
    - name: contextDir
      description: the context dir within source
      default: .                            ◁──┐ Sets the default value if the
  resources:                                    │ parameter isn't set externally
    inputs:
      - name: source       ◁──┐ The Git input resource is
        type: git              │ defined with the name source.
  steps:
    - name: maven-build    ◁──┤ Steps definition
    ...
```

After arriving at this point, you might be wondering two things:

1 Where do you set the Git project repository?
2 Where is the project cloned?

To answer the first question, the Git repository is configured externally in a Pipeline-Resource object. The second question is easier. The content is cloned at the /workspace/<name> directory, where name is the input name value given in the git type. Hence, the Git resource defined previously is cloned at the /workspace/source directory.

A Task is just the definition, or the description of the steps to execute. To execute it, you need to create a TaskRun object.

TASKRUN

A TaskRun is a Kubernetes object that instantiates and executes a Tekton Task on a cluster. A TaskRun executes each of the steps defined in the Task with the order defined until all of them are executed.

To execute the build-appTask created previously, you need a TaskRun object. This object will reference the Task and set up the input parameters and resources with specific values, as shown in the following listing.

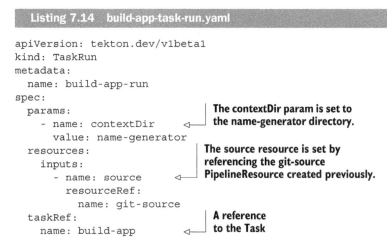

Listing 7.14   build-app-task-run.yaml

```
apiVersion: tekton.dev/v1beta1
kind: TaskRun
metadata:
  name: build-app-run
spec:
  params:
    - name: contextDir          ◁─┘  The contextDir param is set to
      value: name-generator             the name-generator directory.
  resources:                          The source resource is set by
    inputs:                           referencing the git-source
      - name: source          ◁─┘  PipelineResource created previously.
        resourceRef:
          name: git-source
  taskRef:                            A reference
    name: build-app          ◁─┘  to the Task
```

NOTE You might wondering why `contextDir` needs to be set to a specific value instead of being left with its default value (the root of the repository). This is due to the way the https://github.com/lordofthejars/kubernetes-secrets-source.git repository is organized. If you take a close look at the directory hierarchy, you'll notice the repository contains both services (Name and Welcome Message) in a directory:

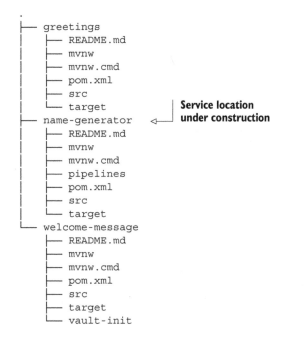

```
.
├── greetings
│   ├── README.md
│   ├── mvnw
│   ├── mvnw.cmd
│   ├── pom.xml
│   ├── src
│   └── target
├── name-generator          ◁─┘  Service location
│   ├── README.md                  under construction
│   ├── mvnw
│   ├── mvnw.cmd
│   ├── pipelines
│   ├── pom.xml
│   ├── src
│   └── target
└── welcome-message
    ├── README.md
    ├── mvnw
    ├── mvnw.cmd
    ├── pom.xml
    ├── src
    ├── target
    └── vault-init
```

Since you are building the Name Generator service, set the Maven's working directory to `name-generator`.

TaskRun is the way to execute a single task. Sometimes you might use them to execute or test a specific task, but most of the time, you want to execute the full `pipeline` with all `tasks` defined on it.

PIPELINE

A `Pipeline` is a Kubernetes object composed of a list of `tasks` connected in a directed acyclic graph. In the `Pipeline` definition, you have full control on the execution order and conditions of `tasks`, making it possible to set up fan-in/fan-out scenarios for running `tasks` in parallel or setting up conditions to a `Task` that should meet before executing it.

Now create a simple `Pipeline` using the `build-app`Task created in the previous section. As with the `tasks`, a `Pipeline` can have input parameters and input resources, making the `pipeline` extendable. For this specific example, only the input parameter (the Git resource) is configurable from outside the `pipeline`, and the `contextDir` parameter value is hardcoded in the `task`. Finally, the `build-app`task is registered as a `pipeline task` with the input parameter and resource set. The `Pipeline` definition should be similar to the one shown in the following listing.

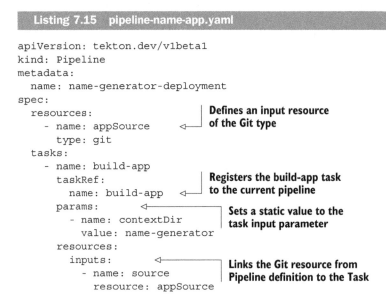

Listing 7.15   pipeline-name-app.yaml

```
apiVersion: tekton.dev/v1beta1
kind: Pipeline
metadata:
  name: name-generator-deployment
spec:
  resources:                          Defines an input resource
    - name: appSource                 of the Git type
      type: git
  tasks:
    - name: build-app
      taskRef:                        Registers the build-app task
        name: build-app               to the current pipeline
      params:                         Sets a static value to the
        - name: contextDir            task input parameter
          value: name-generator
      resources:
        inputs:                       Links the Git resource from
          - name: source              Pipeline definition to the Task
            resource: appSource
```

So far, you've seen how to define a CI pipeline using Tekton, but no execution has happened yet, as the pipeline needs to be instantiated and input parameters and resources need to be provided. In the following section, you'll see how to execute a Tekton `pipeline`.

PIPELINERUN

A `PipelineRun` is a Kubernetes object to instantiate and execute a Tekton `Pipeline` on a cluster. A `PipelineRun` executes each of the defined `tasks` in the `Pipeline`, automatically creating a `TaskRun` for each of them, as shown in the following listing.

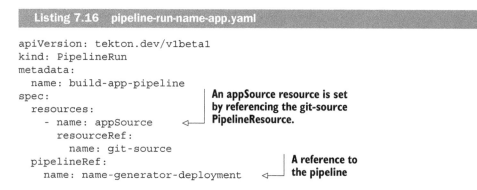

```
apiVersion: tekton.dev/v1beta1
kind: PipelineRun
metadata:
  name: build-app-pipeline
spec:
  resources:
    - name: appSource
      resourceRef:
        name: git-source
  pipelineRef:
    name: name-generator-deployment
```

An appSource resource is set by referencing the git-source PipelineResource.

A reference to the pipeline

Figure 7.6 summarizes the basic Tekton elements and how they are related to one another.

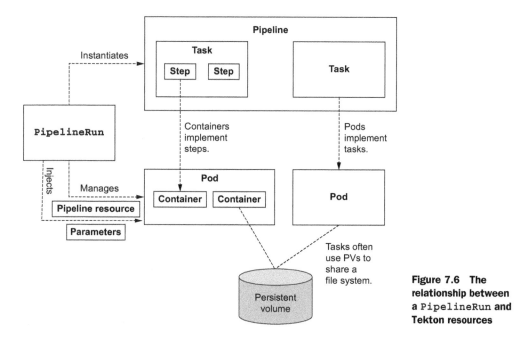

Figure 7.6   The relationship between a PipelineRun and Tekton resources

You've now seen the most important Tekton resources for building a basic CI pipeline, but this is far from a real pipeline.

7.3   Continuous integration for a welcome message

A real CI pipeline in Kubernetes needs at least the following steps:

- Checking out of the code using a Tekton Git resource
- Defining an Apache Maven container in a Tekton step to build and test the application
- Setting the container registry credentials as Kubernetes Secrets and defining a Buildah container in a Tekton step to build and push the container

The application used in this chapter is a simple service architecture composed of two services producing a welcome message:

- *A name generator service*—A service that randomly selects a name from a list of names, as shown in the following listing.

Listing 7.17   NameGeneratorResource.java

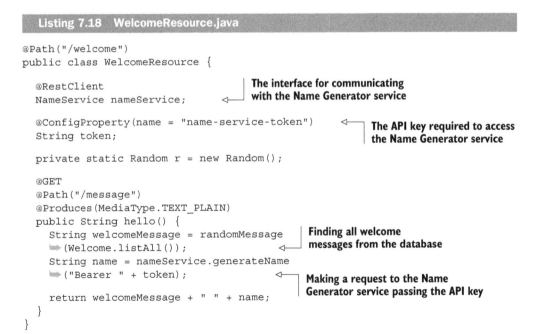

```
@Path("/generate")
public class NameGeneratorResource {                              List of names

  private static final String[] NAMES = new String[] {
    "Ada", "Alexandra", "Burr", "Edson", "Kamesh", "Sebi", "Anna", "Gavina"
  };

  private static final Random r = new Random();

  @GET
  @Path("/name")
  @Produces(MediaType.TEXT_PLAIN)              Securing the method, so only
  @RolesAllowed("Subscriber")                  a user with the Subscriber
  public String generate() {
    return NAMES[generateRandomIndex()];             Generating a random
  }                                                  name((COl8-3))
}
```

- *A welcome message service*—A service that randomly chooses the welcome message from a database and delegates to the name of the person to whom you dedicate the greeting to a name service, as shown in the following listing.

Listing 7.18   WelcomeResource.java

```
@Path("/welcome")
public class WelcomeResource {

  @RestClient                        The interface for communicating
  NameService nameService;           with the Name Generator service

  @ConfigProperty(name = "name-service-token")    The API key required to access
  String token;                                   the Name Generator service

  private static Random r = new Random();

  @GET
  @Path("/message")
  @Produces(MediaType.TEXT_PLAIN)
  public String hello() {
    String welcomeMessage = randomMessage     Finding all welcome
    ➥(Welcome.listAll());                     messages from the database
    String name = nameService.generateName
    ➥("Bearer " + token);                Making a request to the Name
                                          Generator service passing the API key
    return welcomeMessage + " " + name;
  }
}
```

Figure 7.7 shows an overview of the application.

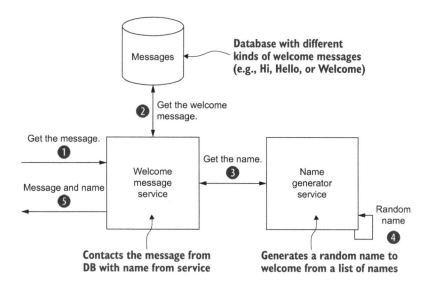

Figure 7.7 Overview of the interactions between Welcome and Name services

The following considerations are taken to maximize security:

- You need to provide an API key to access the Name Generator service. This API key is a secret and is stored in the HashiCorp Vault instance.
- The database credentials of the Welcome Message service are managed by HashiCorp Vault dynamic database credentials.
- Services authenticate against HashiCorp Vault using the Kubernetes authentication method.

Figure 7.8 shows an overview of these elements.

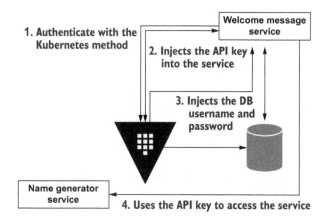

Figure 7.8 Security elements

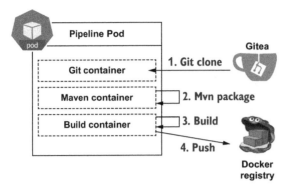

Figure 7.9   A list of the containers running inside a Pod for the Welcome Message service

We'll assume you have some experience with CI/CD as well as basic knowledge of Git and Linux containers. The principles described in this chapter apply to whichever technology you may end up choosing.

The pipeline excution for Tekton and Kubernetes elements is shown in figure 7.9. A Pod is created with three containers; the first one clones the project from the Gitea server, the project is packaged in the second container, and the Linux container with the service is built and pushed to container registry in the third container. The three containers with commands that are executed are shown in figure 7.9.

Each of these steps are implemented as a Tekton step. Let's implement them in the following sections.

7.3.1   Compiling and Running tests

You've already seen how to compile and run tests in the previous section using Apache Maven. The Welcome Message service is developed in Java, and Apache Maven is used as a building tool.

Listing 7.19   Building a service Tekton `step`

```
- name: maven-build
  image: docker.io/maven:3.6.3-jdk-11-slim
  command:
    - mvn
  args:
    - -DskipTests
    - clean
    - install
  workingDir: "/workspace/source/$(inputs.params.contextDir)"
```

7.3.2   Building and Pushing the container image

Building a container image inside a running container (remember that each step is executed inside a container) is a bit complicated because a Docker daemon is required to build a container image. To avoid having to deal with the Docker-inside-Docker problem or to build container images within environments where you can't run a Docker host, such as a Kubernetes cluster, easily, there are some Dockerless tools that permit building container images without depending on a Docker daemon. *Buildah* (https://buildah.io/), for example, is a tool for building container images from a `Dockerfile` inside a container without requiring a Docker daemon.

In the `step` definition shown in listing 7.20, Buildah is used to build and push the Welcome Message container to the container registry. The container name, in the form of `registry:group:name:tag`, and the location of the `Dockerfile` are provided as parameters.

Listing 7.20 Building and pushing a container image Tekton `step`

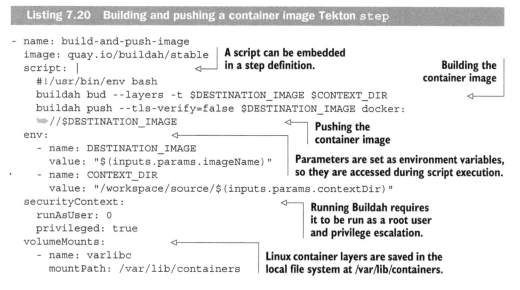

```
- name: build-and-push-image
  image: quay.io/buildah/stable
  script: |
    #!/usr/bin/env bash
    buildah bud --layers -t $DESTINATION_IMAGE $CONTEXT_DIR
    buildah push --tls-verify=false $DESTINATION_IMAGE docker:
    //$DESTINATION_IMAGE
  env:
    - name: DESTINATION_IMAGE
      value: "$(inputs.params.imageName)"
    - name: CONTEXT_DIR
      value: "/workspace/source/$(inputs.params.contextDir)"
  securityContext:
    runAsUser: 0
    privileged: true
  volumeMounts:
    - name: varlibc
      mountPath: /var/lib/containers
```

- A script can be embedded in a step definition.
- Building the container image
- Pushing the container image
- Parameters are set as environment variables, so they are accessed during script execution.
- Running Buildah requires it to be run as a root user and privilege escalation.
- Linux container layers are saved in the local file system at /var/lib/containers.

Create a new file named `welcome-service-task.yaml` containing both `steps` defined previously, as shown in the following listing.

Listing 7.21 welcome-service-task.yaml

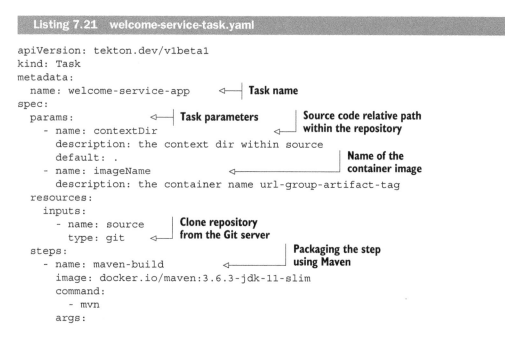

```
apiVersion: tekton.dev/v1beta1
kind: Task
metadata:
  name: welcome-service-app
spec:
  params:
    - name: contextDir
      description: the context dir within source
      default: .
    - name: imageName
      description: the container name url-group-artifact-tag
  resources:
    inputs:
      - name: source
        type: git
  steps:
    - name: maven-build
      image: docker.io/maven:3.6.3-jdk-11-slim
      command:
        - mvn
      args:
```

- Task name
- Task parameters
- Source code relative path within the repository
- Name of the container image
- Clone repository from the Git server
- Packaging the step using Maven

```
      - clean
      - install
    workingDir: "/workspace/source/$(inputs.params.contextDir)"

  - name: build-and-push-image
    image: quay.io/buildah/stable
    script: |
      #!/usr/bin/env bash
      buildah bud --layers -t $DESTINATION_IMAGE $CONTEXT_DIR
      buildah push --tls-verify=false $DESTINATION_IMAGE docker:
         //$DESTINATION_IMAGE
    env:
      - name: DESTINATION_IMAGE
        value: "$(inputs.params.imageName)"
      - name: CONTEXT_DIR
        value: "/workspace/source/$(inputs.params.contextDir)"
    securityContext:
      runAsUser: 0
      privileged: true
    volumeMounts:
      - name: varlibc
        mountPath: /var/lib/containers
volumes:
  - name: varlibc
    emptyDir: {}
```

Creation of Container image step ← (annotation for the build-and-push-image step)

Execute the following command to register the Task into the Kubernetes cluster.

Listing 7.22   Registering the task

```
kubectl apply -f welcome-service-task.yaml
```

← **Registering the Tekton task definition**

7.3.3   *The PipelineResource*

The Welcome Message service repository is stored in the local Git server (Gitea) deployed in the Kubernetes cluster. Set the Git location of the service in a `Pipeline-Resource`. Create a new file named `welcome-service-resource.yaml`, as shown in the following listing.

Listing 7.23   welcome-service-resource.yaml

```
apiVersion: tekton.dev/v1alpha1
kind: PipelineResource
metadata:
  name: welcome-service-git-source
spec:
  type: git
  params:
    - name: url
      value: http://gitea:3000/gitea/
         kubernetes-secrets-source.git
```

← **Points to the internal repository**

Execute the following command to register the `PipelineResource` into the Kubernetes cluster.

Listing 7.24 Registering the `pipeline` resource

```
kubectl apply -f welcome-service-resource.yaml
```
◁─┐ **Registering the Tekton pipeline resource**

7.3.4 *Pipeline*

The last step is defining a `pipeline` to implement the CI pipeline for the Welcome Message service. Create a new file named `welcome-service-pipeline.yaml`, as shown in the following listing.

Listing 7.25 welcome-service-pipeline.yaml

```
apiVersion: tekton.dev/v1beta1
kind: Pipeline
metadata:
  name: welcome-deployment
spec:
  resources:
    - name: appSource
      type: git
  params:
    - name: imageTag
      type: string
      description: image tag
      default: v1
  tasks:
    - name: welcome-service-app
      taskRef:
        name: welcome-service-app
      params:
        - name: contextDir
          value: welcome-message
        - name: imageName
          value: "registry:5000/k8ssecrets/
            welcome-message:$(params.imageTag)"
      resources:
        inputs:
          - name: source
            resource: appSource
```

Execute the following command to register the `Pipeline` into the Kubernetes cluster.

Listing 7.26 Registering the `Pipeline`

```
kubectl apply -f welcome-service-pipeline.yaml
```
◁─┐ **Registering the Tekton pipeline definition**

Figure 7.10 shows the relationship between `Pipeline` and `Task` parameters.

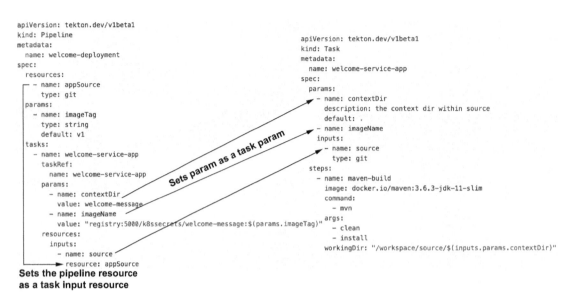

```
apiVersion: tekton.dev/v1beta1
kind: Pipeline
metadata:
  name: welcome-deployment
spec:
  resources:
    - name: appSource
      type: git
  params:
    - name: imageTag
      type: string
      default: v1
  tasks:
    - name: welcome-service-app
      taskRef:
        name: welcome-service-app
      params:
        - name: contextDir
          value: welcome-message
        - name: imageName
          value: "registry:5000/k8ssecrets/welcome-message:$(params.imageTag)"
      resources:
        inputs:
          - name: source
            resource: appSource
```

**Sets the pipeline resource
as a task input resource**

```
apiVersion: tekton.dev/v1beta1
kind: Task
metadata:
  name: welcome-service-app
spec:
  params:
    - name: contextDir
      description: the context dir within source
      default: .
    - name: imageName
  inputs:
    - name: source
      type: git
  steps:
    - name: maven-build
      image: docker.io/maven:3.6.3-jdk-11-slim
      command:
        - mvn
      args:
        - clean
        - install
      workingDir: "/workspace/source/$(inputs.params.contextDir)"
```

Sets param as a task param

Figure 7.10   Relationship between the `Pipeline` and `Task` parameters

7.3.5   *PipelineRun*

Create a `PipelineRun` to trigger the `welcome-deploymentpipeline` defined in the previous step. In this `PipelineRun`, in addition to setting the Git repository location, the container image tag is also provided.

Listing 7.27   welcome-service-pipeline-run.yaml

```
apiVersion: tekton.dev/v1beta1
kind: PipelineRun
metadata:
  name: welcome-pipeline-run
spec:
  params:
    - name: imageTag
      value: "1.0.0"          ⟵  Sets the image tag
                                  to version 1.0.0.
  resources:
    - name: appSource
      resourceRef:
        name: welcome-service-git-source
  pipelineRef:
    name: welcome-deployment
```

Figure 7.11 shows the relationship between the `PipelineRun` and `PipelineResource` parameters.

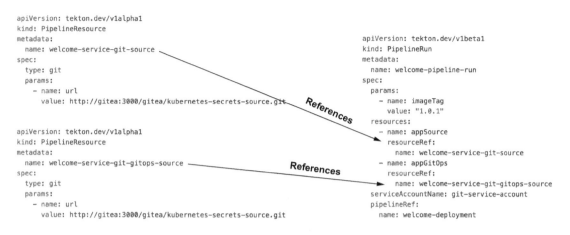

```
apiVersion: tekton.dev/v1alpha1
kind: PipelineResource
metadata:
  name: welcome-service-git-source
spec:
  type: git
  params:
    – name: url
      value: http://gitea:3000/gitea/kubernetes-secrets-source.git

apiVersion: tekton.dev/v1alpha1
kind: PipelineResource
metadata:
  name: welcome-service-git-gitops-source
spec:
  type: git
  params:
    – name: url
      value: http://gitea:3000/gitea/kubernetes-secrets-source.git
```

```
apiVersion: tekton.dev/v1beta1
kind: PipelineRun
metadata:
  name: welcome-pipeline-run
spec:
  params:
    – name: imageTag
      value: "1.0.1"
  resources:
    – name: appSource
      resourceRef:
        name: welcome-service-git-source
    – name: appGitOps
      resourceRef:
        name: welcome-service-git-gitops-source
  serviceAccountName: git-service-account
  pipelineRef:
    name: welcome-deployment
```

References

References

Figure 7.11   The relationship between `PipelineRun` and `PipelineResource`

Execute the following command to trigger the `Pipeline` into the Kubernetes cluster.

Listing 7.28   Registering the `PipelineRun`

```
kubectl apply -f welcome-service-pipeline-run.yaml    ⟵┤ Starts the pipeline
```

At this point, a `TaskRun` is automatically created and executed for each `task` defined in the `tasks` section of the `Pipeline` object. To list them, run the following command in a terminal window.

Listing 7.29   Listing all `TaskRuns`

```
tkn tr list     ⟵┤ List all TaskRuns
```

The output provides a list of all `TaskRuns` executed in the Kubernetes cluster with its status:

```
NAME                                              STARTED       DURATION STATUS
welcome-pipeline-run-welcome-service-app-l2zns 1 minute ago --- 	      Running
```

`tkn` allows us to inspect the logs of a `TaskRun` and, in case of a failure, find the error cause. In a terminal, run the following command, with the `-f` option used to stream live logs of the current execution.

Listing 7.30   Streaming logs from `PipelineRun`

```
tkn tr logs welcome-pipeline-run-welcome-service-app-l2zns -f          ⟵
```

**Changing the TaskRun ID to the correct
one showed in the previous command**

You'll see the `pipeline` logs in the console:

> **The Maven process is started for building the service.**

```
[maven-build] Downloaded from central: https://repo.maven.apache.org/
➥maven2/io/quarkus/quarkus-narayana-jta-deployment/1.11.3.Final/
➥quarkus-narayana-jta-deployment-1.11.3.Final.jar (8.4 kB at 19 kB/s)
Downloaded from central: https://repo.maven.apache.org/maven2/io/
➥quarkus/quarkus-agroal-deployment/1.11.3.Final/
➥quarkus-agroal-deployment-1.11.3.Final.jar (13 kB at 30 kB/s)
➥[maven-build] Downloading from central: https://repo.maven.apache.org/
➥maven2/io/quarkus/quarkus-hibernate-orm-deployment/1.11.3.Final/
➥quarkus-hibernate-orm-deployment-1.11.3.Final.jar
```

> **Buildah builds the container image.**

```
...
[build-and-push-image] STEP 11: ENTRYPOINT [ "/deployments/run-java.sh" ]
[build-and-push-image] STEP 12: COMMIT test.org/k8ssecrets/
➥welcome-message:1.0.0
[build-and-push-image] --> abab5f4192b
[build-and-push-image] abab5f4192b3a5d9317419d61553d91baf0dfc4df16
➥b9ad58d2489f71ee0a30a
[build-and-push-image] Getting image source signatures
[build-and-push-image] Copying blob sha256:f0b7ce40f8b0d5a8e10eecc86
➥06f43a8bfbb48255da7d1ddc5e3281434f33b20
[build-and-push-image] Copying blob sha256:ba89bf93365092f038be159229ea
➥fbbc083ff8ffdfd2007e24c4c612e82871ee
[build-and-push-image] Copying blob sha256:04a05557bbadc648beca5cf01b71
➥b152ce7890a454381877144ac7e63b968874
[build-and-push-image] Copying blob sha256:821b0c400fe643d0a9f146c9ab8
➥ec12d8abe59eddd00796673b3154005515b26
[build-and-push-image] Copying blob sha256:7a6b87549e30f9dd8d25021fef3
➥c15626617941f83322ba5f6b1988cade6b1cf
[build-and-push-image] Copying config sha256:abab5f4192b3a5d9317419d61
➥553d91baf0dfc4df16b9ad58d2489f71ee0a30a
[build-and-push-image] Writing manifest to image destination
[build-and-push-image] Storing signatures
```

> **Pushing the container image to the container registry**

Remember that `Task` is executed as a Pod, and each `step` is executed inside a container within that Pod. This can be seen when running the following command.

Listing 7.31   Get all Pods

```
kubectl get pods          Gets all Pods created during
                          the pipeline execution
NAME                                  READY    STATUS      RESTARTS   AGE
welcome-pipeline-run-welcome-         0/3      Completed   0          6m22s
➥service-app-l2zns-pod-98b2l
```

Since the `welcome-service-app`task is composed of three `steps` (Git clone, Maven build, and Docker build/push), three containers were created during the `task` execution, as seen in the `READY` column.

The CI pipeline cycle finishes when the container image is published to the container registry. But the service is not deployed, nor is it released yet to the Kubernetes cluster. In the following chapter, you'll see how to use continuous deployment and GitOps methodology to deploy and release the service to the cluster.

Summary

- Kubernetes Secrets are used either in the application code (e.g., usernames, passwords, and API keys) and in the CI pipelines (e.g., usernames and passwords of external services).
- Continuous integration secrets need to be protected, like any other secret. You can use `SealSecrets` in Tekton and Argo CD to store encrypted secrets in Git. Enable Kubernetes data encryption at rest to store encrypted secrets inside Kubernetes.
- Tekton is the Kubernetes-native platform for implementing the CI pipeline.
- Git is used as a single source of truth—not only for the source code but also for the `pipeline` scripts.

Kubernetes-native continuous delivery and Secrets

This chapter covers

- Introducing continuous delivery and deployment methodology
- Implementing a Kubernetes-native continuous deployment pipeline using GitOps methodology
- Showing ArgoCD as a Kubernetes-native solution for implementing GitOps

In the previous chapter, you saw how to manage secrets during the CI phase, build the application, create a container image, and publish it to the container registry. But the service is neither deployed nor released yet to the Kubernetes cluster. In this chapter you'll see how to deliver the application securely.

In this chapter, you'll see how to use continuous deployment and GitOps methodology to deploy and release services to a Kubernetes cluster, using Argo CD to deliver quality applications rapidly, while managing the secrets correctly throughout the whole pipeline to prevent a leak from occurring in this phase of development.

8.1 Introduction to continuous delivery and deployment

Continuous Delivery is a methodology that involves releasing software faster and more frequently. This methodology helps reduce the cost, time, and risk of delivering changes that potentially affect the user experience. Because delivery of the application is performed continuously and with incremental updates, it's easier to capture feedback from the end user and react accordingly.

The central concept of CD is the *deployment pipeline.* As the name suggests, it is a set of steps or procedures through which the application must pass to be released for production. The deployment pipeline may be changed, depending on the process you choose to follow when releasing the application, but one typical pipeline is composed of the following stages:

- *Commit stage*—The first part of the release process, which is triggered after a team member commits something to the SCM server. This stage is the continuous integration phase shown in the previous chapter.
- *Acceptance tests*—This stage tests that the application meets expectations from a business standpoint. Some of these tests might be automatic, but others not, such as exploratory testing.
- *Release*—Based on feedback from each stage, key users decide whether to release to production or drop the version.

Notice that a release process in continuous delivery implies a manual decision to perform the actual release. On the other hand, continuous deployment automatically releases every change to production on a successful build. Figure 8.1 shows the stages of the CI/CD pipelines.

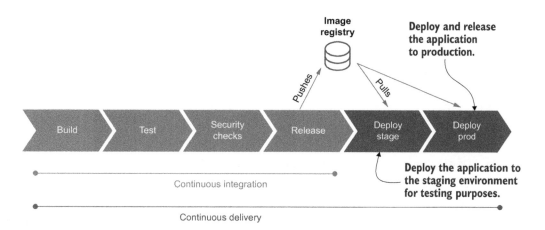

Figure 8.1 Continuous integration vs continuous delivery stages

In the following sections, you will focus on the service's release process, deploying it automatically to the Kubernetes cluster, and keeping the involved secrets protected using the DevOps methodology.

8.2   Continuous delivery for the welcome message

In this chapter you will deploy the same application used in the previous chapter to a Kubernetes cluster. It picks up where the CI phase left off (the Welcome Message container pushed to a container registry) and delivers it to the production environment. As a reminder, figure 8.2 shows an overview of the application and the parts it is composed of.

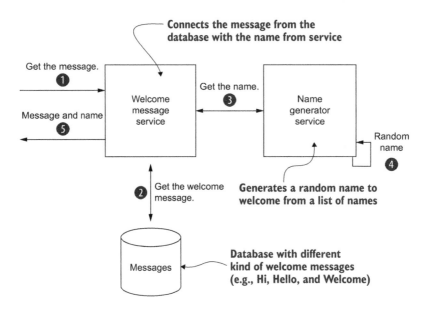

Figure 8.2   Overview of the interactions between Welcome and Name services

Now that you have an overview of the application to deploy, show the Kubernetes resources files to deploy it.

8.2.1   Deploying the Name Generator service

This chapter focuses on applying CD principles in the Welcome Message service to deploy it in the Kubernetes cluster, using GitOps methodology automatically. Although this is an example for one specific service, the same approach can be applied to any other service, including a payment service, stock service, or user management service. To keep things simple, deploy the Name Generator service manually using the following deployment file.

Listing 8.1   src/main/kubernetes/deployment.yml

```
---
apiVersion: v1
kind: Service
metadata:
  labels:
    app.kubernetes.io/name: name-generator
    app.kubernetes.io/version: 1.0.0
  name: name-generator          ⟵┐   Creating a Kubernetes Service for
spec:                           │   the Name Generator service
  ports:
  - name: http
    port: 8080
    targetPort: 8080
  selector:
    app.kubernetes.io/name: name-generator
    app.kubernetes.io/version: 1.0.0
  type: ClusterIP
---
apiVersion: apps/v1
kind: Deployment
metadata:
  labels:
    app.kubernetes.io/version: 1.0.0
    app.kubernetes.io/name: name-generator
  name: name-generator
spec:
  replicas: 1
  selector:
    matchLabels:
      app.kubernetes.io/version: 1.0.0
      app.kubernetes.io/name: name-generator
  template:
    metadata:
      labels:
        app.kubernetes.io/version: 1.0.0
        app.kubernetes.io/name: name-generator
    spec:
      containers:
      - env:
        - name: KUBERNETES_NAMESPACE
          valueFrom:
            fieldRef:
              fieldPath: metadata.namespace
        image: quay.io/lordofthejars/name-generator:1.0.0   ⟵┐   Deploying the name-
        imagePullPolicy: Always                              ┘   generator container
        name: name-generator
        ports:
        - containerPort: 8080
          name: http
          protocol: TCP
```

With the deployment file created, run the following command.

Listing 8.2   Deploying the name generator service

```
kubectl apply -f src/main/kubernetes/deployment.yml     ◁─┐   Creating a service and
                                                            a deployment for the
service/name-generator created                              name generator service
deployment.apps/name-generator created
```

With the Name Generator service up and running, deploy and release the Welcome
Message service using GitOps methodology.

8.2.2   *DevOps and GitOps*

DevOps is a set of practices that automates and helps integrate the processes of software
development and IT teams, so applications are built, tested, and released faster and
more reliably. DevOps isn't only about developer and operator team; it involves the
whole organization. Every team should be a part of the software lifecycle from the planning phase until the application is released in the production environment (figure 8.3).

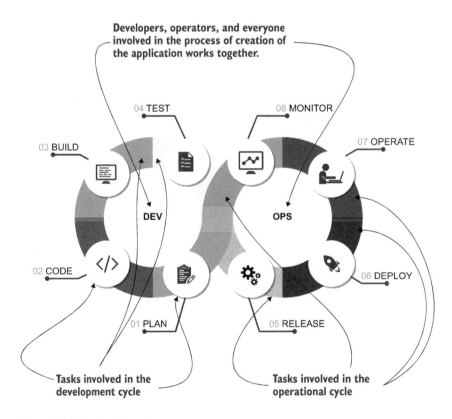

Figure 8.3   DevOps lifecycle

GitOps is a way of implementing DevOps methodology, based on the assumption that Git is the one and only source of truth. Not only is the source code of the application stored in Git, but the scripts and pipeline definitions that build the application and infrastructure code to release and update the application is stored in Git as well. This implies that all parts of the application are versioned, branched, and, of course, they can be audited.

In summary GitOps principles include the following:

- Git is the single source of truth.
- Treat everything as code.
- Operations come about through Git workflows.

One of the important aspects of GitOps is that any update on the Git repository related to the infrastructure must trigger an update to the environment to meet the desired state of the application. When there is a divergence between the desired state (set in the Git repo) and the observed state (the real state in the cluster), the convergence mechanism is executed to drive the observed state toward the desired state defined in the version control. There are two ways to cause a divergence:

1 If a human operator manually updates the Kubernetes cluster, the desired and observed state will be different and the convergence mechanism will update the Kubernetes cluster to the desired state defined in Git.
2 If a file is updated in Git (e.g., a new container image needs to be released), the desired and observed state will be different, and the Kubernetes cluster state will be updated to the new state defined in Git.

Let's see how to update a Kubernetes cluster via Git using Argo CD, a GitOps continuous delivery tool for Kubernetes.

8.3   *Argo CD*

Now it's time to deploy the Welcome Message service to the Kubernetes cluster using Argo CD and following GitOps methodology. As previously mentioned, the source code of the application is stored in Git as well as the scripts and pipeline definitions for building the application and the infrastructure code for releasing and updating the application.

Argo CD has three major components:

- *API server*—The ArgoCD backend exposes the API to Web UI, CLI, or any other system. The main responsibilities of this component are application management, security concerns, and managing Git webhook events.
- *Repository server*—This is an internal service for maintaining the local cache of the Git repositories.
- *Application controller*—This is implemented as a Kubernetes controller that continuously monitors the manifests placed at the Git repository and compares them with the live state on the cluster. Optionally it takes corrective actions.

Figure 8.4 shows each of these parts and how they are related.

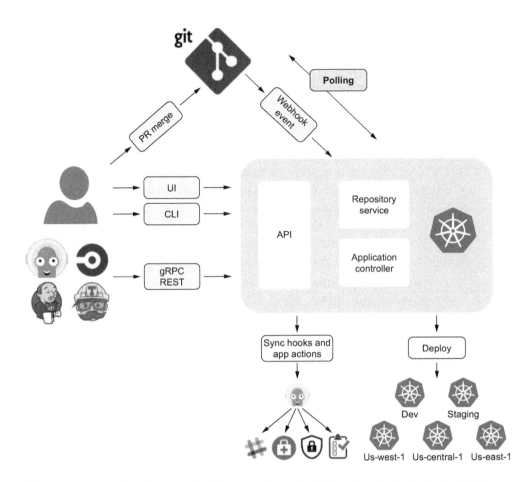

Figure 8.4   Interactions between ArgoCD elements and the Kubernetes cluster for deploying an application

8.3.1   *Installation of ArgoCD*

To install ArgoCD 1.8.7, create a new Kubernetes namespace, and apply the Argo CD resource to the Kubernetes cluster, as shown in the following listing.

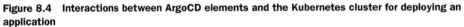

Listing 8.3   Installing ArgoCD

```
                                              ┌── Creating the argocd
kubectl create namespace argocd      ◁────┘   namespace
kubectl apply -n argocd -f https://raw.githubusercontent.com/argoproj/
  argo-cd/v1.8.7/manifests/install.yaml  ◁──┐ Installing Argo CD from official
                                             │ resources at the argocd namespace
```

```
customresourcedefinition.apiextensions.k8s.io/applications.argoproj.io
➥created
customresourcedefinition.apiextensions.k8s.io/appprojects.argoproj.io
➥created
serviceaccount/argocd-application-controller created
serviceaccount/argocd-dex-server created
serviceaccount/argocd-redis created
serviceaccount/argocd-server created
role.rbac.authorization.k8s.io/argocd-application-controller created
role.rbac.authorization.k8s.io/argocd-dex-server created
role.rbac.authorization.k8s.io/argocd-redis created
role.rbac.authorization.k8s.io/argocd-server created
clusterrole.rbac.authorization.k8s.io/argocd-application-controller created
clusterrole.rbac.authorization.k8s.io/argocd-server created
rolebinding.rbac.authorization.k8s.io/argocd-application-controller created
rolebinding.rbac.authorization.k8s.io/argocd-dex-server created
rolebinding.rbac.authorization.k8s.io/argocd-redis created
rolebinding.rbac.authorization.k8s.io/argocd-server created
clusterrolebinding.rbac.authorization.k8s.io/argocd-application-controller
➥created
clusterrolebinding.rbac.authorization.k8s.io/argocd-server created
configmap/argocd-cm created
configmap/argocd-gpg-keys-cm created
configmap/argocd-rbac-cm created
configmap/argocd-ssh-known-hosts-cm created
configmap/argocd-tls-certs-cm created
secret/argocd-secret created
service/argocd-dex-server created
service/argocd-metrics created
service/argocd-redis created
service/argocd-repo-server created
service/argocd-server created
service/argocd-server-metrics created
deployment.apps/argocd-dex-server created
deployment.apps/argocd-redis created
deployment.apps/argocd-repo-server created
deployment.apps/argocd-server created
statefulset.apps/argocd-application-controller created
```

TIP argocd CLI is a command-line utility used to interact with Argo CD. To install it, just visit https://github.com/argoproj/argo-cd/releases/tag/ v1.7.14, download the package for your platform, uncompress the archive, and copy the argocd file into a PATH directory, so it's accessible from any directory.

Next expose the Argo CD server by changing the Argo CD Kubernetes Service to the LoadBalancer type using the patch command shown in listing 8.4.

Listing 8.4 Exposing ArgoCD server

```
kubectl patch svc argocd-server -n argocd -p
➥'{"spec": {"type": "LoadBalancer"}}'          ⟵── Changing the Kubernetes
                                                     Service type to LoadBalancer
```

To use the `argocd` CLI tool, you need the external IP and the Argo CD server exposed port. You can get them by running the commands shown in the following listing.

Listing 8.5   Argo CD access IP and port

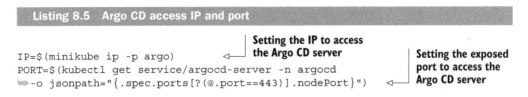

```
IP=$(minikube ip -p argo)
PORT=$(kubectl get service/argocd-server -n argocd
    -o jsonpath="{.spec.ports[?(@.port==443)].nodePort}")
```

Setting the IP to access the Argo CD server

Setting the exposed port to access the Argo CD server

The last step before configuring Argo CD is logging in to the Argo CD server using the CLI tool. By default, the username is `admin`, and the initial password is autogenerated to be the Pod name of the Argo CD API server. The password is retrieved with the command shown in the following listing.

Listing 8.6   Getting the Argo CD password

```
kubectl get pods -n argocd -l app.kubernetes.io/name=argocd-server
    -o name | cut -d'/' -f 2
```

Gets the Argo CD Pod name

Run `login` command, as shown in the following listing, to log in to the Argo CD server using the `admin` username and password retrieved in the last step.

Listing 8.7   ArgoCD login

```
argocd login $IP:$PORT
```

Log in to Argo CD.

8.3.2   Welcome service and GitOps

When you installed Gitea in section 7.2.1, a Git repository with the sources required in this chapter were migrated inside. This repo contains two source directories: one for each service and one named `welcome-message-gitops`, where all Kubernetes YAML files related to the deployment of the Welcome Message service and GitOps definitions are placed. The repository layout is shown in the following listing.

Listing 8.8   Repository layout

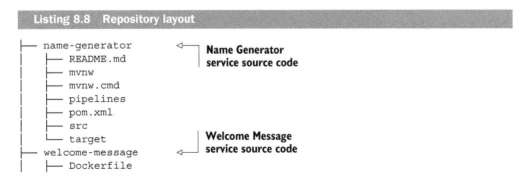

```
├── name-generator
│   ├── README.md
│   ├── mvnw
│   ├── mvnw.cmd
│   ├── pipelines
│   ├── pom.xml
│   ├── src
│   └── target
├── welcome-message
│   ├── Dockerfile
```

Name Generator service source code

Welcome Message service source code

```
|     ├── README.md
|     ├── mvnw
|     ├── mvnw.cmd
|     ├── pom.xml
|     ├── src
|     ├── target
|     └── vault-init
└── welcome-message-gitops    ◄──┤ GitOps files        │ Welcome Message
      ├── apps              ◄─────────────────────────┘ Service deployment files
      ├── cluster             ◄──────────────────┐
      └── gitops    ◄──┤ Argo CD definitions      │ One-time operations
                                                    deployment files
```

The `welcome-message-gitops` directory is composed of three directories:

- *apps*—A deployment YAML file for releasing the Welcome Message service to Kubernetes
- *cluster*—YAML files for deploying external dependencies required by the Welcome Message service (PostgreSQL and Vault)
- *gitops*—YAML files required to register the application in Argo CD

```
welcome-message-gitops
├── apps
├── cluster
└── gitops
```

APPS

The apps folder contains the deployment files required to deploy the service into a Kubernetes cluster. In this case, there are two standard Kubernetes `Deployment` and `Service` resources.

```
welcome-message-gitops
├── apps
|     └── app.yml
|     └── service.yml
```

To deploy the Welcome Message service, create the `apps.yaml` file with the content shown in the following listing.

Listing 8.9   apps/apps.yml

```
---
apiVersion: apps/v1
kind: Deployment
metadata:
  labels:
    app.kubernetes.io/name: welcome-message
  name: welcome-message
spec:
  replicas: 1
  selector:
    matchLabels:
```

```
        app.kubernetes.io/name: welcome-message
  template:
    metadata:
      labels:
        app.kubernetes.io/name: welcome-message
    spec:
      containers:
      - env:
        - name: KUBERNETES_NAMESPACE
          valueFrom:
            fieldRef:
              fieldPath: metadata.namespace
        image: quay.io/lordofthejars/welcome-message:1.0.0  <──┐ Deploying first
        imagePullPolicy: Always                                │ version of
        name: welcome-message                                    Welcome Message
        ports:
        - containerPort: 8080
          name: http
          protocol: TCP
```

Create a `service.yml` file to make the Welcome Message accessible with the content shown in the following listing.

Listing 8.10   apps/service.yml

```
---
apiVersion: v1
kind: Service
metadata:
  labels:
    app.kubernetes.io/name: welcome-message
  name: welcome-message
spec:
  ports:
  - name: http
    port: 8080
    targetPort: 8080
  selector:
    app.kubernetes.io/name: welcome-message
  type: LoadBalancer
```

CLUSTER

The cluster folder contains all YAML files required to deploy and configure the external dependencies required by the service—in this case, PostgreSQL as the database and HashiCorp Vault as the secret management system:

```
welcome-message-gitops
├── cluster
│       ├── postgresql.yaml
│       ├── vault-job.yaml
│       ├── vault-secrets.yaml
│       └── vault.yaml
```

The `postgresql.yaml` and `vault.yaml` files are standard deployment files for deploying both of the services to the Kubernetes cluster, but two more files deserve an explanation. The `vault-secrets.yaml` file is a Kubernetes `Secret` object containing secrets required to be stored into HashiCorp Vault and consumed by the application. In this case, these are the token to log in to HashiCorp Vault and the API token used by the Welcome service to authenticate to the Name Generator service. The file is partially shown in the following listing.

> **Listing 8.11 cluster/vault-secrets.yml**

```
apiVersion: v1
kind: Secret
metadata:
  name: vault-secrets
type: Opaque
data:                                              Access token for
  VAULT_LOGIN: cm9vdA==          ◁──┘  HashiCorp Vault
  NAME_SERVICE_TOKEN: ZXlKcmFFXUWlPa........      ◁──┤ API key
```

The `vault-job.yaml` file is a Kubernetes `Job` object configuring the HashiCorp Vault instance. It's applied after the deployment of HashiCorp Vault and enables Kubernetes auth mode and database dynamic secrets, configures policies, and adds the API token into the key–value secrets store. The file is shown partially in the following listing.

> **Listing 8.12 cluster/vault-job.yml**

```
apiVersion: batch/v1
kind: Job
metadata:
  name: init-vault
  annotations:                                          The file is applied after
    argocd.argoproj.io/hook: PostSync      ◁──┘  HashiCorp Vault is deployed.
    argocd.argoproj.io/hook-delete-policy: HookSucceeded
spec:
  template:
    spec:
      volumes:
      - name: vault-scripts-volume
        configMap:
          name: vault-scripts
          defaultMode: 0777
      containers:
      - name: init-vault
        image: vault:1.6.2
        envFrom:                              Secrets are injected as
          - secretRef:        ◁──┘  environment variables.
              name: vault-secrets
        volumeMounts:
```

```
       - mountPath: /vault-scripts
         name: vault-scripts-volume
      command:
       - /bin/ash
       - -c
       - |
         export VAULT_ADDR=http://vault:8200
         vault login $VAULT_LOGIN
         vault auth enable kubernetes
         vault secrets enable database
         vault write database/config/mydb
         ➡plugin_name=postgresql-database-plugin
         ➡allowed_roles=mydbrole ...
         vault write database/roles/mydbrole db_name=mydb ...
         vault policy write vault-secrets-policy
         ➡/vault-scripts/vault-secrets-policy.hcl
         vault kv put secret/myapps/welcome/config
         ➡name-service-token=$NAME_SERVICE_TOKEN
   restartPolicy: Never
 backoffLimit: 2
```

◁⎤ HasiCorp Vault configuration
  ⎦ files are mounted as volumes.

◁⎤ **Job commands for configuring**
  ⎦ **HashiCorp Vault**

IMPORTANT   To keep things simple, vault-secrets.yaml is a standard Kubernetes Secrets file, but it should be protected in any of the ways explained in chapter 3.

GITOPS

The gitops folder contains all files used to register the previous folders as Argo CD applications.

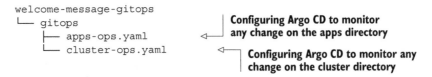

```
welcome-message-gitops
└── gitops
    ├── apps-ops.yaml
    └── cluster-ops.yaml
```

◁⎤ **Configuring Argo CD to monitor**
  ⎦ **any change on the apps directory**

◁⎤ **Configuring Argo CD to monitor any**
  ⎦ **change on the cluster directory**

In the following section, you'll see these files in more detail.

TIP   You could add the application and the external dependencies deployment files into the same directory. However our advice is to keep the files that usually change separated from those that rarely do.

8.3.3   *Creating a Welcome Message service from a Git repository*

An Argo CD *application* is a group of Kubernetes resources used to deploy the application to the target environment and keep it in the desired state. An application is defined in an Argo CD custom resource definition (CRD) file, where you specify parameters like Git repository, the path of Kubernetes resources, or the target where the application will be deployed. Figure 8.5 shows the schema of what is deployed by cluster-ops and apps-ops Argo CD applications.

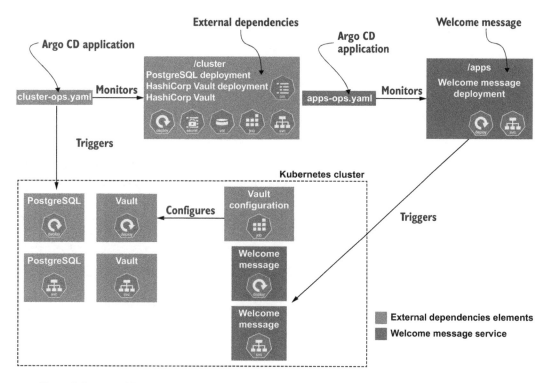

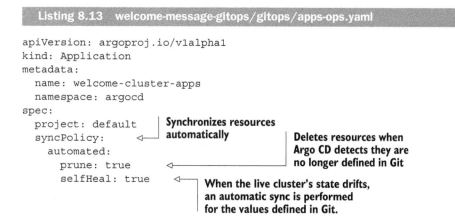

Figure 8.5   Argo CD application deployments

Listing 8.13 shows how to define an Argo CD application that clones the Git repo defined in Gitea, listens to any change in the welcome-message-gitops/apps directory, and applies these changes to meet the desired state. As we said before, the apps directory contains the resources to deploy the Welcome Message service to the Kubernetes cluster. Create the apps-ops.yaml file in the welcome-message-gitops/gitops folder.

Listing 8.13   welcome-message-gitops/gitops/apps-ops.yaml

```
apiVersion: argoproj.io/v1alpha1
kind: Application
metadata:
  name: welcome-cluster-apps
  namespace: argocd
spec:
  project: default          Synchronizes resources
  syncPolicy:               automatically
    automated:                                Deletes resources when
      prune: true                             Argo CD detects they are
                                              no longer defined in Git
      selfHeal: true
                            When the live cluster's state drifts,
                            an automatic sync is performed
                            for the values defined in Git.
```

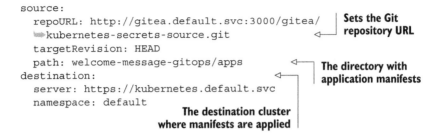

```
source:
  repoURL: http://gitea.default.svc:3000/gitea/
  ⮡kubernetes-secrets-source.git
  targetRevision: HEAD
  path: welcome-message-gitops/apps
destination:
  server: https://kubernetes.default.svc
  namespace: default
```

Sets the Git repository URL

The directory with application manifests

The destination cluster where manifests are applied

In a similar way, the cluster directory is added as an Argo CD application. Create the `cluster-ops.yaml` file in the welcome-message-gitops/gitops folder.

Listing 8.14   welcome-message-gitops/gitops/cluster-ops.yaml

```
apiVersion: argoproj.io/v1alpha1
kind: Application
metadata:
  name: welcome-cluster-ops
  namespace: argocd
spec:
  project: default
  syncPolicy:
    automated:
      prune: true
      selfHeal: true
  source:
    repoURL: http://gitea.default.svc:3000/gitea/
    ⮡kubernetes-secrets-source.git
    targetRevision: HEAD
    path: welcome-message-gitops/cluster
  destination:
    server: https://kubernetes.default.svc
    namespace: default%
```

Directory with manifests for external dependencies

Apply the cluster-ops.yaml resource to install and configure the external dependencies required by the Welcome Message service. In a terminal window, run the command shown in the following listing.

Listing 8.15   Registering the cluster application

```
kubectl apply -f welcome-message-gitops/gitops/
⮡cluster-ops.yaml
```

Registering the cluster application

The previous execution registers the cluster directory as the Argo CD application. Since it's the first time, and the `syncPolicy` parameter is set to `automated`, Argo CD automatically applies the resources defined there. Validate that PostgreSQL and Vault are deployed by getting Pods of the default namespace using the command shown in the following listing.

Listing 8.16 Getting all pods

```
kubectl get pods -n default                                              PostgreSQL
                                                                         is deployed.

NAME                                    READY   STATUS    RESTARTS   AGE
gitea-deployment-7fbbf9c8b-bbcjq        1/1     Running   1          2d17h
name-generator-579ccdc5d5-mhzft         1/1     Running   2          2d23h
postgresql-59ddd57cb6-tjrg2             1/1     Running   0          6m30s   ⟵┐
registry-deployment-64d49ff847-hljg9    1/1     Running   2          2d23h
vault-0                                 1/1     Running   0          6m30s   ⟵
welcome-message-55474d6b78-g9l5w        1/1     Running   0          2m1s

                                                                      Vault statefulset
                                                                      is deployed. │
```

The argocd CLI tool also lets you review the status of the deployment using the command shown in the following listing.

Listing 8.17 Listing ArgoCD applications

```
argocd app list               ⟵┐ Lists current Argo
                                 │ CD applications
NAME                 CLUSTER                              NAMESPACE   PROJECT
welcome-cluster-ops  https://kubernetes.default.svc       default     default
⟿STATUS   HEALTH    SYNCPOLICY   CONDITIONS
   Synced   Healthy   Auto-Prune   <none>
⟿REPO
   https://github.com/lordofthejars/kubernetes-secrets-source.git
⟿PATH                            TARGET
   welcome-message-gitops/cluster  HEAD
```

The status field shows the current status of the resources. When it's set to Synced, the cluster is aligned with the state specified with the Git repository. To deploy the Welcome Message service, apply the apps-ops.yaml file created in the previous step using the command shown in the following listing.

Listing 8.18 Registering the service application

```
kubectl apply -f welcome-message-gitops/gitops/apps-ops.yaml   ⟵┐ Registering the
                                                                 │ apps application
```

The Welcome Message service is deployed when its Pod is in the running state using the command shown in the following listing.

Listing 8.19 Getting all pods

```
kubectl get pods -n default

NAME                              READY   STATUS    RESTARTS   AGE
gitea-deployment-7fbbf9c8b-bbcjq  1/1     Running   1          2d17h
name-generator-579ccdc5d5-mhzft   1/1     Running   2          2d23h
```

```
postgresql-59ddd57cb6-tjrg2              1/1    Running    0        6m30s
registry-deployment-64d49ff847-hljg9     1/1    Running    2        2d23h
vault-0                                  1/1    Running    0        6m30s
welcome-message-55474d6b78-g9l5w         1/1    Running    0        2m1s     ◁─┐
```

**The Welcome Message
service is deployed.**

8.3.4   *Updating the Welcome service*

So far you've learned how to build the Welcome Message service using Tekton and how to deploy it the first time automatically, using the Argo CD project. But what happens when the service is already deployed and a new version needs to be released?

Aside from packaging the new version of the service, building a container, and pushing it to the container registry, as explained in section 7.3, now the CI pipeline needs to update the Welcome Message service Kubernetes Deployment file with the new container tag and push the update to the Git repository to start the rolling update of the service. Figure 8.6 shows how Tekton (Continuous Integration part) and Argo CD (Continuous Delivery part) work together to implement a CD pipeline.

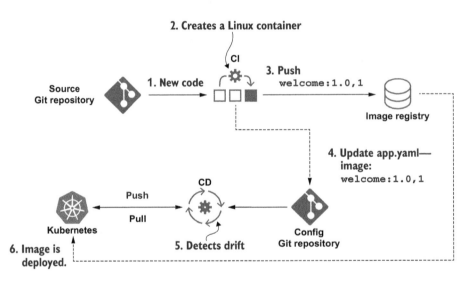

Figure 8.6   Interrelationship between Tekton and Argo CD

To implement these two remaining steps, some changes need to be made to Tekton resources.

PIPELINERESOURCE FOR GITOPS REPOSITORY

The first thing to register is a new PipelineResource registering the GitOps repository location. This repository is the place Argo CD is listening for changes. The definition is shown in the following listing.

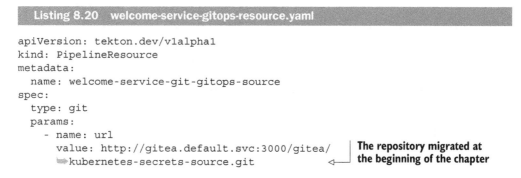

Listing 8.20 welcome-service-gitops-resource.yaml

```
apiVersion: tekton.dev/v1alpha1
kind: PipelineResource
metadata:
  name: welcome-service-git-gitops-source
spec:
  type: git
  params:
    - name: url
      value: http://gitea.default.svc:3000/gitea/          The repository migrated at
      ⇒kubernetes-secrets-source.git                       the beginning of the chapter
```

In a terminal window, apply the resource using the command shown in the following listing.

Listing 8.21 Registering the GitOps repository

```
kubectl apply -f welcome-service-gitops-resource.yaml          Regsitering the
                                                               pipline resource
```

You need to set the username and password to push the changes made in the deployment file to the previous repository. This is done by creating a Kubernetes Secret and service account with the content shown in the following listing.

Listing 8.22 git-secret.yaml

```
---
apiVersion: v1
kind: Secret
metadata:
  name: git-auth
  annotations:                                                    Setting the URL of the
    tekton.dev/git-0: http://gitea.default.svc:3000               service to authenticate
type: kubernetes.io/basic-auth                                    (gitea host)
stringData:                              The username and password used    Configuring the
  username: gitea                        in the Basic Auth mechanism       authentication schema.
  password: gitea1234
---
apiVersion: v1
kind: ServiceAccount
metadata:
  name: git-service-account
secrets:                                 The service account with
  - name: git-auth                       the created secret
```

IMPORTANT Remember to manage these secrets correctly using any of the techniques shown in chapter 3.

In a terminal window apply the resource using the command shown in the following listing.

Listing 8.23   Registering the Gitea secret

```
kubectl apply -f git-secret.yaml          ◁──┐  Creating
                                              │  the secret
```

UPDATING THE TEKTON TASK TO UPDATE THE CONTAINER IMAGE

About yq

yq is a lightweight and portable command-line YAML processor. It can be used to query YAML documents or modify them. The yq tool uses the following structure:

```
yq eval [flag] [expression] [yaml_file]
```

Given the following YAML document:

```
apiVersion: apps/v1
kind: Deployment
metadata:
  labels:
    app: myboot
  name: myboot
spec:
  replicas: 1
  selector:
    matchLabels:
      app: myboot
  template:
    metadata:
      labels:
        app: myboot
    spec:
      containers:
      - image: quay.io/rhdevelopers/myboot:v1
```

You can refer to the image field by using the following expression: .spec.template .spec.containers[0].image. Run the following to update the image field to a new value using yq:

```
yq eval -i '.spec.template.spec.containers[0].image =
  "quay.io/rhdevelopers/myboot:v2"' deployment.yml
```

Before configuring the pipeline, you need to modify the task defined previously with two new additions:

- Defining a new resource for the GitOps repository, so it's automatically cloned
- Defining a step that updates the deployment definition with the container image tag created in the previous step

```
apiVersion: tekton.dev/v1beta1
kind: Task
metadata:
  name: welcome-service-app
```

```
spec:
  params:
    ...
  resources:
    inputs:
      - name: source
        type: git                    ┐  Defining the GitOps input
      - name: gitops        ◁────────┘  resource with gitops name
        type: git
  steps:
    - name: maven-build
      ...

    - name: build-and-push-image
      ...

    - name: update-deployment-file                      ┐  Custom image with
      image: quay.io/lordofthejars/image-updater:1.0.0  ◁─┘  git and yq installed
      script: |
        #!/usr/bin/env ash
                                        ┐  Moving into the
        cd /workspace/gitops    ◁───────┘  cloned repository
                                                     ┐  Creating a new branch
        git checkout -b newver        ◁──────────────┘  for the update

        git config --global user.email "alex@example.com"   ◁─┐  Configuring
        git config --global user.name "Alex"                  │  the Git user

        yq eval -i '.spec.template.spec.containers[0].image
        ➡= env(DESTINATION_IMAGE)'                      ┐  Updating the deployment
        ➡welcome-message-gitops/apps/app.yml    ◁───────┘  file with the new container

        git add .                          ◁───────┐  Committing and pushing the
        git commit -m "Update to $DESTINATION_IMAGE" │  changes to the repository
        git push origin newver:master
      env:
        - name: DESTINATION_IMAGE
          value: "$(inputs.params.imageName)"
  volumes:
    - name: varlibc
      emptyDir: {}
```

The following listing shows the full version of the Task.

Listing 8.24   welcome-service-task.yaml

```
apiVersion: tekton.dev/v1beta1
kind: Task
metadata:
  name: welcome-service-app
spec:
  params:
    - name: contextDir
      description: the context dir within source
      default: .
```

```
    - name: imageName
      description: the container name url-group-artifact-tag
resources:
  inputs:
    - name: source
      type: git
    - name: gitops
      type: git
steps:
  - name: maven-build        ⟵──┘ Apache Maven task to
    image: docker.io/maven:3.6.3-jdk-11-slim    package the application
    command:
      - mvn
    args:
      - clean
      - install
    workingDir: "/workspace/source/$(inputs.params.contextDir)"

  - name: build-and-push-image
    image: quay.io/buildah/stable                    The Buildah
    script: |                                    command to build
      #!/usr/bin/env bash                          the container
      buildah bud --layers -t $DESTINATION_IMAGE $CONTEXT_DIR    ⟵──┘
      buildah push --tls-verify=false
      ➥$DESTINATION_IMAGE docker://$DESTINATION_IMAGE    ⟵── The Buildah command
    env:                                                    to push the container to
      - name: DESTINATION_IMAGE                             the container registry
        value: "$(inputs.params.imageName)"
      - name: CONTEXT_DIR
        value: "/workspace/source/$(inputs.params.contextDir)"
    securityContext:
      runAsUser: 0
      privileged: true
    volumeMounts:
      - name: varlibc
        mountPath: /var/lib/containers
  - name: update-deployment-file
    image: quay.io/lordofthejars/image-updater:1.0.0
    script: |
      #!/usr/bin/env ash          Moving to the              Updating the
      cd /workspace/gitops    ⟵── gitops repository         deployment YAML
      git checkout -b newver                                 file with the new
      git config --global user.email "alex@example.com"      container image tag
      git config --global user.name "Alex"
      yq eval -i '.spec.template.spec.containers[0].image
      ➥= "$DESTINATION_IMAGE"' welcome-message-gitops/apps/app.yml    ⟵──┘
      git add .
      git commit -m "Update to $DESTINATION_IMAGE"
      git push origin newver:master    ⟵── Committing and pushing the
    env:                                    change to the Git repository
      - name: DESTINATION_IMAGE
        value: "$(inputs.params.imageName)"
volumes:
  - name: varlibc
    emptyDir: {}
```

Creating a
new branch ┌──►

In a terminal window, apply the resource executing the command shown in the following listing.

Listing 8.25   Upating the Welcome service task

```
kubectl replace -f welcome-service-task.yaml
```

Updating the task from the previous chapter

IMPORTANT   Substitute `replace` with `apply` if you didn't apply the Tekton task in the previous section.

UPDATING THE PIPELINE DEFINITION

The `pipeline` definition requires an update on the resources part, as shown in the following listing to register the GitOps repository.

Listing 8.26   welcome-service-pipeline.yaml

```
apiVersion: tekton.dev/v1beta1
kind: Pipeline
metadata:
  name: welcome-deployment
spec:
  resources:
    - name: appSource
      type: git
    - name: appGitOps        ◁──┐  Defining a new
      type: git                 │  Git resoure
    ...
  tasks:
    - name: welcome-service-app
      ...
      resources:
        inputs:
          - name: source
            resource: appSource
          - name: gitops           ┌─  Setting the resource
            resource: appGitOps  ◁─┘   to the task
```

In a terminal window apply the resource executing the command shown in the following listing.

Listing 8.27   Updating the Welcome service pipeline

```
kubectl replace -f welcome-service-pipeline.yaml
```

IMPORTANT   Substitute `replace` with `apply` if you didn't apply the Tekton task in the previous section.

UPDATING PIPELINERUN

Finally, create a new `PipelineRun` with the following changes:

- Increase the image tag number.

- Set the reference of the new `PipelineResource`.
- Configure the service account running the Pipeline.

The new `PipelineRun` is shown in the following listing.

Listing 8.28   welcome-service-gitops-resource-2.yaml

```
apiVersion: tekton.dev/v1beta1
kind: PipelineRun
metadata:
  name: welcome-pipeline-run-2          ◁──┐ The new
spec:                                         │ PipelineRun
  params:
    - name: imageTag
      value: "1.0.1"          ◁──┐ The version of the
  resources:                       │ container is increased.
    ...
    - name: appGitOps
      resourceRef:                                    ┐ A new GitOps
        name: welcome-service-git-gitops-source   ◁──┘ resource is registered.
  serviceAccountName: git-service-account   ◁──┐ The serviceAccount
  pipelineRef:                                     │ with gitea credentials
    name: welcome-deployment
```

In a terminal window, apply the resource executing the command shown in the following listing.

Listing 8.29   Registering PipelineRun

```
kubectl apply -f welcome-service-gitops-resource-2.yaml   ◁──┐ Registering the
                                                               │ new PipelineRun
```

INSPECTING THE OUTPUT

After applying the previous `PipelineRun`, a new `Pipeline` instance is started. It executes the following steps in Tekton:

- Clones the service Git repository and GitOps repository from `gitea`
- Builds the service
- Creates a container image and pushes it to the container `registry` instance
- Updates the deployment file with the new image
- Pushes the deployment file to the GitOps repository

To view the currently executing log lines, run the command shown in the following listing.

Listing 8.30   Listing the PipelineRun

```
tkn pr logs -f     ◁──┐ Showing the logs of
                        │ the current PipelineRun
```

The steps are shown in the following log lines:

```
[welcome-service-app : git-source-source-8xjvv] {
➥"level":"info","ts":1618242546.5564516,"caller":"git/git.go:165",
➥"msg":"Successfully cloned
➥http://gitea:3000/gitea/kubernetes-secrets-source.git @
➥841cd108640cc2aef9b52250e0ed8f5bf53ec973 (grafted, HEAD)
➥in path /workspace/source"}
[welcome-service-app : git-source-source-8xjvv] {
➥"level":"info","ts":1618242546.5845127,"caller":"git/git.go:203",
➥"msg":"Successfully initialized and updated submodules
➥in path /workspace/source"}                          ◄─┐ The Welcome service
                                                          │ Git repo is cloned.

[welcome-service-app : git-source-gitops-v6f2q] {
➥"level":"info","ts":1618242546.842591,"caller":"git/git.go:165",
➥"msg":"Successfully cloned
➥http://gitea:3000/gitea/kubernetes-secrets-source.git @
➥841cd108640cc2aef9b52250e0ed8f5bf53ec973 (grafted, HEAD)
➥in path /workspace/gitops"}
[welcome-service-app : git-source-gitops-v6f2q] {
➥"level":"info","ts":1618242546.8661046,"caller":"git/git.go:203",
➥"msg":"Successfully initialized and updated submodules
➥in path /workspace/gitops"}                          ◄─┐ The Welcome service
                                                          │ GitOps repo is cloned.

[welcome-service-app : maven-build] [INFO]
➥Scanning for projects...         ◄─┐ Building the Welcome
                                     │ service Java project
....

[welcome-service-app : maven-build] [INFO] BUILD SUCCESS
[welcome-service-app : maven-build] [INFO] --------------------------------
[welcome-service-app : maven-build] [INFO] Total time:  01:12 min
[welcome-service-app : maven-build] [INFO] Finished at: 2021-04-12T15:50:22Z
[welcome-service-app : maven-build] [INFO] --------------------------------

[welcome-service-app : build-and-push-image] STEP 1: FROM
➥registry.access.redhat.com/ubi8/ubi-minimal:8.3                    ◄──┐
[welcome-service-app : build-and-push-image] Getting image source signatures │
                                                                            │
....                                                         Building the Welcome
                                                             service Linux container

[welcome-service-app : build-and-push-image]
➥Writing manifest to image destination
[welcome-service-app : build-and-push-image]  ┌ Pushing the Linux container
➥Storing signatures                       ◄─┘ to the container registry

[welcome-service-app : update-deployment-file]
➥Switched to a new branch 'newver'   ◄─┐ Updating the Welcome
                                        │ service deployment file
....

[welcome-service-app : update-deployment-file]
➥To http://gitea:3000/gitea/kubernetes-secrets-source.git
[welcome-service-app : update-deployment-file]              ┌ Pushing the Deployment
➥841cd10..472d777  newver -> master         ◄─────────────┘ file to the GitOps repo
```

After these steps are executed, Argo CD will detect the change on the `welcome-message-gitops/apps/app.yml` Deployment file. It will apply these changes, triggering a rolling update of the service to the new version.

IMPORTANT   The Argo CD controller can detect and sync the new manifests using a webhook or polling every three minutes. The polling strategy is the default one.

After waiting up to three minutes, Argo CD will detect the change and start the synchronization process, applying the new deployment file. Suppose you continuously monitor the status of the Pods. In that case, you'll see how the old Welcome Message Pod is terminated, and a new one is started automatically with the container created in the Tekton process. Execute the command shown in the following listing continuously to inspect the change.

Listing 8.31   Getting all pods

```
kubectl get pods                                          The new version of the
                                                          service is deployed.

NAME                                       READY  STATUS       RESTARTS  AGE
gitea-deployment-7fbbf9c8b-xc27w           1/1    Running      0         16m
name-generator-579ccdc5d5-mhzft            1/1    Running      2         3d5h
postgresql-59ddd57cb6-tjrg2                1/1    Running      0         5h34m
registry-deployment-64d49ff847-hljg9       1/1    Running      2         3d5h
vault-0                                    1/1    Running      0         5h34m
welcome-message-55799f7dc9-c5j24           1/1    Running      0         13s    ←
welcome-message-6778c7978b-tqxkv           1/1    Terminating  0         8m58s  ←
welcome-pipeline-run-welcome
-service-app-mj5z6-pod-mkkpx               0/5    Completed    0         6m17s
```

The PipelineRun is completed.   The old version of the
                                                                      service is undeployed.

Describing the newly deployed Pod like listing 8.32 shows the new container is used.

Listing 8.32   Describing the new Welcome service pod

```
kubectl describe pod welcome-message-55799f7dc9-c5j24   ←  Changing the pod name
                                                           to the correct one
....
Controlled By:  ReplicaSet/welcome-message-55799f7dc9
Containers:                                                         The version
 welcome-message:                                                   tag is updated.
  Container ID:
  →docker://fa8b45f46311819adb0fcfc5c8d8a17e4626792aac38f0e6a116d71cb0571718
    Image:        registry:5000/k8ssecrets/welcome-message:1.0.1   ←
....
```

Figure 8.7 shows a screenshot of the Argo CD dashboard, where the Welcome Message status is shown. If you look closely, you'll see that `rev:2` is the current deployment, as the service has been updated.

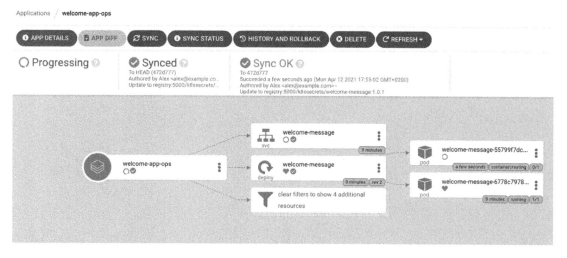

Figure 8.7 Argo CD dashboard

Summary

- Kubernetes Secrets are used in the application code (e.g., usernames, passwords, and API keys) and the CI/CD pipelines (e.g., usernames and passwords of external services).
- Enable Kubernetes data encryption at rest to store encrypted secrets inside Kubernetes.
- CD secrets need to be protected like any other secret. Use `SealSecrets` in Argo CD to store encrypted secrets in Git.
- Git is used as a single source of truth for the source code and deploying scripts.
- Argo CD is a Kubernetes controller that allows you to implement GitOps in Kubernetes.

appendix A
Tooling

To deploy and manage a Kubernetes environment on your machine, several tools need to be installed and configured.

A.1 Minikube

Minikube is a local Kubernetes cluster, focusing on making it easy to learn and develop for Kubernetes in a local environment. It relies on container/virtualization technology, such as Docker, Podman, HyperKit, Hyper-V, KVM, or VirtualBox to boot up a Linux machine with Kubernetes installed. The VirtualBox virtualization tool is used for simplicity and because it is a generic installation that works in the most-used operating systems (Microsoft Windows, Linux, and Mac OS).

To install VirtualBox (if you haven't done it yet), open the following URL in a browser: https://www.virtualbox.org/. When the webpage is opened, click the Downloads link located in the left menu, as shown in figure A.1.

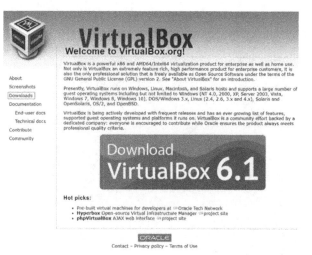

Figure A.1 The VirtualBox home page annotating the Downloads section

Then select your package based on the operating system to run the examples, as shown in figure A.2.

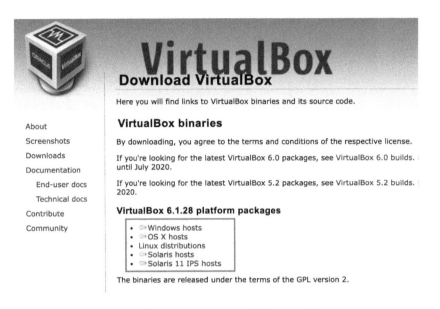

Figure A.2   The VirtualBox Downloads page with different packages

The downloading process will start storing the package on your local disk. When this process is finished, click the downloaded file to start the installation process, as shown in figure A.3.

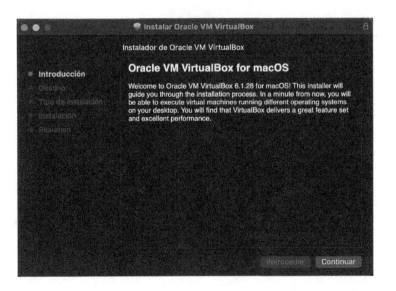

**Figure A.3
The VirtualBox
installation window**

You can use the default VirtualBox configuration values provided by the installation process or adapt them to your requirements. After the installation finishes, you can validate that VirtualBox has been installed correctly by opening it. See figure A.4 for an example of the opening screen of VirtualBox with three machines installed.

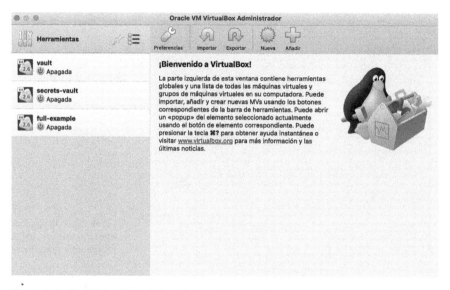

Figure A.4   The VirtualBox status window with three instances

A.2   *Kubectl*

To interact with a Kubernetes cluster, you will need to install the kubectl CLI tool. The best way to download and install kubectl is visiting the following URL: https://kubernetes.io/docs/tasks/tools/. When the webpage is opened, click on the installation link corresponding to your platform, as shown in figure A.5.

**Figure A.5
The kubectl
homepage**

You will install Kubernetes 1.19.0; for this reason, it's essential to download kubectl CLI version 1.19.0. To download a specific version, scroll down the page until you see a Note heading that discusses installing a particular version instead of the latest stable. Figure A.6 shows the part with an explanation on downloading a specific version.

Install kubectl binary with curl on macOS

1. Download the latest release:

Intel   Apple Silicon

```
l -LO "https://dl.k8s.io/release/$(curl -L -s https://dl.k8s.io/release/stable.txt)/bir
```

Note:
To download a specific version, replace the `$(curl -L -s https://dl.k8s.io/release/stable.txt)` portion of the command with the specific version.

For example, to download version v1.22.0 on Intel macOS, type:

```
curl -LO "https://dl.k8s.io/release/v1.22.0/bin/darwin/amd64/kubectl"
```

And for macOS on Apple Silicon, type:

```
curl -LO "https://dl.k8s.io/release/v1.22.0/bin/darwin/arm64/kubectl"
```

Figure A.6   Downloading a specific kubectl version; replacing v1.22.0 with v1.19.0

With VirtualBox and kubectl installed, you can start downloading minikube version 1.17.1 to boot up the Kubernetes cluster.

Open the following URL in a browser: https://github.com/kubernetes/minikube/releases/tag/v1.17.1. When the webpage is loaded, unfold the Assets menu to find the minikube release specific to your platform. Figure A.7 shows the GitHub Release page of minikube 1.17.1.

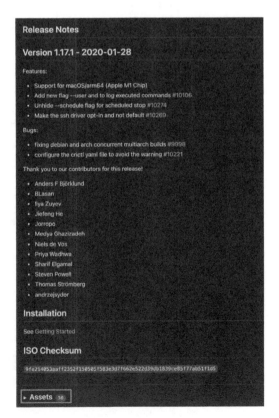

Figure A.7   Minikube is relased as a GitHub release in the Assets section

When the Assets menu is unfolded, click the minikube link corresponding to your platform. Figure A.8 shows the list of releases.

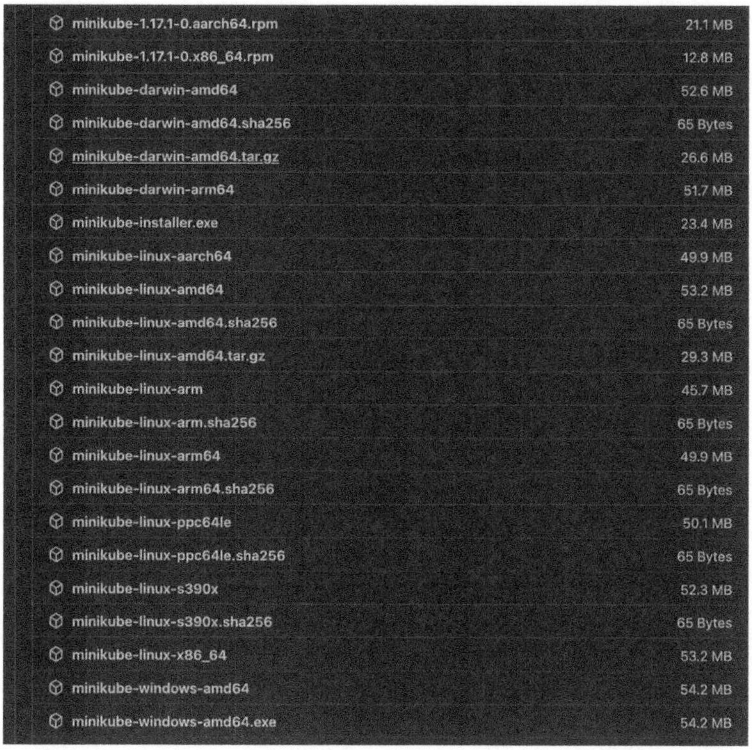

minikube-1.17.1-0.aarch64.rpm	21.1 MB
minikube-1.17.1-0.x86_64.rpm	12.8 MB
minikube-darwin-amd64	52.6 MB
minikube-darwin-amd64.sha256	65 Bytes
minikube-darwin-amd64.tar.gz	26.6 MB
minikube-darwin-arm64	51.7 MB
minikube-installer.exe	23.4 MB
minikube-linux-aarch64	49.9 MB
minikube-linux-amd64	53.2 MB
minikube-linux-amd64.sha256	65 Bytes
minikube-linux-amd64.tar.gz	29.3 MB
minikube-linux-arm	45.7 MB
minikube-linux-arm.sha256	65 Bytes
minikube-linux-arm64	49.9 MB
minikube-linux-arm64.sha256	65 Bytes
minikube-linux-ppc64le	50.1 MB
minikube-linux-ppc64le.sha256	65 Bytes
minikube-linux-s390x	52.3 MB
minikube-linux-s390x.sha256	65 Bytes
minikube-linux-x86_64	53.2 MB
minikube-windows-amd64	54.2 MB
minikube-windows-amd64.exe	54.2 MB

Figure A.8 Minikube is released for several platforms; download the one that fits yours

When the file is downloaded, rename it `minikube`, as the filename also contains the platform and the architecture. For example, `minikube-linux-amd64` is the minikube version for Linux for the 64-bits architectures. With VirtualBox installed and the minikube file renamed, create a Kubernetes cluster by running the following command in a terminal window:

```
minikube start --kubernetes-version='v1.19.0'        Starting a
    --vm-driver='virtualbox' --memory=8196           Kubernetes cluster
```

The output lines should be similar to the following:

```
?  [vault] minikube v1.17.1 en Darwin 11.6
?  Kubernetes 1.20.2 is now available. If you would like to upgrade,
specify: --kubernetes-version=v1.20.2
?  minikube 1.24.0 is available! Download it:
https://github.com/kubernetes/minikube/releases/tag/v1.24.0
?  Using the virtualbox driver based on existing profile
```

```
?   To disable this notice, run:
'minikube config set WantUpdateNotification false'

?   Starting control plane node vault in cluster vault
?   Restarting existing virtualbox VM for "vault" ...
?   Preparando Kubernetes v1.19.0 en Docker 20.10.2...
?   Verifying Kubernetes components...
?   Enabled addons: storage-provisioner, default-storageclass

?   /usr/local/bin/kubectl is version 1.21.3, which may have
incompatibilites with Kubernetes 1.19.0.
    ? Want kubectl v1.19.0? Try 'minikube kubectl -- get pods -A'
?   Done! kubectl is now configured to use "" cluster and "default"
namespace by default
```

appendix B
Installing and
configuring yq

Most operating systems have built-in support for manipulating text within the terminal, such as sed and awk. These tools are great for fairly simple text manipulations but can become cumbersome when working with structured serialization languages, such as YAML. yq (https://mikefarah.gitbook.io/yq) is a command-line tool that provides support for querying and manipulating YAML-based content and can be helpful when interacting with Kubernetes environments, as the majority of the resources are expressed in YAML format. A similar and popular tool, called jq, provides similar capabilities for JSON-formatted content, which is described in chapter 4. This appendix describes the installation of yq, along with several examples to confirm the successful installation of the tool.

B.1   Installing yq

yq is supported on multiple operating systems and can be installed using a variety of methods, including a package manager or as a direct binary download from the project website (https://github.com/mikefarah/yq/releases/latest). The direct binary option is the most straightforward option, as there are no external dependencies or prerequisites needed. Be sure to locate version 4 or higher of the tool, as there was a significant rewrite from prior versions. The Releases page will allow you to choose between downloading a compressed archive or the direct binary. Alternatively, you can use the terminal to download the binary to your local machine.

> **WARNING**   There is another tool, also called yq, which is available as a Python package and performs similar capabilities. Installing the incorrect tool will cause errors, as there are differences in the syntax and functionality between the two tools.

The following command can be used to download the yq binary and place the binary in a directory on the PATH:

```
sudo curl -o /usr/bin/yq
  https://github.com/mikefarah/yq/releases/download/${VERSION}/${BINARY}   ◁──┐
  && \                                                                        │
     sudo chmod +x /usr/bin/yq                    VERSION refers to the tagged release version,
                                                   while BINARY is a combination of the name of
                                                     the yq binary, the name of the operating
                                                     system, and the architecture. An example for
                                                      AMD64 Linux is yq_linux_amd64.
```

The installation was successful if the following command succeeds:

```
yq --version
```

If the command does not succeed, confirm the file was downloaded successfully, placed in a directory on the operating system PATH, and that the binary is executable.

B.2   *yq by example*

yq can perform actions against YAML-formatted content, such as querying and manipulating values, and is useful when working with Kubernetes manifests. kubectl has the functionality to output in a variety of formats, such as JSONPath or Go templates. However, certain advanced features, like piping, are not available and require a more full-purpose, dedicated tool.

To showcase some of the ways yq can be used to manipulate YAML content, create a file called book-info.yaml containing a resource that we are familiar with: a Kubernetes Secret.

```
apiVersion: v1
metadata:
  name: book-info
stringData:
  title: Securing Kubernetes Secrets
  publisher: Manning
type: Opaque
kind: Secret
```

yq has two primary modes: evaluating a single document (with the evaluate or e subcommand) or multiple documents (with the eval-all or ea subcommand). Evaluating a single document is the most common mode, so you can use it to query the contents of the book-info.yaml file created in listing B.2.

Operations against YAML files use *expressions* to determine the specific actions to take. Since most YAML content uses nested content, these properties can be accessed using dot notation. For example, to extract the contents of the `title` field underneath `stringData`, the expression `.stringData.title` is used. The combination of the type of action to perform, such as `evaluate`, the expression, and the location of the YAML content are three components needed when using yq. Now use the following command to extract the `title` field:

```
yq eval '.stringData.title' book-info.yaml
```

More complex expressions can also be used to perform advanced operations. *Pipes* ('|') can be used to chain expressions together, so the output from one expression becomes the input to another expression. For example, to determine the length of the `publisher` field underneath `stringData`, a pipe can be used to take the output of the `.stringData.publisher` expression and feed it into the `length` operator:

```
yq eval '.stringData.publisher | length' book-info.yaml
```

The result of the command should have returned 7. In addition to extracting properties, yq can also be used to modify YAML content. Now add a new property underneath `stringData` called `category` with a value of `Security`. The yq expression to accomplish this task is `'.stringData.category = "Security"'`. Execute the following command to add the `category` field:

```
yq eval '.stringData.category = "Security"' book-info.yaml
```

The following listing should have been returned as a result of the command.

Listing B.3 The output of updating YAML content using `yq`

```
apiVersion: v1
metadata:
  name: book-info
stringData:
  title: Securing Kubernetes Secrets
  publisher: Manning
  category: Security          ◁──┐ A new category
type: Opaque                      │ field is added.
kind: Secret
```

Even though the output of the execution resulted in the addition of the new `category` field, it is important to note the content of the `book-info.yaml` file was not modified. To update the content of the `book-info.yaml` field, the `-i` option must be used, which will instruct yq to perform an in-place update of the file. Execute the following command to perform an in-place file update:

```
yq eval -i '.stringData.category = "Security"' book-info.yaml
```

Confirm the changes have been applied to the file. The capabilities provided by yq to extract and manipulate make it a versatile tool and useful to have in your arsenal when working with any YAML-formatted content.

appendix C
Installing and configuring pip

Like most other programming languages, Python includes support for enabling reusable portions of code, such as statements and definitions, that can be included in other applications. These pieces of reusable code are known as *modules*. Multiple modules can be organized together and included in a *package*. The Standard Python library contains an array of modules and packages, which are fundamental to any application. However, the contents of the Standard Python Library do not cover every possible use case imaginable. This is where user defined packages and modules come in. As more and more individuals create customized packages, it becomes important that there is a way to easily distribute and consume these Python packages. The Python Package Index (PyPi) (https://pypi.org/) attempts to provide a solution to enable a centralized location for storing and discovering Python packages shared by the Python community. Python packages from either the centralized Python Package Index or a self-hosted instance can be managed using *pip*, a package manger that facilitates the discovery, downloading, and lifecycle management for Python packages.

C.1   Installing pip

Python packages located in the Python Package Index can be managed using the pip executable. Most recent distributions of Python (>=2.9.2 for Python 2 and >=3.4 for Python 3) using binary installations have pip preinstalled. If Python was installed via another method, such as a package manager, pip may not be included. You can check whether pip is installed by attempting to execute pip if you are on Python version 2 or pip3 if you are on Python version 3. If an error is returned when executing the prior commend, pip must be installed.

There are several ways pip can be installed:

- The `ensurepip` Python 3 module
- The `get-pip.py` script
- A package manager

Let's install pip using the `ensurepip` Python module, since it makes use of native Python constructs that are applicable across the majority of platforms. Execute the following command to install pip:

```
python -m ensurepip --upgrade
```

Confirm pip was installed by executing the `pip` command:

```
pip
```

If the command returned without error, pip was successfully installed.

> **NOTE** On some systems, an alias or symbolic link may be used to link `python3` and `python` executables to provide backward compatibility or simplify the interaction with Python; the same applies to `pip`. Specifying the `--version` flag when executing either `python`, `python3`, `pip` or `pip3` will confirm the specific version being used.

C.2 Basic pip operations

Before starting to work with pip, it is recommended you, along with a few of the supporting tools, update it to its latest version. Obtaining the latest updates will ensure appropriate access to any required source archives. Execute the following command to update pip, along with the `setuptools` and `wheel` packages, to its latest version:

```
python -m pip install --upgrade pip setuptools wheel
```

With the necessary tool up to date, let's start working with pip.

One of the first steps for anyone using a package manager is determining the software component to install. This may be known upfront, or it could be queried from the list of available components. The best location to search for packages is on the PyPi website (https://pypi.org/), which details each available package, their history, and any dependencies.

There are countless packages available to install from the Python Index, and choosing the correct package can be a challenge. One of the most common use cases for Python developers is making HTTP-based requests. While Python does provide modules, such as `http.client`, constructing simple queries can be complex. The `requests` module attempts to simplify the use of HTTP-based invocations.

Details related to the Requests module can be found on the PyPi website, but let's use pip to install the package. Execute the following command to install the `requests` package using `pip`:

```
pip install requests
```

Information related to the installed package can be viewed using the `info` subcommand:

```
pip show requests
```

The response from the command is as follows:

```
Name: requests
Version: 2.26.0
Summary: Python HTTP for Humans.
Home-page: https://requests.readthedocs.io
Author: Kenneth Reitz
Author-email: me@kennethreitz.org
License: Apache 2.0
Location: /usr/local/lib/python3.9/site-packages
Requires: certifi, charset-normalizer, idna, urllib3
Required-by:
```

With the `requests` package installed, a simple Python interactive session can be used to illustrate how it can be used. Execute the following command to first start a Python interactive session:

```
python
```

Now import the requests, query a remote address, and print the HTTP status.

Listing C.1 Using the requests package to query a remote server

```
import requests                                    Import the
                                                   requests package.
response = requests.get("https://google.com")      Perform
                                                   a request.
print(response.status_code)                        Print the HTTP status
                                                   from the request.
```

A 200 response code should be returned, indicating a successful query to the remote HTTP server. Type `exit()` to exit the Python interactive console.

Installed Python packages can also be installed via pip. The `pip list` command can be used to determine which packages are currently installed. Once the desired package for removal has been identified, it can be removed by using the `pip uninstall` command. To remove the requests package previously installed, execute the following command.

Listing C.2 Removing the requests package

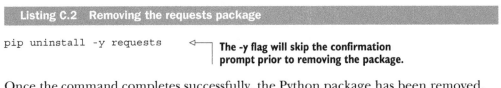

```
pip uninstall -y requests        The -y flag will skip the confirmation
                                 prompt prior to removing the package.
```

Once the command completes successfully, the Python package has been removed.

appendix D
Installing and configuring Git

Git has become the de facto VCS for tracking the changes in files and is used frequently when working with Kubernetes content. It gained popularity due to its simplified branch management capabilities in comparison with other version control systems. Before beginning to use Git on a local machine, there are a series of steps that must first be completed.

D.1 Installing Git

To start working with Git content, the `git` executable must be installed. Support is available for `git` on most operating systems, including Linux, OSX, and Windows, and the steps are available on the Git website (https://git-scm.com/book/en/v2/Getting-Started-Installing-Git).

When installing `git` on Linux, the easiest method is using a package manager, such as `apt` or `dnf`. On a Debian-based Linux operating system, execute the following command in a terminal to install Git:

```
apt install git-all
```

On an RPM-based operating system, such as Fedora or Red Hat Enterprise Linux, execute the following command in a terminal to install Git:

```
dnf install git-all
```

Confirm Git was installed successfully by checking the version:

```
git --version
```

If the version was returned, Git was successfully installed. If an error occurs, confirm the steps associated with the installation method were completed fully.

D.2   *Configuring Git*

Even though Git can be used immediately after installation, it is recommended to take a few additional steps to customize the Git environment. Certain capabilities, such as committing code, will not be available without additional actions.

The `git config` subcommand is available for retrieving and setting configuration options. These options can be specified at one of three levels:

- At a system level and specified within the [path]/etc/gitconfig file.
- At a user profile level in the ~/.gitconfig. This level can be targeted by specifying the --global option using the `git config` subcommand.
- At a repository level within the .git/config file. This level can be targeted by specifying the --local option using the `git config` subcommand.

While there is an array of configurable options available in Git, there are two options that should be defined whenever Git is installed:

- Username
- Email address

These values will be associated with any commits you perform. Failure to configure these values will result in the following error while attempting to perform a commit.

Listing D.1   Error message produced when no Git identity is configured

```
Author identity unknown

*** Please tell me who you are.

Run

  git config --global user.email "you@example.com"    ◁──┐  Indicates the variables that
  git config --global user.name "Your Name"              │  should be configured

to set your accounts default identity.
Omit --global to set the identity only in this repository.

fatal: unable to auto-detect email address (got 'root@machine.(none)')
```

As the error in listing D.1 describes, both the user.email and user.name variables should be configured. While these variables can be configured separately within each repository, for simplicity's sake, it is more straightforward to define at a global level and make appropriate modifications within individual repositories.

Execute the following commands to set the user.email and user.name to configure the required variables substituting your user details as appropriate:

```
git config --global user.name "Your Name"
git config --global user.email "you@example.com"
```

Confirm the values are set appropriately by listing all global configurations:

```
git config --global -l
```

The following values should be returned:

```
user.name=Your Name
user.email=you@example.com
```

At this point, your machine is ready to start fully interacting with the Git ecosystem.

appendix E
Installing GPG

GNU Privacy Guard (GPG) is an open standards implementation of the proprietary Pretty Good Privacy (PGP) encryption scheme and is commonly used to encyrpt and decrypt emails and filesystem content. The combination of symmetric-key cryptography and public-key cryptography enables a rapid and secure method of exchanging messages. Users must first generate a public–private key pair using GPG tooling to enable the encryption and decryption of messages. The private key is used during the encryption process, while the public key is used at decryption time. Public keys are shared with anyone who needs to decrypt the encrypted message and can also be hosted on internet key servers to simplify how encrypted content is decrypted by a wider audience. The creation of the public–private key pair as well as encrypting and decrypting message is facilitated through the use of GPG tooling—specifically, the gpg command-line interface.

E.1 Obtaining the GPG tools

The GPG tools along with the gpg command-line interface can be installed on most major operating systems and are available either as a direct download or from a package manager, such as apt, dnf, or brew.

On a Debian-based Linux operating system, execute the following command in a terminal:

```
apt install gnupg
```

On an RPM-based operating system, such as Fedora or Red Hat Enterprise Linux, execute the following command in a terminal:

```
dnf install gnupg
```

On an OSX operating system, execute the following command in a terminal:

```
brew install gpg
```

Confirm the gpg CLI was installed successfully by using the --version flag to assess the version of the tool.

Listing E.1 Displaying the GPG Version

```
gpg (GnuPG) 2.2.20
libgcrypt 1.8.5
Copyright (C) 2020 Free Software Foundation, Inc.
License GPLv3+: GNU GPL version 3 or later
<https://gnu.org/licenses/gpl.html>
This is free software: you are free to change and redistribute it.
There is NO WARRANTY, to the extent permitted by law.

Home: /root/.gnupg           ◁───────────────┐  The directory containing
Supported algorithms:                        │  GPG files
Pubkey: RSA, ELG, DSA, ECDH, ECDSA, EDDSA
Cipher: IDEA, 3DES, CAST5, BLOWFISH, AES, AES192, AES256, TWOFISH,
        CAMELLIA128, CAMELLIA192, CAMELLIA256
Hash: SHA1, RIPEMD160, SHA256, SHA384, SHA512, SHA224
Compression: Uncompressed, ZIP, ZLIB, BZIP2
```

If a response similar to listing E.1 is displayed, the GPG tools were successfully installed.

E.2 Generating a public–private key pair

Prior to being able to encrypt content, a key pair must be generated. The process of generating a key pair was also discussed in chapter 3 but will be addressed here again for completeness.

GPG keys can be created using the gpg CLI using one of the following flags:

- --quick-generate-key—Generates a key pair with the user providing a USER-ID along with expiration and algorithm details
- --generate-key—Generates a key pair while prompting for a real name and email details
- --full-generate-key—Dialogs for all of the possible key pair generation options

The option you choose depends on your own requirements. The --generate-key and --full-generate-key options support batch mode, which enables a noninteractive method for key pair creation.

Create a new GPG key pair using the --generate-key flag:

```
gpg --generate-key
```

As soon as this command is executed, a home directory for GPG files is created within the .gnupg folder in your home directory. This location can be changed by specifying the GNUPGHOME environment variable.

Provide your name and email address at the prompts. You will then be asked to confirm the details. Press 0 to confirm the details.

Then you are prompted to provide a passphrase to protect your key. The exercise in chapter 3 advised not to create one to promote simplicity in integrating each of the security tools that were being used. However, when creating GPG key pairs for other uses, it is recommended that a passphrase is provided. Once a passphrase has been provided, a new key pair will be generated, and details related to the key will be presented, as shown in the following listing.

Listing E.2 Displaying the GPG version

```
pub    rsa2048 2020-12-31 [SC] [expires: 2022-12-31]
       53696D1AB6954C043FCBA478A23998F0CBF2A552
uid            [ultimate] John Doe <jdoe@example.com>
sub    rsa2048 2020-12-31 [E] [expires: 2022-12-31]
```

You can confirm that the name and email were added correctly from the values provided, along with the algorithm, key size, and expiration. Now that the key pair has been generated, messages can be encrypted using the GPG set of tools.

index